With the publication of *Linguistic Imperialism* in 1992 Robert Phillipson provided a provocative but timely account of English as an international language, a book which has become essential reading for anyone involved in English teaching or education worldwide. *Linguistic Imperialism Continued* provides a collection of some of Phillipson's most important and influential work, which reflects his thinking on the expansion of English since the publication of his seminal book. Phillipson's work is not only thought-provoking and ground-breaking, but it gets to the very heart of some of the key issues around the global dominance of English in the world. It provides a major contribution to our understanding of the role of English in the contemporary world.

Peter Martin
University of East London

The scholarly work of Robert Phillipson has made, and continues to make, a major contribution to our understanding of the social construction of English as a 'world language' as representing potent symbolic capital within the global cultural economy. This anthology comprising some of his key writings lays bare the discursive political, cultural, economic and social inequalities intrinsic to the idea and ideal of pursuing English as medium of communication to the exclusion of other languages historically grounded in different cultures and societies. *Linguistic Imperialism Continued* underscores the fact that English language, historically, and in the contemporary world represents a power/knowledge discourse par excellence.

Naz Rassool
University of Reading

Robert Phillipson's present book represents his continued understanding and interest in the way policies which ensure the global dominance of English in all domains of power are maintained and legitimated. It is a fascinating work which manifests how humanistic values can be blended with erudition and analytical incisiveness to create the kind of scholarship which can transcend the mere description of reality our research methods enforce upon us.

Tariq Rahman
Quaid-i-Azam University
Islamabad

In this major contribution to critical sociolinguistics, Phillipson describes 'Global' English as 'a normative project, not a reality but a vision that powerful forces are keen to bring about'. At the heart of this *project*, Phillipson argues, is a *process* of 'accumulation of linguistic capital by dispossession' oriented towards a *product* packaged as the already attained of 'Global' English. He brings to bear on the study of this project/ process/ product a social science perspective that maps the variably conscious agency and objectification of the many actors in this drama. His approach scrutinizes the stage on which these actors stand to find where some features of this stage itself constrain what neoliberal doctrine portrays as unfettered informed choices by free individuals. A compelling engagement with some of the central sociolinguistic forces in today's world.

Probal Dasgupta
Linguistic Research Unit
Indian Statistical Institute
Kolkata

Linguistic Imperialism Continued

Robert Phillipson

Routledge
Taylor & Francis Group

NEW YORK AND LONDON

ORIENT BLACKSWAN PRIVATE LIMITED

Registered Office
3-6-752 Himayatnagar, Hyderabad 500 029 (A.P.), INDIA
e-mail: centraloffice@orientblackswan.com

Distributed in India, Pakistan, Bangladesh, Sri Lanka, Nepal, Bhutan and Maldives by
Orient Blackswan Private Limited.

Other Offices
Bangalore, Bhopal, Bhubaneshwar, Chennai, Ernakulam, Guwahati,
Hyderabad, Jaipur, Kolkata, Lucknow, Mumbai, New Delhi, Patna

Distributed in the rest of the world by
Routledge, Taylor and Francis Group, 270 Madison Avenue, New York 10016, USA

Library of Congress Cataloging-in-Publication Data

Phillipson, Robert.
Linguistic imperialism continued / Robert Phillipson.
    p. cm.
Includes index.
ISBN 978-0-415-87201-0 (pbk)
1. English language--Political aspects--Developing countries.
2. English language--Study and teaching--Foreign speakers. 3. English
language--Political aspects--Foreign countries. 4. English
language--Social aspects--Developing countries. 5. English
language--Social aspects--Foreign countries. 6. Imperialism. I. Title.

PE2751.P53 2010
420.9--dc22
                                    2009026297

© Robert Phillipson, 2009   **1006400123**
First published 2009

Typeset in 11/13 pt Garamond by
System Graphics (India) Pvt. Ltd., New Delhi

Published by
Orient Blackswan Private Limited
3-6-752 Himayatnagar, Hyderabad 500 029
Email: hyderabad@orientblackswan.com

Contents

Acknowledgements

Sources and permissions, which are gratefully acknowledged.

'Linguistic imperialism'. Entry in *Encyclopedia of Language and Linguistics*, Second edition. Keith Brown (ed.), volume 10, 44-47 (under 'Linguistic pragmatics', section edited by Jacob Mey, ms 4309). Oxford: Elsevier, 2006. © Elsevier.

'English in the new world order: variations on a theme of linguistic imperialism and "world" English'. In *Ideology, politics and language policies: Focus on English*, ed. Thomas Ricento. Amsterdam: John Benjamins, 87-106, 2000. © John Benjamins.

'Language policy and linguistic imperialism'. In *An introduction to language policy. Theory and method*, ed. Thomas Ricento. Oxford: Blackwell, 346-361, 2006. © Wiley-Blackwell.

'Linguistic imperialism: a conspiracy, or a conspiracy of silence?' *Language policy*, 6/3-4, 377-383, 2007. © Springer Science and Business Media.

'English, no longer a foreign language in Europe?' In *International Handbook of English Language Teaching*, Part 1, ed. Jim Cummins and Chris Davison. New York: Springer, 123-136, 2007. © Springer Science and Business Media.

'The linguistic imperialism of neoliberal empire'. *Critical Inquiry in Language Studies*, 5/1, 2008, 1-43, 2008. © Taylor and Francis Group, LLC.

'Lingua franca or lingua frankensteinia? English in European integration and globalization'. *World Englishes*, 27/2, 'Forum' , 250-284, 2008. © Wiley-Blackwell.

Book review of A.L. Khanna, Mahendra K. Verma, R.K. Agnihotri and S.K. Sinha 1998. *Adult ESOL learners in Britain*, Clevedon: Multilingual Matters. *Journal of Multilingual and Multicultural Development*, 22/5, 2001, 454-456. © Taylor and Francis Group, LLC.

Book review of Ulrich Ammon (ed.) 2001. *The dominance of English as a language of science. Effects on other languages and language communities*. Berlin: Mouton de Gruyter. *Journal of Language, Identity, and Education*, Vol. 1, no. 2, 2002, 163-169. © Taylor and Francis Group, LLC.

Review article, English in globalization: three approaches (books by de Swaan, Block and Cameron, and Brutt-Griffler). *Journal of Language, Identity, and Education*, Vol. 3/1, 73-84, 2004. © Taylor and Francis Group, LLC.

Book review of Michael Cronin 2004. *Translation and globalization*. London: Routledge, 2003. *Language policy* 5, 2006, 227-232. © Springer Science and Business Media.

Book review of Viv Edwards 2004. *Multilingualism in the English-speaking world. Pedigree of nations*, Oxford: Blackwell. *World Englishes*, 24/3, 2005, 395-397. © Wiley-Blackwell.

Book review of Angel M.Y. Lin and Peter W. Martin (eds) 2005. *Decolonisation, globalisation: Language-in-education policy and practice*. Clevedon: Multilingual Matters, 2005. *Studies in Second Language Acquisition* 29/1, 2007, 139-141. © Cambridge University Press.

Linguistic imperialism—an introductory encyclopedia entry

The study of linguistic imperialism focuses on how and why certain languages dominate internationally, and on attempts to account for such dominance in an explicit, theoretically founded way. Language is one of the most durable legacies of European colonial and imperial expansion. English, Spanish, and Portuguese are the dominant languages of the Americas. In Africa, the languages of some of the colonizing powers, England, France, and Portugal are more firmly entrenched than ever, as English is in several Asian countries.

The study of linguistic imperialism can help to clarify whether the winning of political independence led to a linguistic liberation of Third World countries, and if not, why not. Are the former colonial languages a useful bond with the international community and necessary for state formation and national unity internally? Or are they a bridgehead for Western interests, permitting the continuation of a global system of marginalization and exploitation? What is the relationship between linguistic dependence (continued use of a European language in a former non-European colony) and economic dependence (the export of raw materials and import of technology and know-how)? In a globalizing world, has English shifted from serving Anglo-American interests into functioning as an instrument for more diverse constituencies? Or does US dominance in the neoliberal economy constitute a new form of empire that consolidates a single imperial language?

Imperialism has traditionally been primarily concerned with economic and political aspects of dominance (Hobson 1902). Later theorists have been concerned with analyzing military, social, communication, and cultural activities, and the underlying structures and ideologies that link powerful countries, the 'Center,' with powerless countries, the 'Periphery,' and the structure of exploitation from which rich countries benefit and poor countries suffer (Galtung 1980). Resources are distributed unequally internally within each country, which has its own Center and Periphery, which in Marxist analysis is seen in terms of class (Holborrow 1999). Linguistic imperialism was manifestly a feature of the way nation-states privileged one language, and often sought actively to eradicate others, forcing their speakers to shift to the dominant language. It was a also a feature of colonial empires, involving a deeper degree of linguistic penetration in settler countries (e.g., Canada, New Zealand) than in exploitation and extraction colonies (e.g., Malaya, Nigeria). Linguistic imperialism presupposes an overarching structure of asymmetrical, unequal exchange, where language dominance dovetails with economic, political and other types of dominance. It entails unequal resource allocation and communicative rights between people defined in terms of their competence in specific languages, with unequal benefits as a result, in a system that legitimates and naturalizes such exploitation (Phillipson, 1992).

Linguistic imperialism can be regarded as a subcategory of cultural imperialism, along with media imperialism (e.g., news agencies, the world information order), educational imperialism (the export of Western institutional norms, teacher training, textbooks, etc., and World Bank policies privileging Center languages in education systems; Mazrui, 2004), and scientific imperialism (e.g. dissemination of paradigms and methodologies from the Center, which controls knowledge about the Periphery). Linguistic imperialism may dovetail with any of these, as for instance when English as the dominant language of science marginalizes other languages, English as 'Lingua Tyrannosaura' (Swales 1997, Ammon 2001, Phillipson 2002).

The mechanisms of linguistic imperialism are documented in works that link linguistics with colonialism (Calvet 1974 refers to linguistic racism, confirming the interlocking of 19th century philology with European racist thought), relate the promotion of English in educational 'aid' to the economic and political agendas of Center countries (Phillipson 1992), and discuss the effect of literacy on the local languages ecology, including the role of missionaries (Mühlhäusler 1996). Linguistic dominance has invariably been buttressed by ideologies that glorify the dominant language: as the language of God (Arabic, Dutch, Sanskrit), the language of reason, logic, and human rights (French over several centuries), the language of the superior ethonational group as advocated by imperialist racism (German in Nazi ideology), the language of modernity, technological progress, and national unity (English in much postcolonial discourse). A Ghanaian sociolinguist describes linguistic imperialism as

> The phenomenon in which the minds and lives of the speakers of a language are dominated by another language to the point where they believe that they can and should use only that foreign language when it comes to transactions dealing with the more advanced aspects of life such as education, philosophy, literature, governments, the administration of justice, etc....Linguistic imperialism has a way of warping the minds, attitudes, and aspirations of even the most noble in a society and preventing him from appreciating and realizing the full potentialities of the indigenous languages (Ansre 1979, 12).

There are studies that focus on the discourses accompanying linguistic hierarchies (Pennycook 1994), and the ambivalent role of English in contemporary India (Rajan 1992). English in Africa is seen as 'an imperial language, the language of linguistic Americanization, a language of global capitalism, ...creating and maintaining social divisions serving an economy dominated primarily by foreign economic interests and, secondarily, by a small aspiring African bourgeoisie' (Mazrui 2004, 30, 40, 50), though English is simultaneously appropriated for Afrocentricity in Africa and in the United States. The tension between the need to learn English for local empowerment alongside local languages, and the adequacy of our theories for addressing these issues has been explored (Canagarajah 1999, several contributions in Ricento 2000).

Fishman et al. (1996) is an anthology on *Post-Imperial English: Status Change in Former British and American Colonies, 1940–1990*, with contributions from many countries, who were asked to assess linguistic imperialism in each context. The editors see the need for English to be 'reconceptualized, from being an imperialist tool to being a multinational tool...English... being postimperial (as the title of our books implies, that is in the sense of not directly serving purely Anglo-American territorial, economic, or cultural expansion) without being postcapitalist in any way.' Fishman, in a 'summing-up and interpretation' of the contributions to the book, correlates the status of English with hard data on the use of English in the media, education, studies abroad, technology, administration, etc., and more subjective assessments. He tabulates the degree of 'anglification' in each state. His assessment is that the 'socioeconomic' factors that are behind the spread of English in former colonies is 'related more to their engagement in the modern world economy than to any efforts derived from their colonial masters' (1996: 639). Fishman seems to ignore the fact that 'engagement in the modern world' means a Western-dominated globalization agenda set by the transnational corporations, the international Monetary Fund, and the World Trade Organization, with the US military intervening whenever 'vital interests' are at risk. Although some contributors conclude that linguistic imperialism is not present, they have no difficulty in using the concept in country studies, and none question its validity or utility.

Others are more robust in distancing themselves from a linguistic imperialism approach, when reassessing the language policies of the colonial period and in theorizing about the role of English in the modern world (Brutt-Griffler 2002) and when describing the global constellation of languages (de Swaan 2001), on which see Phillipson (2004). English plays a supremely important role in the ongoing processes of globalization, which is seen by some scholars as synonymous with Americanization. English is playing an increasingly prominent role in continental European countries and in the institutions of the European Union, though in principle and law these are committed to maintaining linguistic diversity and the equality of the languages of the member states (Phillipson 2003). Increased European integration and market forces are, however, potentially leading to all continental European languages becoming second-class languages. This concern has led to the advocacy of Europe-wide policies to strengthen foreign language learning, but few European states (probably Sweden and Finland are those most active) have elaborated language policies to ensure the continued strength of national languages alongside competence in English and full respect for linguistic human rights.

One symptom of market forces is the major effort by 'English-speaking' states to expand their intake of foreign students. Higher education is increasingly seen as a market opportunity, a sector that the British government seeks to expand by 8 per cent per year between 2004 and 2020. The British economy benefits by £11 billion directly and a further £12 billion indirectly (British Council). Over half a million foreign students attend language schools in Britain each year. The English Language Teaching business is of major significance for the British economy. These figures reveal something of the complexity of the supply and demand elements of English as a commodity and cultural force. They also demonstrate the need for the analysis of linguistic dominance to shift from a colonial and postcolonial perspective to contemporary patterns that are maintained by more subtle means of control and influence, language playing an increasingly important role in the internationalization of many domains.

Thus in the teaching and marketing of 'communication skills,' a shift from linguistic imperialism to communicative imperialism can be seen: "Language becomes a global product available in different local flavours …. The dissemination of 'global' communicative norms and genres, like the dissemination of international languages, involves a one-way flow of expert knowledge from dominant to subaltern cultures" (Cameron 2002, 70). A focus on communication skills may well entail the dissemination of American ways of speaking and the forms of communication, genre, and style of the dominant consumerist culture, which globalization is extending worldwide.

In *Empire*, Hardt and Negri (2000) draw together many threads from political, economic, and cultural theory and philosophy and astutely unravel the role of communication in global social trends, and the ways in which language constitutes our universe and creates subjectivities. They reveal how the hegemonic power imposes or induces acceptance of its dominion. They show why it has been so important for the corporate world not only to dominate the media but also education, which is increasingly run to service the economy and to produce consumers rather than critical citizens. Linguistic dominance as such is not pursued in their book, and it is also largely neglected in social and political science. Linguistic imperialism, or linguistic dominance in the sense of the maintenance of injustice and inequality by means of language policies, is invariably connected to policies in commerce, science, international affairs, education, culture, and the media, all of which involve material resources and attitudes, and all of which evolve dynamically.

Bibliography

Ammon, Ulrich (ed.) 2001. *The Dominance of English as a Language of Science. Effects on other Languages and Language Communities.* Berlin: Mouton de Gruyter.

Brutt-Griffler, Janina 2002. *World English. A Study of its Development.* Clevedon: Multilingual Matters.

British Council. http://www.britishcouncil.org.

Calvet L-J (1974). *Linguistique et colonialisme: petit traité de glottophagie.* Paris: Payot.

Cameron, Deborah 2002. 'Globalization and the teaching of "communication" skills.' In David Block and Deborah Cameron (eds.) 2002. *Globalization and Language Teaching.* London: Routledge, 67–82.

Canagarajah, Suresh A. 1999. *Resisting Linguistic Imperialism in English Teaching.* Oxford: Oxford University Press.

de Swaan, Abram 2001. *Words of the World. The Global Language System.* Cambridge: Polity.

Fishman, Joshua, A., Andrew Conrad and Alma Rubal-Lopez (eds.) 1996. *Post-Imperial English: Status Change in Former British and American Colonies, 1940–1990.* Berlin: Mouton de Gruyter.

Galtung, J. 1980. *The True Words: A Transnational Perspective.* New York: Free Press.

Hardt, D. and Negri, Antonio 2000. *Empire.* Cambridge, MA: Harvard University Press.

Hobson, J. A. 1902. *Imperialism, A Study.* London : Allen & Unwin.

Holborrow, M. 1999. *The Politics of English. A Marxist View of Language,* London: Sage.

Mazrui, Alamin A. 2004. *English in Africa: After the Cold War.* Clevedon: Multilingual Matters.

Mühlhäusler, Peter 1996. *Linguistic Ecology. Language Change and Linguistic Imperialism in the Pacific Region.* London: Routledge.

Pennycook, Alastair 1994. *The Cultural Politics of English as an International Language.* Harlow: Longman.

Phillipson, Robert 1992. *Linguistic Imperialism*. Oxford: Oxford University Press.

Phillipson, Robert 2002. Review of Ammon 2001. *Journal of Language, Identity and Education*, 163–169.

Phillipson, Robert 2003. *English-Only Europe? Challenging Language Policy*. London: Routledge.

Phillipson, Robert 2004. 'English in globalization: three approaches (review of de Swaan, 2001, Block and Cameron, 2002, and Brutt-Griffler, 2002)'. *Journal of Language, Identity and Education*, Vol. 3, No. 1, 73–84.

Rajan, Rajeswari Sunder (ed.) 1992. *The Lie of the Land. English Literary Studies in India*. Delhi: Oxford University Press.

Ricento, Thomas (ed.) 2000. *Ideology, Politics and Language Policies: Focus on English*, Amsterdam: John Benjamins.

Swales, J. M. 1997. 'English as Tyrannosaurus Rex'. *World Englishes* Vol. 16, No. 3, 373–382.

Chapter 1

The study of continued linguistic imperialism

This book contains an encyclopedia entry on linguistic imperialism, seven articles that I have written since the appearance of my book *Linguistic Imperialism* in 1992, and six book reviews on closely related topics. It therefore reflects the way my thinking about the expansion of English worldwide has evolved over two decades. The scholarly study of 'global' English, language policy, language planning, language ideologies and sociolinguistics has expanded hugely in recent years. The global language map and the geopolitics of language are never static, so there is a constant need to fine-tune how linguistic imperialism can be approached, and evidence for or against it analysed.

There appears to be plenty of evidence for the continued relevance of the 1992 book. Oxford University Press authorised its publication in Shanghai, China in 2001; a South Asian edition was published by Oxford in Delhi in 2007; and a translation into Arabic will appear in 2009. The book itself was a first attempt to explore in a theoretically informed, multi-disciplinary way how and why English was strengthened worldwide in recent decades, and the role of language professionals and educators. Many found the work stimulating, others found it disturbing or disagreed with its conclusions. I am fully aware that the book is not the last word on linguistic imperialism, whether of English or other dominant languages. There is a need for a completely new study of linguistic imperialism in the 21st Century—which, alas, I can see no imminent prospect of—so I am delighted that this volume makes material that I have written in recent years easily available.

The articles and book reviews have been reprinted in the chronological order in which they were written.

- The first appeared in a volume entitled *Ideology, Politics and Language Policies: Focus on English* (Ricento 2000). It reviews several approaches to 'world' English, stresses the need for conceptual clarification when assessing language in globalisation, and demonstrates how linguistic imperialism persists. It reviews work by Crystal, Fishman, and Graddol that has been influential in positioning 'global' and 'post-imperial' English and in predicting the future of the language. Ricento's volume also included articles by scholars with related interests but with a different focus: Pennycook, who stresses discourse analysis and postcolonial uses of English (some of his points of criticism are discussed in the third section of this chapter), and Canagarajah, whose work has demonstrated how linguistic imperialism can be resisted through appropriation in a Sri Lanka context.

- The second article appeared in *An Introduction to Language Policy. Theory and Method* (Ricento 2006), in which my approach to linguistic imperialism is presented alongside that of others working in the rapidly expanding field of language policy. The article exemplifies how English is accommodating to and constitutes a neoimperial, US dominated world, leading possibly to a global linguistic apartheid.

- The third article rebuts an interpretation of linguistic imperialism as a 'conspiracy'.

- In the fourth article, ideas are explored in relation to contemporary developments in Europe.

- More global issues are dealt with in the fifth and sixth articles, which are longer and draw on new historical evidence.

- The seventh, as yet unpublished, article deals with university language policy and the trend towards English serving as the medium of instruction in higher education in an increasing number of countries worldwide. Should this be seen as a positive development, a panacea, or as a threat to other cultures and languages, a pandemic?

- The analysis of whether English is a *lingua franca* or a *lingua frankensteinia* was published in the journal *World Englishes* as a lead article in a Forum to which seven scholars were invited to contribute. They have kindly agreed to their Comments being reproduced in this book.

- The book reviews deal with topics that are not significantly addressed elsewhere in this anthology: how English is taught to immigrants in Britain, the dominance of English as a language of science worldwide, alternative analyses of the global language system and 'world English', globalization and language teaching, translation and globalization, multilingualism in the English-speaking world, and the impact of decolonization and globalization on language-in-education policy and practice in a range of countries.

A brief word on what the book does not include. It makes little reference to two of my major concerns of the past two decades. The first is *linguistic human rights*, a language policy topic on which I have edited three books, two of them with colleagues (Skutnabb-Kangas and Phillipson 1994; Kontra, Phillipson, Skutnabb-Kangas and Várady 1999, Phillipson 2000). The second is the increasing role of English in European Union, explored in *English-only Europe? Challenging language policy* (Phillipson 2003). A summary of this book and a number of articles are available for downloading from my homepage, <www.cbs. dk/staff/phillipson>. I have also chosen not to include any of the responses I wrote to book reviews of *Linguistic Imperialism* that I felt needed a reply (Phillipson 1993, 1995, 1996, 1997, 1999), since these are of a more ephemeral nature. Nor have I included a retrospective interview (Phillipson 2005).

What this introduction aims at is not to anticipate or sum up the analysis presented throughout the book but to

- provide some 2009 glimpses of English as a centrally significant component of Anglo-American attempts to 'rule the world' (Engler 2008), in English of course,

- present two tabulations of the many factors that are currently strengthening English, and

- comment on some critiques of *Linguistic Imperialism* that are not taken up in the articles.

English is in great *demand* worldwide. The British are also keen to promote the *supply* side—books, dictionaries, textbooks, educational know-how, advisers—and to ensure that the learning of English is to the benefit of Britain economically, culturally and politically. On the occasion of Gordon Brown's first visit to China and India as Prime Minister he announced a plan to make British English the global language of 'choice'.[1] The British Council, the government-funded body responsible for promoting Britain and English worldwide, states on its website[2] that Brown's project involves 'a boost to English language learning, teaching and training facilities for people throughout the world. We will help develop a new website to offer learners and teachers around the world ready access to the materials, resources and qualifications they need to develop their skills in English. Gordon Brown announced how the British Council will be starting a programme in India to recruit "Master Trainers" charged with developing the skills of 750,000 teachers of English over a five-year period. These initiatives are being developed by our teams in China, India and the UK.'

One wonders what role the Indians and Chinese have in this project, and whether the high-profile British initiative has evolved from any concerted effort to assess what language learning needs are the most urgent ones in Asia (on promoting multilingual education worldwide, including India and Nepal, see Mohanty et al, 2009). The popular 'demand' for English-medium schools or instruction reflects awareness that success in English opens doors, but has little to do with insight into what has to be in place in education to ensure successful learning – meaning, in particular, well qualified teachers and the cognitive development of children in the mother tongue. Equally uninformed is the blind faith in such Asian countries as China, Japan, Korea and Thailand that by importing thousands of native speakers of English, the effective learning of English will be assured—which is educational nonsense. Such faith reflects a continued belief in what I formulated in *Linguistic Imperialism* (1992, chapter 7) as the five tenets:

- English is best taught monolingually
- The ideal teacher of English is a native speaker
- The earlier English is taught, the better the results
- The more English is taught, the better the results
- If other languages are used much, standards of English will drop.

The book documents in considerable detail that each principle is absolutely false:

- the monolingual fallacy
- the native speaker fallacy
- the early start fallacy
- the maximum exposure fallacy
- the subtractive fallacy.

Adherence to the five tenets is fundamental to the British English teaching business. The British Council's corporate plan 2008–2011 anticipates an income of over £100 million from English teaching activities in 50 countries in the first year, and an equivalent amount from the administration of British exams. Priority areas for strengthening cultural links with Britain are trouble spots like the Middle East and Central Asia, plus the 'emergent economies' of India, China and Brazil. The higher education market for foreign students is big business for the USA, Australia, and New Zealand as well as the UK, and the skills learned through the language are central to the functioning of the contemporary world economy.

It would be naïve to assume that the Brown initiative represents altruistic 'aid'. The Rupert Murdoch-owned British tabloid the *Sun* declared that Brown believes his scheme will 'add a staggering £50billion a year to the UK economy by 2010.' Imperialism, including linguistic imperialism, has always been about profit. One of the British Council's primary functions is to ensure that the English language 'industry' will continue to thrive, despite geopolitical changes affecting the many functions and forms of English worldwide (see Graddol

2006), through setting agendas that will strengthen British economic and cultural interests. Brown's strategy is to influence globalization through English, and to cash in on it. The term globalization is deceptive, since it reveals nothing of who the winners and losers are in this phase of global economic relations.

Mainstream 'development aid' to education has an appalling track record, which ought to make one sceptical about whether the British English Language Teaching (ELT) sector can solve educational learning problems in India or anywhere else. Most British people are notoriously monolingual. ELT qualifications in the major 'English-speaking' countries typically do not require evidence of successful foreign language learning or experience of multilingualism. Educational language projects in Asia in the 1990s are surveyed in the papers in *Language and Development. Teachers in a Changing World* (Kenny and Savage 1997). It contains a fund of reflective analysis of the factors contributing to the triumphs and, more frequently, the failures of development aid projects. What is striking is that the title of the book itself seems to assume that English is a panacea. 'Language' refers exclusively to English. All 'teachers' in our changing world are apparently teachers of English. This invisibilisation of the rest of the relevant languages is a re-run of much colonial and postcolonial language-in-education policy, which, as is well known, has served European languages well and other languages much less well. It reflects investment being put into English, an infrastructure and ideology that discursively construct English as the handmaiden of globalisation, the universal medium. The interlocking of language with cultural and economic globalisation is lucidly and insightfully explored in Naz Rassool's *Global Issues in Language, Education and Development* (2007).

In the 21st century, 'empire' has increasingly figured in the political discourse of advocates and critics. In *How to Rule the World. The Coming Battle over the Global Economy* (Engler 2008), a clear distinction is made between the *corporate globalization* of the final decades of the 20th century and its successor, imperial globalization based on military dominance. While the two clearly overlap, Bush II's policies represent a paradigm shift in how US world empire is asserted, with corporate interests divided about the desirability of this change. Engler makes a case for *democratic globalization*, which he hopes will emerge from the groundswell of popular resistance to disastrous military policies and to unjust economic policies. The major changes in Latin America, with many countries attempting to resist US dominance, are also grounds for optimism.

From the time of the USA declaring its independence, it has seen itself as a model for the world, with a divine mission to impose its values. George Washington saw the United States as a 'new empire' and a 'rising empire', and in 1786 wrote that, 'However unimportant America may be considered at present...there will assuredly come a day when this country will have some weight in the scale of empires.' The address was read out in its entirety in Congress every February until the mid-1970s' (Roberts 2008, 68[3]).

Roberts (2008, 144) also cites Rudyard Kipling, who wrote in his autobiography that he 'never got over the wonder of a people who, having extirpated the aboriginals of their continent more completely than any other modern race had done, honestly believed they were a godly New England community, setting examples to brutal Mankind.'

US national identity was forged through massive violence, the dispossession and extermination of the indigenous peoples, the myth of unoccupied territory, the surplus value extorted from slave labour, and an active process of national imagination to form a common identity, one deeply permeated by religion (Hixson 2008). The nationalist revolt of 1776 and the ensuing state formation and constitution privileged white male slave-owning Euro-Americans. These founding fathers devised a constitution in which ' "We, the people" elided hierarchies of race, class, and gender.' (ibid., 39), the Other being stigmatised as sub-human and therefore exterminable. The architects of the American Revolution were highly literate, 75 per cent were English-speaking, seeing themselves as involved in 'a sacred event ordained by God for the redemption of all of mankind. Even Benjamin Franklin, the leading scientific rationalist, declared, "Our cause is the cause of all mankind, and we are fighting for their liberty in defending our own. It is a glorious task assigned us by Providence"' (ibid., 37). This Myth of America has been echoed continuously over three centuries, notably in the rhetoric of Bush II, with active support from several European leaders.[4]

Think tanks are promoting closer links between English-speaking countries, with India included as an English-speaking country (Bennett 2004). A central message, at least in the USA but probably elsewhere, is that 'Multiculturalism and bilingualism should be abandoned, and assimilation and learning of English should become national policies' (Bennett 2007, 85). This exemplifies how the massive forces behind imperial globalisation are being advocated and legitimated, in ways that are directly or indirectly connected to how English functions locally. We need to be aware of the agendas, often hidden ones, at both the global and local levels.

In his book *Critical Applied Linguistics*, Pennycook (2001, 59–63) relates linguistic imperialism to other approaches to the global role of English, both more celebratory ones and more critical ones. He correctly notes that linguistic imperialism is one type of linguicism,[5] with material and ideological dimensions that presuppose an understanding of language as power. However, he distances himself from my approach in several ways:

- Pennycook rightly raises the question (without answering it) of how English linguistic imperialism (which he reductively restricts to 'the promotion of English') 'creates the forms of imperialism' rather just reflecting them. As I see it, one of the major challenges of work within a linguistic imperialism approach is to specify precisely the role that language policy plays in constituting and maintaining relations of unequal dominance. The articles in this book hopefully show how this can be done.

- Pennycook falsely states that my approach entails a principle that one should 'teach English sparingly' (ibid., 59). I have never in my writings suggested that people should not learn English optimally —that would be silly and counter-productive in the modern world. What I have insisted on is that English should not be learned or used in ways that serve to subjugate or obliterate other languages, for instance through a monolingual approach, which is educationally unsound and installs or reinforces an inequitable language hierarchy.

- Pennycook considers that a linguistic imperialism approach entails an excessive focus on structural power that fails to explain why people choose to learn and use English; he suggests that my analysis underplays agency, resistance and appropriation. Canagarajah also stresses the need for more focus on how competition between English and other languages is experienced at the grassroots level, the 'micropolitics of language use' (cited ibid., 63). I would claim that the two levels, micro and macro, global and local, do not exclude each other, quite the opposite. A valid approach to the analysis of English must do justice to both the micro and macro levels and their interlocking. It is therefore false to claim (ibid., 59) that linguistic imperialism is 'Too powerful a model of structural power; strong on structure, weak on potential effects'—though clearly the over-arching concept 'linguistic imperialism' is a very broad one. The effects of linguistic imperialism are only too visible, with English invariably at the summit of linguistic hierarchies, parents anxious for their children to benefit from English-medium education, and proficient users of English often at an advantage vis-à-vis others. The language is naively seen as a panacea, though the reality of the conditions that need to be met for creating educational success, or symmetrical equitable communication, and for maintaining a balanced ecology of languages in any given context is far more complex than meets the eye, with the structural power of English and the forces behind it not immediately apparent.

- Pennycook states that linguistic imperialism is 'first and foremost an economic model, with the nations at the *center* exploiting the nations in the *periphery*' (ibid., 62), which he sees as reductive of global relations and inadequate for dealing with culture. I consider this an invalid objection, since the values and beliefs that are ascribed to English are part and parcel of its institutionalisation in education (e.g. in the five ELT fallacies, see above) and other domains of cultural life. These ideological traits are in a dialectic relationship with the resources that are invested in one language rather than others (university degrees, teacher training, school time, etc). In addition the relationships between centre and periphery change over time: for linguicism to be in force in any given postcolonial periphery context or in continental Europe (Phillipson 2003) presupposes the willing complicity of local elites and professionals. The dilemma that this puts the periphery in, is captured insightfully by Thiru Kandiah of Sri Lanka. He sees countries in the postcolonial world as trapped in a major contradiction. On the one hand, they need the 'indispensable global medium' for pragmatic purposes, even for survival in the global economy. On the other there is the fact that the medium is not culturally or ideologically neutral, far from it, so that its users run the 'apparently unavoidable risk of co-option, of acquiescing in the negation of their own understandings of reality and in the accompanying denial or even subversion of their own interests' (Kandiah 2001, 112). What is therefore needed in relation to English is 'interrogating its formulations of reality, intervening in its modes of understanding, holding off its normalising tendencies, challenging its hegemonic designs and divesting it of the co-optive power which would render it a reproducing discourse' (ibid.). Kandiah advocates authentic local projections of reality, and emancipatory action.

These issues are difficult and challenging. The need to critically evaluate how English is used and learned, and to decolonise our minds, is as much a task for the centre as it is for the periphery. There are thoughtful reflections on the interconnections between the global English teaching profession and its ideological foundations in the contributions to *(Re-)Locating TESOL in an Age of Empire* (Edge, ed., 2006). As researchers we need to ensure that the ethical principles and value judgements that underpin our activities are made clear, as a necessary foundation for valid, objective and enlightened analysis. Each of us should aim at being an 'interpretative specialist', whose 'virtues consist of passionate conviction, uncompromising intellectual integrity, and, most important of all, a Socratic knowledge of one's own self'—to cite the scholarly principles espoused by one of the key founders of social science research, Max Weber (see Sung Ho Kim 2007, 130-131). What we have to avoid is unreflective positivism and academic exhibitionism (ibid.), which unfortunately a great deal of applied linguistic research suffers from.

Ashis Nandy expresses the issue very insightfully: 'colonized Indians do not remain in these pages simple-hearted victims of colonialism; they become participants in a moral and cognitive oppression' (1988, xiv) that can only be shaken off by a 'recovery of self'. As a Westerner, what one needs to appreciate is that 'liberation ultimately had to begin from the colonized and end with the colonizers. As Gandhi was so clearly to formulate through his own life, freedom is indivisible, not only in the popular sense that the oppressed of the world are one but also in the unpopular sense that the oppressor too is caught in the culture of oppression' (ibid., 63). Language plays a central role in the processes of creating and counteracting linguistic imperialism. We therefore have a moral duty to combat the culture of linguistic oppression.

Many factors are involved in the expansion of English, supply and demand, push and pull factors. In my book on what currently is happening to the linguistic map of Europe (Phillipson 2003), one chapter is devoted to global trends impacting on language policy, with sub-sections on commerce, science, culture and education. In it I tabulate many of the factors, grouping them crudely as either structural or ideological (op.cit., 64-65).

Table 1. Factors contributing to the increased use of English in Europe

A. Structural

1. English is an integral dimension of ongoing globalisation processes in commerce, finance, politics, military affairs, science, education, and the media. The adoption of English as the key corporate, institutional, and scholarly language for such activities

is symptomatic of this trend. The frequent use of English in networking, NGOs (Non-Governmental Organisations), subcultural youth groups, and the internet consolidates the language at the grassroots level.

2. The Americans and British have invested heavily in promoting their language globally since the mid-1950s.

3. Higher education in the USA, the UK and Australia attracts increasing numbers of students from all over the world, including continental Europe, in part because the language of instruction is English.

4. There has been substantial investment in the teaching of English in the education systems of continental European countries.

5. Levels of foreign language competence vary widely, but there tend to be more people who are proficient in English in the demographically small countries.

6. In continental Europe there is an increasing tendency for universities to offer courses and degrees taught in English. This is a general trend, particularly at graduate level in the north of Europe, and in such fields as Business Studies. In some schools the trend is to teach a content subject through the medium of English.

7. There is a poor scholarly infrastructure at European universities and research institutes for the analysis of language policy, multilingualism, and language rights, reflecting a lack of investment in this field.

8. Responsibility for language policy in each country tends to be shared between ministries of foreign affairs, education, culture, research, and commerce. They each tend to have little expertise in language policy, and between them there is inadequate coordination, if any. In countries with a federal structure, responsibility is even more diffuse.

9. As English is used extensively by native and non-native speakers from different parts of the world, there is no simple correlation between English and the interests of a particular state. The connection of English to the dominant economic system and to

global networking remains.

10. The mobility of labour, more extensive international links, and cross-cultural marriages reinforce a pattern of language shift towards dominant languages, particularly English.

B. Ideological

11. Major differences in the ideologies underpinning the formation of states, and in the role ascribed to language in these (*jus sanguinis*, Herder, e.g. Germany v. *jus soli*, citizenship, e.g. France) mean that language issues are understood differently in different countries, this impeding a shared understanding of language policy issues.

12. Attitudes to multilingualism are affected by people's exposure to and use of foreign languages and minority languages. These affect people's awareness of linguistic diversity and language rights, and their motivation for learning additional languages.

13. Levels of awareness about language policy issues range widely between and within each EU country. They tend to be relatively high in, for instance, Finland and Greece, and low in Denmark and England.

14. There is a popular demand for English that is strongly connected to a language that is projected in advertising and the media as connoting success, influence, consumerism, and hedonism.

15. Ranking languages for their purported qualities or limitations, through processes of glorification and stigmatization, correlates with language hierarchies and their hegemonic rationalization.

Many of the factors may be equally relevant in other parts of the world. Empirical studies can analyse whether the learning or use of English is additive or subtractive, whether it increases the linguistic repertoire of the group and the individual, or on the contrary, constrains it, triggering language attrition and in its most extreme forms, the annihilation of languages.

Many of these dimensions are brought together in two paradigms that have been elaborated by my wife and frequent co-author, Tove Skutnabb-Kangas (2008, 657):

Table 2. The Diffusion of English and Ecology of Languages paradigms

1. monolingualism and linguistic genocide	1. multilingualism, and linguistic diversity
2. promotion of subtractive learning of dominant languages	2. promotion of additive foreign/second language learning
3. linguistic, cultural and media imperialism	3. equality in communication
4. Americanization and homogenization of world culture	4. maintenance and exchange of cultures
5. ideological globalization and internationalization	5. ideological localisation and exchange
6. capitalism, hierarchization	6. economic democratisation
7. rationalization based on science and technology	7. human rights perspective, holistic integrative values
8. modernization and economic efficiency; quantitative growth	8. sustainability through promotion of diversity; qualitative growth
9. transnationalization	9. protection of local production and national sovereignties
10. growing polarization and gaps between haves and never-to-haves	10. redistribution of the world's material resources

Given the crucial role of English in maintaining the global system, and if we wish to work for best-case scenarios and a pluralist global language ecology, how can sociolinguists and language in education people contribute? We have a long way to go, if English is to strengthen linguistic diversity.

Governments in many countries are constraining academic freedom step by step, through budgetary control, through evaluation exercises, and through creating a climate of opinion in which conformity to dominant political and economic agendas grinds academics into defensiveness and passivity. The results of this can be seen in the way universities are being turned into mass production machines that do not generate critical thinking.

The journalist John Pilger (2002) interprets the relatively 'apolitical' stance of academics as meaning that they accept and condone state terrorism. This can be seen in escapism in the humanities and in such social science subjects as political science, which is subservient to the dominant political system, an archetypal product of American university thinking:

> Humanities departments—the engine rooms of ideas and criticism- are close to moribund…The task of liberal realists is to ensure that western imperialism is interpreted as crisis management, rather than the cause of the crisis and its escalation. By never recognising western state terrorism, their complicity is assured.

This does not mean that individual academics have accepted what the British and U.S. governments have chosen to do in Iraq, or World Bank policies that increase the gaps between global haves and have-nots. But it may mean that our disciplines and activities are so self-contained and marginal that they underpin an unethical world order and implicitly accept it. This is why we need to relate our professional concerns to the evidence of English in the wider society, in an uncertain world with shifts of power balances (towards China, India, Brazil), and an unsustainable global economy and ecology.

There is a small measure of duplication in the articles which I would ask the reader to be patiently tolerant of. In particular some of my 'favourite' quotations recur. This reflects the fact that the articles were initially published separately, and since the anthology consists of reproductions of the original articles, it has not been possible to adjust the text. I trust that this is a minor inconvenience.

Notes

[1]   The Prime Minister's Press Release of 17 January 2008, http://www.
number-10.gov.uk/output/Page14289.asp. By May the text appears
to have been removed.

[2]   http://www.britishcouncil.org/home-about-us-world-of-difference-
india-english-language-teaching.htm?mtklink=india-english-language-
teaching-world-of-difference-clickthrough-link.

[3]   Citing Warren Zimmermann 2002. *First Great Triumph: How Five
Americans Made their Country a Great power*, New York.

[4]   The British connection, articulated by Tony Blair and Gordon Brown,
is explored in the article on neoliberal empire. Other cheer-leaders
include Berlusconi and the Danish prime minister, Anders Fog
Rasmussen, who stated (in an interview for the newspaper *Information*
on 28 June 2008) that European powers have a duty to attempt to
spread and market their values worldwide: 'we have to go out and
fight for them.'

[5]   Linguicism is defined as ideologies, structures and practices which
are used to legitimate, effectuate, regulate and reproduce an unequal
division of power and resources (both material and immaterial)
between groups which are defined on the basis of language. See
definition boxes 1.1 and 5.4 in Skutnabb-Kangas 2008.

References

Bennett, James C. 2004. *The Anglosphere Challenge. Why the English-Speaking
Nations will Lead the Way in the Twenty-First Century.* Lanham, MD:
Rowman and Littlefield.

Bennett, James C. 2007. *The Third Anglosphere Century; The English-
Speaking World in an Era of Transition.* www.heritage.org/bookstore/
anglosphere

Canagarajah, Suresh A. 1999. *Resisting Linguistic Imperialism in English
Teaching.* Oxford: Oxford University Press.

Edge, Julian (ed.) 2006. *(Re-)Locating TESOL in an Age of Empire.*
Basingstoke: Palgrave Macmillan.

Engler, Mark 2008. *How to Rule the World. The Coming Battle over the Global
Economy.* New York: Nation Books.

Graddol, David 2006. *English Next. Why Global English May Mean the End of 'English as a Foreign Language'.* London: British Council.

Hixson, Walter L. 2008. *The Myth of American Diplomacy. National Identity and U.S. Foreign Policy.* New Haven: Yale University Press.

Kandiah, Thiru 2001. 'Whose Meanings? Probing the Dialectics of English as a global language'. In Robbie Goh et al. (eds.) *Ariels – departures and returns: A festschrift for Edwin Thumboo.* Singapore: Oxford University Press.

Kenny, Brian and William Savage (eds.) 1997. *Language and Development. Teachers in a Changing World.* Harlow and New York: Addison Wesley Longman.

Kim, Sung Ho 2007. *Max Weber's Politics of Civil Society.* Cambridge: Cambridge University Press.

Miklós Kontra, Robert Phillipson, Tove Skutnabb-Kangas and Tibor Várady (eds.) 1999. *Language, a Right and a Resource. Approaching Linguistic Human Rights.* Budapest: Central European University Press.

Mohanty, Ajit, Minati Panda, Robert Phillipson and Tove Skutnabb-Kangas (eds.) 2009. *Multilingual Education for Social Justice: Globalising the Local.* Delhi: Orient Blackswan.

Also published in a slightly modified version as: Skutnabb-Kangas, Tove, Ajit Mohanty, Minati Panda and Robert Phillipson (eds.) 2009. *Social Justice through Multilingual Education.* Bristol: Multilingual Matters.

Nandy, Ashis 1988. *The Intimate Enemy. Loss and Recovery of Self under Colonialism.* New Delhi: Oxford University Press (first published 1983).

Pennycook, Alastair 2001. *Critical Applied Linguistics: A Critical Introduction.* Mahwah, NJ: Lawrence Erlbaum Associates.

Phillipson, Robert 1992. *Linguistic Imperialism.* Oxford: Oxford University Press.

Phillipson, Robert 1993. Reply to Five Book Reviews, Symposium on Linguistic Imperialism. *World Englishes* Vol. 12, No. 3, 365–373.

Phillipson, Robert 1995. Response to John Honey's review of *Linguistic Imperialism. RASK,* Vol. 3, 137–140.

Phillipson, Robert 1996. 'Linguistic imperialism—African Perspectives'. *English Language Teaching Journal,* Vol. 50, No. 2, 160–167.

Phillipson, Robert 1997. 'Realities and Myths of Linguistic Imperialism'. *Journal of Multilingual and Multicultural Development*, Vol. 18, No. 3, 238–247.

Phillipson, Robert 1999. 'Linguistic Imperialism Re-Visited—or Re-Invented. A Rejoinder to a Review Essay'. *International Journal of Applied Linguistics*, Vol. 9, No. 1, 135–137; and 'A closing word', 142.

Phillipson, Robert (ed.) 2000. *Rights to Language: Equity, Power and Education.* New York: Lawrence Erlbaum Associates.

Phillipson, Robert 2003. *English-Only Europe? Challenging Language Policy.* London: Routledge.

Phillipson, Robert 2005. 'Linguistic imperialism 10 years on. Sohail Karmani interviews Robert Phillipson'. *ELT Journal*, Vol. 59, No. 3, 244–249.

Pilger, John 2002. *The New Rulers of the World.* London and New York: Verso.

Rassool, Naz 2007. *Global Issues in Language, Education and Development: Perspectives from Postcolonial Countries.* Clevedon: Multilingual Matters, and New Delhi: Orient Blackswan, 2009.

Roberts, Andrew 2008. *A History of the English-Speaking Peoples Since 1900.* New York: Harper Perennial (first published 2006).

Skutnabb-Kangas, Tove 2008. *Linguistic Genocide in Education—Or Worldwide Diversity and Human Rights?* New Delhi: Orient Longman (originally published by Lawrence Erlbaum Associates, 2000).

Skutnabb-Kangas, Tove and Robert Phillipson (eds, in collaboration with Mart Rannut) 1994. *Linguistic Human Rights: Overcoming Linguistic Discrimination.* Berlin: Mouton de Gruyter.

English in the new world order: variations on a theme of linguistic imperialism and 'world' English

Chapter 2

Approaches to 'world' English

This paper considers some of the new forms that linguistic imperialism is taking in the contemporary world, suggests how the dominance of English and inequality can be approached, and reviews three recent books on English as a 'world' language (Crystal 1997, Fishman, Conrad and Rubal-Lopez 1996, and Graddol 1997). Analysis of English in the new world order presupposes agreement on the two objects in focus, the language English, and the globalization processes that characterize the contemporary post-cold-war phase of aggressive casino capitalism, economic restructuring, McDonaldization and militarization on all continents. There is a considerable literature on both phenomena, on English in all its diversity, and on globalization and a posited new world order. By contrast there is an alarming absence of literature that brings the two together.

The huge literature on English includes excellent portrayals of the history of how and why the language expanded (Bailey 1991, Mühlhäusler 1996), and many descriptions of its diversity in different parts of the world. There are also radical-critical analyses by scholars in the South who challenge Western professional orthodoxies. Dasgupta (1993), for instance, convincingly demonstrates that English is not in an organic relationship with Indian languages or the mass of Indian people; Parakrama (1995) explores the distinctiveness of Sri Lankan English and its distance from an Anglo norm; and Rajan (1992) laments the continuing dependence in India on Western content in higher education, not least in the subject English, and its irrelevance to the needs of most Indians.

These *cris de coeur* from globally peripheral cultures have affinities to critiques of linguistics for failing to address the role of language in societal reproduction. Bourdieu (1991) shows how linguists working in a Saussurean tradition cut themselves off from social reality when focussing on a standard language but simultaneously ignoring the processes of state formation that have led to 'a unified linguistic market, dominated by the official language' (ibid., 45). In similar vein Mufwene (1997) demonstrates that the concepts and terminology used in relation to English, 'new Englishes', and creoles, involve biassed processes of hierarchization of 'legitimate and illegitimate offspring of English', and are fundamentally flawed and ethnocentric. There are therefore basic epistemological and methodological questions that need to be addressed: they relate to what it is we are analysing, and to the adequacy and validity of our concepts and procedures. When analysing English worldwide the crux of the matter is whose interests English serves, and whose interests scholarship on English serves. Ngũgĩ wa Thiong'o, the Kenyan novelist, and a key thinker in the study of linguistic oppression, encapsulates the issues vividly as follows:

> A new world order that is no more than a global dominance of neo-colonial relations policed by a handful of Western nations ... is a disaster for the peoples of the world and their cultures ... The languages of Europe were taught as if they were our own languages, as if Africa had no tongues except those brought there by imperialism, bearing the label MADE IN EUROPE. (Ngũgĩ 1993, xvi, 35)

In additional to critical voices from the South, there is in the North Pennycook's work (1994) on the cultural politics of English as an international language, inspired by Foucault and critical pedagogy, and my own linguistic imperialism (Phillipson 1992), which looks particularly at the role of applied linguistics in maintaining North–South inequity, and attempts to develop a theoretical framework for the analysis of linguistic hierarchisation. Such work in critical applied linguistics represents a challenge to specialists in English to reconsider their/our professional identities. Though this is an uncomfortable process, the evidence from many professional fora seems to be that many are willing to engage in it.

My title refers to English rather than Englishes, though I approve of the principle of celebrating the multiplicity of Englishes, and liberating the languages from narrow conceptions of ownership (McArthur 1998). It is legitimate and valid to consider local uses and functions of English as forming a distinct language. There may be strategic or political reasons for linguistic declarations of independence. Noah Webster blazed this trail two centuries ago, the Australians followed suit about twenty years ago, and any English-using nation-state could have strong reasons for doing the same. This could permit education in post-colonial contexts such as Nigeria or India to build on internal, local uses and forms of English, and to leave the acquisition of internationally intelligible forms of English until a later stage. When considering globalization, however, it is important to look at English as one language, because we are abstracting from a multiplicity of forms in order to situate English in the wider linguistic ecology, in processes of hierarchization of languages, in the realities of structural power nationally and supra-nationally.

Conceptual clarification

We can begin the process of decolonizing our minds by critically evaluating our concepts. What does 'English as a world language' refer to? Only a tiny fraction of the population of most countries in the world, including those often described as 'English-speaking' countries in Africa and Asia, actually speaks English, meaning that terms like 'English as a world language' grossly misrepresent the reality of the communication experience of most of the world's population. More seriously, such terms as 'global English', 'anglophone Africa', or reference to English as a 'universal' *lingua franca* conceal the fact that the use of English serves the interests of some much better than others. Its use includes some and excludes others.

Language 'spread' is another apparently innocuous term that refers to a seemingly agentless process, as though it is not people and particular interests that account for the expansion of a language.

And what is 'international' communication? The label 'international language' was applied to planned languages like Esperanto long before English, Russian and other dominant languages were referred to as 'international'. Probal Dasgupta (1997, 2000) suggests that communication between people of different nationalities would be more appropriately designated as 'inter-local' since the language they use permits communication between people from different local cultures, and is in this sense inter-cultural. In much person-to-person communication, one's national or international identity is not in focus, unlike many other aspects of one's identity. Nations do not speak unto nations, except in the slogans of missionary societies, bodies that had great difficulty in distinguishing between preaching the word of God and promoting the political and economic interests of their countries of origin. This was as true of missionaries 200 years ago as it is today.

There are thus many terms in the sociology of language that are grounded in implicit, covert value judgements. We need to be constantly vigilant in reflecting on the ideological load of our concepts, and how they relate to, and probably serve to underpin and legitimate a hierarchical linguistic order.

The expansion of English in recent decades has occurred simultaneously with a widening gap between haves and have-nots, and with a consolidation of wealth and power globally in fewer hands. I am not suggesting a direct causal link between English and processes of global enrichment and impoverishment, but to suggest that the two are not connected, which is basically Crystal's position (1997), seems to me to be irresponsible. His book is entitled 'English as a Global Language', a seemingly neutral designation that appears to presuppose that the term 'global' is unproblematical, and that we all know what it refers to. Neither premise is correct. The sociology of language has to do better than that. And you don't have to be a sociologist to register that our world is increasingly dominated by Coca Cola, CNN, Microsoft and the many transnational corporations for whom the key language is English, and who through processes of McDonaldization (see below) are seeking to create and imagine, in Benedict Anderson's sense (1983), a global consumerist culture, a single market.

Globalization has economic, technological, cultural and linguistic strands to it. The globalization of English in diverse contexts, post-colonial, post-communist and western European, is one such interconnected strand in asymmetrical flows of products, ideas and discourses. Thus we live in a world in which 80% of films shown in western Europe are of Californian origin, whereas 2% of films shown in North America are of European origin (Hamelink 1994: 114). The trend towards the creation of the impression of a global culture through production for global markets, so that products and information aim at creating 'global customers that want global services by global suppliers' can be termed McDonaldization (Ritzer 1996), which means 'aggressive round-the-clock marketing, the controlled information flows that do not confront people with the long-term effects of an ecologically detrimental lifestyle, the competitive advantage against local cultural providers, the obstruction of local initiative, all converge into a reduction of local cultural space' (Hamelink 1994, 112).

In the contemporary world the imagined community of the nation-state is being superseded by global and regional alliances and governmental, non-governmental and private organizations. It is now the world that is being imagined and shaped by media magnates, transnational companies, drafters of human rights documents, and a variety of grassroots interests (for instance internet, music, amateur radio, Preisler 1999). At the heart of globalization is the 'tension between cultural homogenization and cultural heterogenization' (Appadurai 1990, 295).

Globalization and Englishization are discreetly penetrating a mass of economic, political, and cultural domains in complex ways (Phillipson and Skutnabb-Kangas 1999). As well as being a means of communication and a marker of identity, English is a big commodity, second in importance to the British economy after North Sea oil. Commodities are marketed in a range of ways, some overt, some more covert. English has powerful advocates. One example: at an informal lunch at our university (Roskilde) in March 1997, the American ambassador to Denmark, Mr Elton, who has a background in the corporate world, stated that the most serious problem for the European Union (EU) was that it had so many languages, this preventing real integration and development of the Union. No prize for guessing which language he thinks would solve all the EU's problems.

English linguistic imperialism

The expansion of English was not left to chance on either side of the Atlantic. Language professionals have willingly contributed to it: Ogden, the inventor of BASIC English (BASIC = British American Scientific International Commercial) promoted his 'auxiliary' language in the belief that 'what the world needs is about 1000 more dead languages—and one more alive' (written in 1934, cited in Bailey 1991, 210). He was not thinking of a democratic language like Esperanto, which has come to life in ways that I find fascinating and challenging for anyone concerned with language policy and equity. He was thinking of a simplified form of English as a stepping-stone to the language proper. Randolph Quirk's 'Nuclear English' is a more recent variation on this theme, which fits well with his insistence on a single standard for global English, one that by his own admission only the few can hope to master, and that he describes and prescribes. The 'Comprehensive' grammar of English that he co-authored (Quirk, Greenbaum, Leech and Svartvik 1985) is only comprehensive in relation to standardized forms.

To effectuate the spread of English, teachers of English were needed. A key policy document for the post-colonial age was written by an adviser to the British Council in 1941 outlining the case: 'a new career service is needed, to lay the foundations of a world-language and culture based on our own...an army of linguistic missionaries... a central office in London, from which teachers radiate all over the world' (Routh 1941: 12-13). When I graduated from an elite British university at a tender age I was commissioned into this 'army', i.e. into the British Council version of cultural diplomacy. This was at the height of the cultural cold war (Saunders 1999). After a couple of months of pitifully inadequate training I found myself in Algeria and later Yugoslavia in posts referred to as that of an 'English Language Officer'. The militaristic terminology is not coincidental. Nowadays such rank would be graded in such favourably loaded terms as 'adviser' or 'expert', implying high status on a professional hierarchy of the kind that Illich warns against:

> Professional imperialism triumphs even where political and economic domination has been broken...The knowledge-capitalism of professional imperialism subjugates people more imperceptibly than and as effectively as international finance and weaponry...The possibility of a convivial society depends therefore on a new consensus about the destructiveness of imperialism at three levels: the pernicious spread of one nation beyond its boundaries; the omnipresent influence of multinational corporations; and the mushrooming of professional monopolies over production. Politics for convivial reconstruction of society must especially face imperialism on this third level, where it takes the form of professionalism. (Illich 1973, 56–7)

The British and American variants of TESOL are significant agents in the spread of English, taking over where colonial education left off. Their origins and formative professional ideologies are now well documented (Phillipson 1992; Pennycook 1994, 1998). The significance and role of the English teaching profession in the current intensive phase of globalization is under-explored and emphatically needs closer scrutiny. Exploring it is a tricky and messy business because of the interlocking of language with so many other dimensions, in education, the media, 'aid', and multiple commodification processes. Also under-explored is the relationship between the British and American variants of the profession, and how these relate to the strong traditions of teaching English as a foreign language in western Europe and in former communist states. Even though my understanding of linguistic imperialism was developed primarily in relation to the experience of the post-colonial world, there is evidence that comparable processes, ideologies and structures are in force in western Europe (Ammon 1996), and in southern Europe. This is the case in Greece, for instance, where English Language Teaching (ELT) is heavily influenced by British linguistic and pedagogical practice:

> There is a systematic construction of reality whereby, by not knowing English, one is excluded from anything of social importance... Greek ELT practitioners persistently evaluate their proficiency in English against the English of the native speaker...This underlying contradiction of a 'culturally neutral' language used in a 'culturally appropriate way'...the claim that the native speaker is the ideal ELT practitioner construes Greek ELT practitioners as 'knowledge

deficient'. The monolingualism legacy of ELT discourse ... positions
Greek EFL teachers as 'information receivers' involved in a process
of 'ideological becoming' in Bakhtinian terms and of selectively
assimilating the [authoritative] word of the other. (Dendrinos 1999,
715–6)

The same pattern is now true of post-communist Europe, which
is the most recent region to have been exposed to the impact of
western interests:

> Until 1989 there was little serious danger of English–American
> cultural and linguistic imperialism in Hungary but today there are
> unmistakable signs of such penetration and voices of concern are
> heard from a growing number of Hungarians ... Most ELT materials
> produced in and exported from the United Kingdom and the United
> States disregard the learners' L1, and in this respect we might question
> their professionalism ... business interests override a fundamental
> professional interest, or: business shapes our profession in ways that
> we know are unprofessional. This puts us, both native and nonnative
> teachers of English into quite a schizophrenic position. This is an
> embarrassment that we'll have to live with for some time to come.
> The challenge that we are faced with is to keep the professionalism
> and get rid of the embarrassment. (Kontra 1997: 83, 87)

The market economy, 'democracy', 'human rights' and English were
marketed in former communist states as soon as the Iron Curtain was
wound down. The present chaos in most of what used to be the Soviet
empire has multiple causes, but English was one of several panaceas
that were explicitly marketed as the solution to the problems of the
economy and civil society in post-communist Europe (explicitly by two
British foreign ministers, Douglas Hurd and Malcolm Rifkind). Sadly
the promise of what might be achieved in and through English was
as much of a hollow sham as it has been in most post-colonial states,
where English is the hallmark of corrupt, self-serving governments
which are in league with transnational corporations.

Whether linguistic imperialism is in force in a given context is an
empirical question. The issue then is whether our concepts are
rigorous and productive enough to match up with the relevant data.
Only in such ways can we go beyond personal impressions to more
informed analyses.

A recent example of cultural globalization aimed at strengthening English and British interests is the 'Blair Initiative', announced on 18 June 1999. This aims at increasing Britain's share of the global market in foreign students. They are to study in English, of course. The massive expansion of British universities into distance education, initially in such fields as accounting and business administration, is a related development. Such initiatives mean jobs for British universities and service industries, and are doubtless also seen as an investment in good will, in fostering favourable attitudes to things British among potentially influential people. The imported foreign students are seen as the successors of Gandhi, Nehru, Kenyatta and Nkrumah, colonial subjects who had their academic training in Britain and the USA. Universities must produce the post-colonial, post-national global citizens who will work for transnational corporations, finance houses, and supra-national bureaucracies. This 'Initiative' is somewhat intriguing and puzzling, when, according to the British government's own figures, one third of all children in Britain are growing up in poverty and derive little benefit from the education system, and Britain, to a greater extent than many of its partners in continental Europe, is a deeply divided society.

Whether foreign students will be received in culturally and linguistically sensitive ways is a question to which there are probably only anecdotal answers, but recent assessments of TESOL are that it is still 'imposing an ethnocentric ideology and inadvertently supporting the essentializing discourse that represents cultural groups as stable or homogeneous entities' (Spack 1997: 773, see also Oda 2004). Such practices perpetuate a colonialist world view in which orientalism operates to position the Other in education:

> When students are considered to have cultures, these tend to be fixed and deterministic. Thus, it is common to talk in terms of Asian, Japanese or Hispanic etc. students having certain characteristics as if these emerged from some preordained cultural order. This tendency to ascribe fixed (and often, though not always, negative) characteristics by dint of membership to a certain culture can be explained in terms of the colonial construction of the Other....Culture has become a category of fixity rather than an engagement with difference. (Pennycook 1998, 188–9)

There are fortunately a number of critical linguists active in exploring our professionalism and deconstructing some of our cherished concepts. Many of the contributions to the book 'Standard English, the widening debate' (Bex and Watts 1999), are concerned not only to pin down a slippery phenomenon but also to pinpoint the ideologies, values and interests that are associated with the concept of standards, in language and broader social processes. There is thus a shift from fixing the language to fixing the structures and processes that certain forms of the language are viscerally involved in.

Critical sociolinguists or applied linguists are here doing what Edward Said, the Palestinian-American, regards as the role of the intellectual, namely

> to raise embarrassing questions, to confront orthodoxy and dogma (rather than to produce them), to be someone who cannot easily be co-opted by governments or corporations ... someone whose whole being is staked on a critical sense, a sense of being unwilling to accept easy formulas, or ready-made clichés, or the smooth, ever-so-accommodating confirmations of what the powerful or conventional have to say, and what they do (Said 1994: 9, 17).

English as a global language

In my view, David Crystal in his book *English as a Global Language* epitomises the powerful and conventional in our professional world. He is a an influential and prolific author. He is on the board of the British Council, a primary function of which is to promote English worldwide, promote British influence, and make money for Britain. Crystal is widely cited, not least for figures for the number of L1 and L2 speakers of English, a tricky statistical exercise where others cite different figures (see Skutnabb-Kangas 2000: 30–46). He is the 'world's leading authority' according to the blurb on the book's cover (which pictures the symbiosis of English and Chinese in Hong Kong, the important Asian connection). The blurb suggests that the book is 'for anyone of any nationality concerned with English', but it was initially commissioned by the US English organization in the United States, a body whose intolerance of linguistic diversity is notorious. Crystal announces this intriguingly in his preface, along with proclaiming twin faiths, a belief in multilingualism, and an equally fundamental belief in a single world language for 'mutual understanding' and 'international cooperation'. As the book in fact focuses on English, multilingualism barely gets a look-in. And why should understanding and cooperation, which are currently mediated in literally thousands of languages, shift in the direction of a 'single world language'? This is a dangerously millenarian notion that is primarily likely to serve the interests of the few who profit from the activities of transnational corporations.

Crystal's book is structured around three basic questions: what makes a world language, why is English the leading candidate, and will it continue to hold that position? There is an introductory general chapter, followed by a historical run-through of the establishment of English worldwide, a chapter on 'the cultural foundation', with sub-sections entitled political developments, access to knowledge, and 'taken for granted'; a chapter on 'the cultural legacy' with sub-sections on international relations, the media, travel, safety, education, and communications, and a concluding section, 'the right place at the right time'; and a final chapter called 'the future of global English', with sub-sections on the rejection of English, new Englishes, fragmentation of the language, and the uniqueness of global English. In fact nearly half of this chapter is devoted to the current debate in the United States about English Only legislation, implying that Crystal's understanding is that the internal affairs of the present-day United States are central to the future of 'global' English. This seems to be inadvertently endorsing what George Bernard Shaw presciently wrote in 1912: 'what has been happening in my lifetime is the Americanisation of the world' (cited in Holroyd 1997: 660).

I have reviewed Crystal's book in detail for various audiences, for applied linguists (Phillipson 1999a), for a South African language policy publication, and for discourse analysts and will merely note here that the book does not seem to be informed by any clear social science principles, nor would the historical focus win the respect of many historians. Even though Crystal's general introduction refers to military conquest, his coverage of English in Africa avoids any upsetting talk of bloodshed or apartheid, let alone that what colonizers saw as triumph involved capitulation and domination for others. There is no reference to the many African scholars who have pleaded for the upgrading of African languages and denounced 'aid' that strengthens European languages. Crystal regards an increased use of English as unproblematical.

His coverage of English in the European Union is marred by several errors of fact, but more importantly it does not raise issues of principle. It is true that the use of English is expanding in the institutions of the EU, but as the EU is supposed to be a confederation of member states with equal rights, it would have been important to assess what language rights there are and how equality or symmetry in communication between speakers of different backgrounds can be achieved. This involves reducing English to equality, to adapt a phrase used first by Neville Alexander, a key figure in South African language policy, in relation to Afrikaans.

While acknowledging the strength of American influence, Crystal is confident that 'the English language has already grown to be independent of any form of social control' (1997, 139). His optimistic scenario is that in 500 years' time everyone is multilingual and will 'automatically be introduced to English as soon as they are born' (ibid.), whereas his pessimistic scenario is a monolingual English-speaking world. My demonstration of the slips and false argumentation (for details see Phillipson 1999a) shows how difficult it is to summarize such a huge variety of complex multilingual settings and issues correctly in a few words, and as the book represents vulgarization, there is no scholarly apparatus of references, which gives Crystal a free hand to select and narrate for the general public as he pleases. His story of globalising English is fundamentally Eurocentric and triumphalist, despite his protestations to the contrary.

English and equality in communication

My impression is that as English expands, users of English as a second language are becoming verbal about their unequal communication rights:

- Ranko Bugarski, a distinguished Yugoslav/Serbian Professor of English and Linguistics, in a review of Crystal's book (1998) writes that 'as a non-native speaker who has used English almost daily for decades I tend to get increasingly reluctant to engage in protracted serious argument with native speakers over subtle non-professional—e.g. philosophical or political—issues … I would not be surprised to learn that other people in my category have at times experienced a similar uneasiness.'

- Ulrich Ammon (2000) reports that the use of English as the dominant language of scientific communication is experienced by Germans as an additional burden. He has collected a range of types of evidence of inequality, such as reports of matched guise experiments that indicate that in the medical world, texts in English are judged as superior to texts in Dutch and Scandinavian languages, and information from professors of English in Germany, who report insecurity about the quality of their own manuscripts in English, which appears to confirm Bugarski's suspicions.

- Yukio Tsuda's experience as a Japanese user of English, and as an observer of inequality between Japanese and English in many contexts, has contributed to his elaboration of two global language policy paradigms, a 'Diffusion of English' paradigm and an 'Ecology of Language' paradigm, which is a productive way of conceptualizing global language policy trends (see Phillipson and Skutnabb-Kangas 1996 and further elaboration in Skutnabb-Kangas 2000). One constituent of his Ecology of Language paradigm is equality in communication.

- Some recent evidence is from my own experience in the summer of 1996 during which I attended two international conferences, a Language Rights conference in Hong Kong (see Benson, Grundy and Skutnabb-Kangas 1998), and a language policy symposium in Prague as part of the Universal Esperanto Association Eighty-First World Congress (see Fettes and Bolduc 1998). At the Hong Kong conference, English was virtually the sole means of communication. In the question time of one of the plenary sessions a South African participant expressed surprise at why those whose competence in English was less than ideal, particularly Asians who had great difficulty in expressing themselves in English, accepted the unequal communication rights imposed on them by the conference organizers. The answer was that the organizers, who were mainly British, had not given the matter any thought, and the non-native speakers were too polite to protest. A few weeks later at the Esperanto symposium it was amazing to experience participants from all over the world communicating confidently in a shared international language, among them a number of Asians who were manifestly at no disadvantage. As this event was my first experience of Esperanto in action (with interpretation provided for us non-Esperantists), it was a vivid and memorable way of seeing at first hand that Esperanto is not merely utopian but a reality for those who have chosen to make it part of their domestic, national and international lives (in inter-local communication in the sense specified earlier). The juxtaposition of the experience of English working badly and inequitably—and the fact that this for once was being discussed openly in public—and Esperanto working well provides appetizing food for thought.

There is a tendency for those not familiar with Esperanto to reject it without seriously investigating whether it might be a more efficient and equitable solution to some problems of international communication or to making foreign language learning in schools more effective (because of its simple, regular, productive grammar). The scholarly study of international communication and practical proposals for the solution of the major problems of international bodies ought to take into consideration the use of Esperanto as an alternative to the juggernaut English, which rides roughshod over the rights of many non-native users of the language. There is an extensive literature on Esperanto (see, for instance, Tonkin 1997), which has opened my eyes in recent years to the potential and the reality of this democratic language.

Contrary to popular myths, English is an extremely difficult language to operate in, not least because it is used in so many different ways. Native speakers are not necessarily a suitable performance model. There is masses of anecdotal evidence of lucid L2 users at conferences being more comprehensible than L1 users, simply because the natives are not as sensitive to audience needs. This is probably related to the fact that many British and American people have not experienced the humbling and exhilarating process of learning a second language to a high level. Monolinguals would do well both to learn a foreign language and to heed Ivan Illich (1973, 41):

> A language of which I know only the words and not the pauses is a continuous offence. It is as the caricature of a photographic negative. It takes more time and effort and delicacy to learn the silence of a people than to learn its sounds.

Inequality is thus not a simple category, but relates to multiple aspects of identity, authenticity, fluency and appropriacy in a given interactional context, i.e. it is relational. To regard native speaker competence as an authoritative norm is likely to contribute to an inequitable hierarchy. To ensure reciprocity between L2 users and monolingual English speakers ought to be a continuous challenge in native/non-native communication. These terms themselves—native/ non-native—are offensive and hierarchical in that they take the native as the norm, and define the Other negatively in relation to this norm. Thus are hierarchies internalized subconsciously and serve hegemonic purposes.

It still intrigues me that the experts on foreign language learning are supposed to be found in the heartland of countries where success in language learning is notoriously thin on the ground, namely the United States and the United Kingdom. This myth is central in TESOL and ELT, and works hand in glove with the myth that the foreign policy of the US and the UK is altruistic. A recent study of British foreign policy since 1945 concludes:

> It appears to be a widely held assumption that Britain (and indeed the Western states as a whole) promotes certain grand principles—peace, democracy, human rights and economic development in the Third World—as natural corollaries to the basic political and economic priorities that guide its foreign policy ... (This is false) ... One basic fact—of perhaps unparalleled importance—has permeated a number of studies and is well understood: the mass poverty and destitution that exist in much of the Third World are direct products of the structure of the international system. Moreover, an elementary truth is that the world's powerful states have pursued policies with regard to the Third World which knowingly promote poverty. (Curtis 1995, 236)

The focus of structural adjustment policies has ensured the west of its supplies of raw materials, but has been a raw deal for countries in the South, or at least for the majority of their citizens. Globalization policies serve to ensure that the role of English is maintained and perpetuated. The key player in educational policy is the World Bank:

> The World Bank's real position ... encourages the consolidation of the imperial languages in Africa ... the World Bank does not seem to regard the linguistic Africanisation of the whole of primary education and beyond as an effort that is worth its consideration. Its publication on strategies for stabilising and revitalising universities, for example makes absolutely no mention of the place of language at this tertiary level of African education. (Mazrui 1997, 39)

Post-apartheid South Africa is being subjected to similar pressures (Heugh 1995). An understanding of North–South relations requires analysis of the relationship between local languages and English, the dominant language of the economic forces that have propelled this language forward. Thus a key issue in language policy in any given country is whether it is local people setting the agenda, or the transnational corporations which are imposing a late capitalist world order that relegates peripheral countries, economies and languages to a subordinate position. In this scenario elites need to be proficient in English in order to serve their own and 'global' interests, and local languages must facilitate internal policing of an export-oriented economy, and attempt to limit social unrest so that this economy can persist. Transnational corporations are increasingly active in determining the content of education worldwide (Spring 1998). This development reflects the predominant interest of corporations in producing consumers rather than critical citizens. Corporations have long dominated advertising and the media. As education is a key site of cultural reproduction, it is logical that the World Bank and the transnational corporations are expanding their influence in education.

Throughout the entire post-colonial world, English has been marketed as the language of 'international communication and understanding', economic 'development', 'national unity' and similar positive ascriptions, but these soft-sell terms obscure the reality of globalization, which is that the majority of the world's population is being impoverished, that natural resources are being plundered in unsustainable ways, that the global cultural and linguistic ecology is under threat, and that speakers of most languages do not have their linguistic human rights respected (Skutnabb-Kangas and Phillipson 1994; Kontra et al 1999). 'Understanding' ought to refer to a dialogic process which respects the cultures and languages of our global diversity. In fact the term tends to be used as a smokescreen for the forces behind globalization. The need therefore is to document and analyse how English contributes to and interlocks with these processes.

Post-imperial English

The contemporary status and uses of English are the topic of Fishman, Conrad and Rubal-Lopez's substantial book entitled *Post-imperial English: Status Change in Former British and American Colonies, 1940–1990* (1996). If English is post-imperial, as the book's title suggests, what sort of world order do its eminent contributors envisage that we live in?

In earlier work, Fishman went to substantial lengths to explore the relationship between language(s) and economic, social and political indicators, and patterns in the use of a former imperial language or local languages in key sectors such as the media, education at various levels and higher education abroad. The 'Post-imperial English' volume begins and ends with Fishman's attempt to bring such work up to date in the light of a statistically-based study of a wealth of such data by one of his collaborators, Rubal-Lopez, and input from the twenty-nine scholars from British and American 'spheres of influence' who contribute to this volume. These were given a pretty free hand, so that each paper is *sui generis* rather than proceeding through a constraining template. Contributors were also invited to assess whether 'linguistic imperialism' in the sense in which I have used the term applies in their context.

The contributors are primarily sociolinguists, but there are also social scientists such as Alamin and Ali Mazrui, who highlight major differences between language policy in Uganda and Kenya. Many of the other contributors use an impressively cross-disciplinary approach. There are also other local and global heavyweights in the line-up of contributors, such as Bamgbose on Nigeria, Yahya-Othman and

Batibo on Tanzania, Chumbow on Cameroon. It is also extremely rewarding to have countries from the British colonial world analysed alongside American colonies. The papers demonstrate the substantial variations on a theme of American dominance (and resistance to it) in Cuba, Mexico, the Philippines, Puerto Rico, Quebec, and, further afield, Saudi Arabia and Israel. Several Asian countries are also well covered, and there is a survey article by Ulrich Ammon on English in the European Union.

Several papers point to the limitations of theory in the fields of language policy and language planning, but few probe deeply into what needs to be done over and above description and analysis, which the book presents a vast amount of, and none venture into theory formation. Fishman comes nearest to this in his introduction, where he speculates on English being 'reconceptualized, from being an imperialist tool to being a multinational tool ... English may need to be re-examined precisely from the point of view of being post-imperial (as the title of our book implies, that is in the sense of not directly serving purely Anglo-American territorial, economic, or cultural expansion) without being post-capitalist in any way' (ibid., 8).

In his characteristically astute 'summing-up and interpretation' of the contributions to the book, Fishman stresses the limitations of our instruments and concepts, but boldly tabulates the degree of 'anglification' in each state on a rough scale and attempts to pull the overall picture into a coherent shape. This is an extremely difficult task in view of the richness and complexity of the national studies, and the various ways in which English co-articulates with elitism, economic success for some, and often the marginalization of (speakers of) other languages, as well as the very different routes along which English has expanded in different countries. 'Post-imperial' has also been understood variously by different contributors, in a purely temporal sense by some and a more structural one by others.

Many of Fishman's reflections are likely to push the analysis of the role of English forward in insightful ways, but I find some of his conclusions debatable. His assessment that the 'socio-economic factors that are behind the spread of English are now indigenous in most countries of the world' and that the continued spread of

English in former colonies is 'related more to their engagement in the modern world economy than to any efforts derived from their colonial masters' (ibid., 639) seems to ignore the fact that 'engagement in the modern world' means a western-dominated globalization agenda set by the transnational corporations and the IMF, and the US military intervening, with or without a mandate from the United Nations, whenever 'vital interests' are at risk. World Bank, NAFTA, and World Trade Organization policies contribute to political instability, and provide less favourable conditions for education, democratization, cultural and linguistic diversity. A world polarized between a minority of English-using haves (whether as L1 or L2) and a majority of have-nots is not likely to provide healthy conditions for people who speak languages other than English to flourish, so I have difficulty in sharing Fishman's restrained optimism about linguistic power-sharing.

The editors of the Fishman volume feel, like Crystal, that since debates about language tend to become emotionally charged, there is a need for scholarship in the area to be 'de-ideologized', almost as if value judgements and paradigms can be avoided. Both books demonstrate that this is a forlorn, self-deluding hope. Crystal seems simply to be unaware of his own ideological biases and of some of the relevant literature on multilingualism, development studies, hegemony, the sociology of language, and social theory. Scholarship on global English needs to be informed by a great deal of relevant work in the humanities and social sciences, such as is brought together with the specific contribution of various disciplines (economics, ethnography, minority education, history, nationalism, political science, social psychology, sociology, etc) in Fishman's edited volume *Handbook of Language and Ethnic Identity* (1999), a book which also has a substantial section on regional perspectives.

What the Fishman et al. volume seems to show is that many studies of the position (the status, in language planning terms) of English in particular countries are insightful and sophisticated, including the role of external and internal factors that influence language policy, whereas the more positivistically oriented studies such as Rubal-Lopez's are weak in their explanatory power and their capacity to generate non-trivial findings. The more hermeneutic approach of the other two editors leads to very broad generalizations (which the 'post-imperial' label encourages), which suggests that there is a need to link micro and macro processes and structures more explicitly, along with critical analysis of the discourses accompanying and realizing them, including those of sociolinguists (a process that book reviews contribute to).

Conrad demonstrates in his paper in this volume that emotional involvement in a topic or in a response to an author's work (in this case, my own) can lead to interpretation that is in flagrant contradiction to the Popperian ideals he otherwise espouses. It is also puzzling that he uses his editorial prerogative to denounce my approach to linguistic dominance while the contributors recruited to write for his book apparently have no qualms about operating with it!

Fishman's final word (ibid., 640) is to the effect that the world has moved beyond imperialism and neo-colonialism in the traditional sense of foreign rule and exploitation. If this is really so, what seems most urgently needed is to explore the role of English locally and globally in our new world order, so as to combat the very real forms of exploitation between states and within states that exist, and to see how English and other languages can be harnessed so as to promote a healthier language ecology. If English is to be a force for democracy and human rights, much needs to change, in North countries as much as in the South, and in North–South relations. Language policy could and should play an important role in such a transition.

English in the future

I will briefly consider another important book, David Graddol's *The Future of English?* (1997), which was commissioned by The British Council. Graddol's 66-page book is divided into sections on English today (history, demography, language hierarchies), Forecasting (futurology, chaos, scenarios), Global trends (demography, economics, technology, globalization, the immaterial economy, cultural flows), Impacts on English (workplace, education and training, media, youth culture, internet, time zones), and English in the future (World English, rival languages, transitions, managing the future). The scope and goals of the work entailed immense pressure to select, condense and unite a large amount of material, and present it in graphs and tables as well as text. Graddol's sources throughout are clearly documented, though the work reflects an unresolved tension between the urge to be scientifically sound and to produce a blueprint for an organization whose purpose it is to maximize the use of English. The work also went through a substantial screening process, with a draft commented on by a substantial number of named individuals (myself included). Even so, there are occasional slips, short-cuts and dubious claims in the text, for instance in terminology and classification in the pyramidical hierarchies of language in India, the European Union and the world.

The book contains a quick run-through of language in the workplace, language learning, new technologies in education and the media, youth consumerism and the internet, all of which demonstrate an increased, but by no means monopolistic expansion of English. English is a polycentric language, which means that a British norm for textbooks or teaching materials is not unchallenged (Modiano 1999). Another worry for British economic interests is that British monolingualism may become a liability in a world of increasingly bilingual or trilingual individuals. The native speaker cachet may lose its charm and prove to be a short-lived asset, with little clout as compared to McDonaldization processes.

A number of key questions are raised in the final section: a consideration of which languages may rival English in the coming century, which factors account for language hierarchies and language death, and questions more specifically related to the health of the British English teaching industry. Graddol and his sponsor, the British Council, deserve real praise for raising the issues in an open, critical spirit, and bringing a concern for the ecology of language and an ethical dimension into language promotion work. One can only hope that policy-makers will heed the call for openness, for commercial interests to be balanced by environmental and ethical principles, and acted on more effectively than the present 'New' Labour's 'ethical' policy on arms sales, which has been a disgraceful sham (not least in Indonesia). The book can serve as a platform for debate on the topics presented, and has in fact been used for just this purpose on internet courses for British Council staff and others.

What evidence is there for Graddol's claim that if the number of speakers of English as a second or foreign language increases, this will upset existing global linguistic hierarchies? Perhaps the answer can be found by exploring the complex web of factors in changed demographies, urbanization, new forms of communication, a global division of labour, and many related factors that influence language choice. Graddol attempts to mesh these with futurology, scenario planning and existing methods for understanding global trends, and stresses the many uncertainties in this pioneer endeavour. The linguistic exemplification may be rather tenuous, and I suspect that the entire exercise is underpinned by a rather unquestioning acceptance of a neo-liberal economic model. There would, in my view, be a need for more probing into how English, the language of many of the global haves, is causally related to the marginalization of non-English-using have-nots. Is it realistic to believe that the global system, which English is so significantly a part of, can administer and alleviate a global share-out by which 20% of the world's population consume 80% of the resources? One cannot help wondering whether Graddol has remained optimistic in view of many appalling economic, political and military crises since his book was written (Kosova, East Timor, the ex-Soviet Union, Central Africa). The notion that globalization entails hybridity would also, it seems to me, need to be connected to fundamental questions about the economic and political forces that are dictating the forms of globalization and McDonaldization—and contributing to the spread of English.

Going beyond analyses of linguistic imperialism

I have commented on three very different books, each of which is concerned, more or less explicitly, with English in the new world order. Crystal's regards English as a panacea, for Fishman et al it is a more or less mixed blessing, and Graddol tells the jury to go away and think—but one suspects that the jury is predominantly white, western and male. For reasons that have to do with the marketing of products such as books, and the forces that drive globalization, Crystal's book is likely to be widely read, Fishman et al's to be found only in well-funded libraries, and Graddol's will mainly serve a restricted audience. This will be a global one geographically, backed up by electronic newsletters, distance education, periodic revision of the text and its translation into several languages. If the book can reach beyond those who are committed to the promotion of English to those with a more open, multilingual agenda, it represents a promising starting-point for disentangling some of the many factors that currently strengthen English and might weaken it. Fishman et al.'s book provides a wealth of documentation, but their story would need to be counter-balanced by more substantial input from critical scholars working with grassroots forms of English and alternatives to English dominance. Crystal foresees the consolidation of 'World Standard Spoken English', which he does not see as replacing other languages or (national) forms of English. For him English has become 'global' because the language happened to be at 'the right place at the right time' (1997, 110), an assessment which detaches it from inequality and injustice.

There are in the contemporary world many ongoing struggles for a greater degree of linguistic justice. This is basically what South African language policy is designed to achieve (LANGTAG 1996). In principle it is also the case in the European Union, which claims to support multilingualism in its institutions and in the education systems of member states. In both cases there exist a number of key policy statements, but there is a substantial gap between rhetoric and implementation. Scholarly study of the issues is still in its infancy, but there are valuable empirical studies which shed light on some aspects of hierarchization and attitudes to languages in the EU (Schlossmacher 1996; Quell 1997). There have also been instructive compilations of research needs (European Cultural Foundation 1999). It is worrying that although the issues are urgent, language policy is seldom given the attention it deserves in political or academic discourse.

Existing scholarly approaches have serious limitations: tabulating variables nationally, sub-nationally and supra-nationally, and correlating linguistic diversity with economic, cultural and many other factors, are necessary but far from sufficient steps in the study of the issues and the elaboration of scenarios.

All that can be attempted here is to suggest a number of pointers that need to be borne in mind in future work, whether in scholarship or in planning and implementation. At the supra-national, European level there is a major need to hammer out principles of language policy that are firmly anchored in the realities of the new world order, but which can serve to ensure that the linguistic vitality of both national and minority languages in each state is maintained and consolidated. In an optimistic scenario, English is learned additively, in top-down ways through the education system, and bottom-up ways that respect grassroots creativity. Here it needs to be recalled that youth culture and the internet are part of McDonaldization processes where MTV and Microsoft represent commercial interests.

Experience worldwide of multilingual education indicates that it is perfectly possible to make children trilingual by the time they leave school if a range of relevant criteria are met (Skutnabb-Kangas 1995). If Europeans are to influence the new world order rather than just being at the receiving end of it, they should therefore ensure that all children leaving school have real competence in the mother tongue, English and one other language, so as to provide a counter-balance to globalization pressures. Likewise in post-colonial and post-communist settings, educational policy should have multilingual aims and means, and build on local resources, rather than being articulated in terms of the false dichotomy between a local language and English.

A key constituent of language in education policy would then be a linguistic human rights approach that sets minimum standards which individuals and groups are entitled to, for instance the right to the mother tongue and one of the official languages of a state in education and public services, and the right not to have language shift imposed on one. A human rights approach attempts to counter-balance the market, to ensure observation of ethical principles, which presupposes accountability, and implementation so that declarations do not remain the posturing of pretty words on paper (see Skutnabb-Kangas 2000, Phillipson 2000).

For us as professionals, it means being attuned to a mass of bottom-up signals and pressures. It presupposes a willingness to subject our own professionalism to scrutiny, otherwise we may be co-opted into new forms of inequitable dominance, which the position of English as the language of global hedonism and success risks making us blind to.

References

Ammon, Ulrich 2000. 'Towards more fairness in international English: linguistic rights of non-native speakers'? In Phillipson (ed.) 2000, 111–116.

Anderson, Benedict 1983. *Imagined Communities. Reflections on the Origins and spread of Nationalism.* London: Verso.

Appadurai, Arjun 1990. Disjuncture and difference in the global cultural economy. *Public Culture,* Vol. 2, No. 2, 1–24.

Bailey, Richard W. 1991. *Images of English: A Cultural History of the Language.* Cambridge: Cambridge University Press.

Benson, Phil, Peter Grundy and Tove Skutnabb-Kangas (eds.) 1998. *Language Sciences,* special number on linguistic human rights, Vol. 20, No. 1.

Bex, Tony and Richard J. Watts (eds) 1999. *Standard English: the Widening Debate.* London: Routledge.

Bugarski, Ranko 1998. Review of Crystal 1997. *Journal of Multilingual and Multicultural Development,* 90-92.

Bourdieu, Pierre 1991. *Language and Symbolic Power.* London: Polity Press.

Christidis, A.-F. (ed.) 1999. *'Strong' and 'weak' languages in the European Union. aspects of linguistic hegemonism.* Proceedings of an international conference, Thessaloniki, 26-28 March 1997. Thessaloniki: Centre for the Greek Language, 2 volumes.

Crystal, David 1997. *English as a Global Language.* Cambridge: Cambridge University Press.

Curtis, Martin 1995. *The Ambiguities of Power. British Foreign Policy Since 1945.* London: Zed Books.

Dasgupta, Probal 1993. *The Otherness of English: India's Auntie Tongue Syndrome.* Delhi and London: Sage.

Dasgupta, Probal 1997. 'Toward a dialogue between the sociolinguistic sciences and Esperanto culture'. In Tonkin (ed.) 1997, 139–170.

Dasgupta, Probal 2000. 'Culture, sharing and language'. In Phillipson (ed.) 2000, 49-51.

Dendrinos, Bessie 1999. 'The conflictual subjectivity of the periphery ELT practitioner'. In Christidis (ed.) 1999, 711–717.

European Cultural Foundation 1999. *Which Languages for Europe?* Report of the conference held at Oegstgeest, the Netherlands, 8–11 October 1998. Amsterdam: European Cultural Foundation.

Fettes, Mark and Suzanne Bolduc, (eds.) 1998. *Al lingva demokratio; Towards linguistic democracy; Vers la démocratie linguistique*, Proceedings of the Nitobe Symposium of International Organizations, Prague, 20–23 July 1996. Rotterdam: Universala Esperanto-Asocio.

Fishman, Joshua A. (ed.) 1999. *Handbook of Language and Ethnic Identity*. Oxford and New York: Oxford University Press.

Fishman, Joshua, A., Andrew Conrad and Alma Rubal-Lopez (eds.) 1996. *Post-Imperial English: Status Change in Former British and American Colonies, 1940–1990*. Berlin and New York: Mouton de Gruyter.

Graddol, David 1997. *The Future of English?* London: The British Council.

Hamelink, Cees 1994. *Trends in World Communication: On Disempowerment and Self-Empowerment*. Penang: Southbound, and Third World Network.

Heugh, Kathleen 1995. 'Disabling and enabling: Implications for language policy trends in South Africa'. In Mesthrie (ed.) 329–350.

Holroyd, Michael 1997. *Bernard Shaw. The One-Volume Definitive Edition*. London: Chatto and Windus.

Illich, Ivan 1973. *Tools for Conviviality*. London: Fontana.

Kontra, Miklós 1997. 'English linguistic and cultural imperialism and teacher training in Hungary'. Report on the Second ELT Conference on Teacher Training in the Carpathian Euro-region, Debrecen, Hungary, 25-27 April 1997. Budapest: British Council, English Language Teaching Contacts Scheme, 83–88.

Kontra, Miklós, Robert Phillipson, Tove Skutnabb-Kangas and Tibor Váradi (eds.) 1999. *Language: A Right and a Resource. Approaching Linguistic Human Rights*. Budapest: Central European University Press.

LANGTAG 1996. *Towards a national language plan for South Africa*. Report of the Language Plan Task Group. Pretoria: Ministry of Arts, Culture, Science and Technology.

Mazrui, Alamin 1997. 'The World Bank, the language question and the future of African education'. *Race and Class*, Vol. 38, No. 3, 35–48.

McArthur, Tom 1998. *The English Languages*. Cambridge: Cambridge University Press.

Mesthrie, Rajend (ed.) 1995. *Language and Social History: Studies in South African Sociolinguistics*. Cape Town: David Philip.

Modiano, Marko 1999. 'Standard English(es) and educational practices for the world's lingua franca'. *English Today* 60, Vol. 15, No. 4, 3–13.

Mufwene, Salikoko 1997. 'The legitimate and illegitimate offspring of English'. *World Englishes 2000*, ed. Larry Smith and Michael L. Forman, Hawaii: University of Hawaii and East-West Center, 182–203.

Mühlhäusler, Peter 1996. *Linguistic Ecology. Language Change and Linguistic Imperialism in the Pacific Region*. London: Routledge.

Ngũgĩ wa Thiong'o 1993. *Moving the Centre. The Struggle for Cultural Freedoms*. London: James Currey, and Portsmouth, NH: Heinemann.

Oda, Masaki 2000. 'Linguicism in action: language and power in academic institutions'. In Phillipson (ed.) 2000, 117–121.

Parakrama, Arjuna 1995. *De-Hegemonizing Language Standards. Learning from (Post) Colonial Englishes about 'English'*. Basingstoke and New York: Macmillan.

Pennycook, Alastair 1994. *The Cultural Politics of English as an International Language*. Harlow: Longman.

Pennycook, Alastair 1998. *English and the Discourses of Colonialism*. London: Routledge.

Phillipson, Robert 1992. *Linguistic Imperialism*. Oxford: Oxford University Press.

Phillipson, Robert 1999a. 'Voice in global English: unheard chords in Crystal loud and clear,' Review article on Crystal 1997. *Applied Linguistics*, Vol. 20, No. 2, 265–276.

Phillipson, Robert 1999b. Review of Fishman, Conrad and Rubal-Lopez (eds.) 1996. *Language*, Vol. 75, No. 2, 165–168.

Phillipson, Robert (ed.) 2000. *Rights to Language: Equity, Power and Education*. Mahwah, NJ: Lawrence Erlbaum Associates.

Phillipson, Robert and Tove Skutnabb-Kangas 1996. 'English only worldwide, or language ecology'. *TESOL Quarterly*, Vol. 30, No. 3, 429–452.

Phillipson, Robert and Tove Skutnabb-Kangas 1999. 'Englishisation: one dimension of globalisation', *English in a changing world, AILA Review,* 13, 17-36, ed. David Graddol and Ulrike Meinhoff.

Preisler, Bent 1999. *Danskerne og det engelske sprog.* Frederiksberg: Roskilde Universitetsforlag-Samfundslitteratur.

Quell, Carsten 1997. 'Language choice in multilingual institutions: A case study at the European Commission with particular reference to the role of English, French and German as working languages'. *Multilingua* Vol. 16, No. 1, 57–76.

Quirk, Randolph, Sydney Greenbaum, Geoffrey Leech and Jan Svartvik 1985. *A Comprehensive Grammar of the English Language.* London and New York: Longman.

Rajan, Rajeswari Sunder (ed.) 1992. *The Lie of the Land. English Literary Studies in India.* Delhi: Oxford University Press.

Ritzer, George 1996. *The McDonaldization of Society.* Thousand Oaks, CA: Pine Forge Press (revised edition).

Routh, R.V. 1941. *The Diffusion of English Culture outside England. A Problem of Post-War Reconstruction.* Cambridge: Cambridge University Press.

Said, Edward 1994. *Representations of the Intellectual.* London: Vintage

Saunders, Frances Stonor 1999. *Who Paid the Piper? The CIA and the Cultural Cold War.* London: Granta.

Schlossmacher, Michael 1996. *Die Amtssprachen in den Organen der Europäische Gemeinschaft.* Frankfurt: Lang.

Skutnabb-Kangas, Tove (ed.) 1995. *Multilingualism for All.* Lisse: Swets and Zeitlinger.

Skutnabb-Kangas, Tove 2000. *Linguistic Genocide in Education – Or Worldwide Diversity and Human Rights?* Mahwah, NJ: Lawrence Erlbaum.

Skutnabb-Kangas, Tove and Phillipson, Robert (eds.) 1994. *Linguistic Human Rights: overcoming Linguistic Discrimination.* Berlin: Mouton de Gruyter (paperback version 1995).

Spack, Ruth 1997. 'The rhetorical constructions of multilingual students'. *TESOL Quarterly,* Vol. 31, No. 4, 765–774.

Spring, Joel 1998. *Education and the Rise of the Global Economy.* Mahwah, NJ: Lawrence Erlbaum Associates.

Tonkin, Humphrey (ed.) 1997. *Esperanto, Interlinguistics, and Planned Language.* Lanham: University Press of America.

Chapter 3

Language policy and linguistic imperialism

'The most serious problem for the European Union is that it has so many languages, this preventing real integration and development of the Union.'
The ambassador of the USA to Denmark, Mr Elton, 1997

'The Union shall respect cultural, religious and linguistic diversity.'
Charter of Fundamental Rights of the European Union,
Article 22, 2000.

The concept of linguistic imperialism resonates with the historical fact of empires as socio-political structures that have risen and fallen over three millennia, and with the analytical exploration of the role of language in the empires that dominated the world scene in recent centuries. The current strength of English, French, Portuguese and Spanish globally reflects the policies that have entrenched use of these languages in colonially occupied territories. The fate of German in Africa and Asia was sealed by German defeat in 1918. Likewise the defeat of Japan in 1945 reversed the impact in several Asian states of Japanese as a language of empire. The demise of Dutch in Indonesia and its decline in southern Africa also flag a reduction of the political power of speakers of Dutch and Afrikaans. The collapse of soviet communism has constrained the use of Russian in central Asia and severely limited its use in eastern Europe. Similar patterns of change are affecting other languages of former empires, such as

Danish in Greenland and Iceland. Worldwide, there is great fluidity and dynamism in the way hierarchies of language are being adjusted. Language policy is torn between top-down pressures to maintain the position of national languages, and bottom-up pressures to secure linguistic diversity and the implementation of language rights. Impacting on both of these trends is the ever-increasing use of English worldwide. The power associated with English also affects the fate of other languages that have been widely used in international relations, in particular French.

I shall confine myself to exploring linguistic imperialism in the contemporary expansion of English. I shall focus on developments globally, and language policy trends in Europe, which are illuminating because the European Union (EU) is officially committed to multilingualism and linguistic diversity, while integrally involved in processes of globalization that are symbiotically linked to English. There is an unresolved tension between many languages being used in running EU affairs and in member states, and the momentum propelling English forward. Related to this is the question of whether the United States is establishing a global empire, different in kind from earlier empires, and if so, what implications follow for language policy. Assessing the adequacy of our theoretical tools for addressing the multiple roles of English and its impact on local language ecologies is needed because of the increasingly rich documentation of languages worldwide. This includes numerous books on English as a 'world' language: recent titles include Block and Cameron (2002), Brutt-Griffler (2002) (see Phillipson 2004), Jenkins (2003), and Maier (2003), as well as synthesizing volumes such as Maurais and Morris's *Languages in a Globalising World* (2003).

From imperial via postimperial to neoimperial

My book on linguistic imperialism (Phillipson 1992) explores how English has retained its dominant role in former colonies, its pivotal role in North-South relations, and the way language pedagogy has consolidated a hierarchy of languages, invariably with English at the top. Some of the strengths and limitations of my approach have been insightfully reviewed (Canagarajah 1999, Pennycook 2001) (see also a range of views on linguistic imperialism and the global role of English in Seidlhofer 2003). In the article 'English in the new world order: variations on a theme of linguistic imperialism and "world" English', in *Ideology, Politics and Language Policies: Focus on English*, (ed. Ricento, 2000), I reviewed three books, one of which, Fishman, Conrad and Rubal-Lopez's *Post-Imperial English: Status Change in Former British and American Colonies, 1940–1990*, has a wealth of empirical description of the functions of English in many contexts. 'Post-imperial' is though a very general label, and I concur with Görlach in a review of the book (1997, 218) that 'the methods underlying the statements on "post-imperial" are not sufficiently defined. If we combine this with the lack of reliable statistics on which arguments are based we see how much thinking, and empirical research, is still needed.'

The 29 contributors to Fishman et al.'s volume were specifically asked to assess whether linguistic imperialism, in the sense in which I have used the term, was in force in the country studies they were responsible for. They all address the issue, but none attempt to refine the concept or to see whether there might be more powerful or precise ways of coming to grips with theorising the dominance of English. It is only Fishman, in his introductory and closing comments, who, as well as tabulating the degree of 'anglification' in each state, speculates on English being 'reconceptualised, from being an imperialist tool to being a multinational tool...English may need to be re-examined precisely from the point of view of being post-imperial (... in the sense of not directly serving purely Anglo-American territorial, economic, or cultural expansion) without being post-capitalist in any way' (Fishman 1996, 8). Corporate activities, which are global, in tandem with the World Bank, the IMF, the World Trade Organization, the United Nations, NATO, and regional economic blocs have made the locus of power more diffuse than in earlier, nation-state imperialism and neocolonialism. In constituting and controlling the current world 'order', English plays a central role, but not one that is isomorphic with the interests of a single state.

Görlach's comment on statistics refers to the absence of reliable data on users of English as a second or foreign language.[2] The same methodological weakness is bewailed in profiling 'francophonie', since most of the statistics on competence in French worldwide are unreliable, if not fraudulent, because they use woolly or no definitions of competence (Chaudenson 2003). However, improved figures for users of English are less significant than identifying which functions English serves, and whether English has the sharpest beak in a pecking order of languages.

Critical sociolinguistics faces a major challenge in teasing out and theorising how globalization dovetails with Americanization and Englishization. Linguistic imperialism entails unequal exchange and unequal communicative rights between people or groups defined in terms of their competence in specific languages, with unequal benefits as a result, in a system that legitimates and naturalizes such exploitation. Linguistic imperialism was manifestly a feature of the way nation-states privileged one language, and often sought actively to eradicate others, forcing their speakers to shift to the dominant language. It was also a feature of colonial empires, with a deeper degree of linguistic penetration in settler countries (e.g. Canada) than exploitation and extraction colonies (e.g. India, Nigeria). Some of the complexities of colonial policies towards English and local languages are being unearthed (Pennycook 1998, Brutt-Griffler 2002), but such studies in no way conflict with the hierarchical world of English linguistic imperialism, even if their authors interpret matters differently (Phillipson 2004). Seeing English from the point of view of both demand and supply is explored in a study of Hong Kong past and present that seeks to go beyond seeing English as an addictive, enfeebling imposition, analogous to opium, preferring the image of English as ginseng, costly, varied, somewhat bitter, but enabling (Li 2002).

Language policies continued largely unchanged into the postcolonial age, as a result of which it is speakers of the former colonial languages who are the dominant group in such states. Postcolonial education systems, particularly due to the influence of the World Bank in recent decades, have tended to give priority to the former colonial language and a marginal status to local languages.

But just as there has never been a close fit between linguistic groups and the states they found themselves in, languages in the globalizing world are no respecters of state borders. Technology permits the instant exchange of financial, commercial, and cultural information in ever more complex networks. The global economy is run from 'global cities' that manage the 'internationalization of capital, production, services, and culture' (Yeung 2000, 24). Thus Hong Kong, Seoul, Singapore and Tokyo are global in the same way as Frankfurt, London, and New York, whereas Delhi and Shanghai are not, since their functions are essentially local ones.

Dominant groups in the military, political, economic, and cultural worlds network with similar groups elsewhere to run a global economy that continues to widen the gulf between haves and have-nots, as unambiguously documented by a World Bank insider (Stiglitz 2002). Constantly recurring military, economic and political crises reveal that the system is chronically unable to deliver to the whole world's population peace, stability and a quality of life that lives up to human rights norms. 'Free' trade liberalism supports the strong against the weak. This might be remedied by a shift to fair trade, but successive WTO meetings from Seattle to Cancun reveal little will on the part of the haves, the US and EU in particular, to move in that direction. Equitable conditions are also needed in our language ecologies, national and international. In both democracies and more repressive systems, particular languages are given more support than others. In most international fora, English is privileged, and attention is seldom paid to ensuring the equality of speakers from different language backgrounds. Is it fair that some should be able to communicate, negotiate, trade, and be culturally productive in their mother tongue, whereas others have to use a second or foreign language? Is it fair that the USA and UK can avoid investing substantially in foreign language education, whereas virtually all other education systems are obliged to in order to access the global economy and cultural industries? Such inequity is largely unrecorded and unquantified, since the structural and ideological underpinning of global linguistic hegemony tends to be regarded as legitimate, despite the massive economic and cultural advantages this gives the English-speaking world.

For example scientific scholarship is increasingly an English-only domain in international communication (journals, reference works, textbooks, conferences, networking), which has a knock-on effect nationally (language shift to English, particularly at graduate level;

funding needed for training, or for translation) and internationally (paradigms from the Anglo-American world being favoured, marginalization of non-native speakers at conferences). In the journal *Discourse and Society*, 8(3), an editorial entitled *The Imperialism of English* (van Dijk,1997) notes that English increasingly intrudes on territory occupied earlier by other languages: 'The language barrier has become a more general scholarly and cultural barrier... The main obstacle to linguistic diversity, also in scholarship, however, is the arrogance of linguistic power in Anglophone countries, and especially the USA' (p. 292).

Resistance and the neoimperial

In several continental European countries, there is major concern about the impact of English on national languages. Thus studies were commissioned in each of the Nordic countries to assess whether domain loss is occurring in Danish, Finnish, Icelandic, Norwegian, and Swedish, in business, the media and other fields, as well as in science. Provisional results have been published in each of the relevant languages (those who only read English possibly need reminding that good work is in fact published in other languages). They confirm that there is a serious problem, hence a need for more proactive language policy formation. The overall picture has been presented in Swedish, in a popularising form, complete with a 15-page English summary (Höglin 2002). As this is a far from precise or correct translation from a Swedish source text, it ironically confirms the existence and nature of the problem of inequity in international communication.

It goes without saying that many factors contribute to the current dominance of English. They can be broadly grouped as structural (the interlocking of English with the global economy, finance, and the military–industrial complex; British and American promotion of English; investment in the teaching of English in education systems) and ideological (imagery of English created through the media, popular and elite culture, connotations of success, necessity etc).[3] The policy-makers of the Bush II administration regard it as their right and duty to impose American values globally.[4]

The unilateralism of the Bush II government represents a break with the more multilateral policies of the Clinton administration, to the point where many scholars talk of an American empire, of the US as hegemon. Language is subordinate to economic and military policies, as noted by the historian, Erik Hobsbawm (in *Le Monde Diplomatique*) in June 2003, soon after the occupation of Iraq: 'Although the US retains some political advantages, it has thrown most of them out of the window in the past 18 months. There are the minor assets of American culture's domination of world culture, and of the English language. But the major asset for imperial projects at the moment is military' (p. 2). Language policy is essential to this mission, as formulated in an article in *Foreign Policy*, by David Rothkopf, Director of the Kissinger Institute, in 1997:

> It is in the economic and political interest of the United States to ensure that if the world is moving toward a common language, it be English; that if the world is moving toward common telecommunications, safety, and quality standards, they be American; and that if common values are being developed, they be values with which Americans are comfortable. These are not idle aspirations. English is linking the world. (p. 45).

Gradual processes of Americanization have gathered speed throughout the twentieth century, and been marketed in recent years as globalization:

> 'Globalisation' serves as a password, a watchword, while in effect it is the legitimatory mask of a policy aiming to universalise particular interests and the particular tradition of the economically and politically dominant powers, above all the United States, and to extend to the entire world the economic and cultural model that favours these powers most, while simultaneously presenting it as a norm, a requirement, and a fatality, a universal destiny, in such a manner as to obtain adherence or at the least, universal resignation. (Bourdieu 2001, 84).

This analysis reveals how the hegemonic power imposes or induces acceptance of its dominion. In their book *Empire*, Hardt and Negri (2000) draw together many threads from political, economic and cultural theory and philosophy, and astutely unravel the role of communication in global social trends, and how language constitutes our universe:

> The great industrial and financial powers thus produce not only commodities but also subjectivities. They produce agentic subjectivities

within the biopolitical[6] context: they produce needs, social relations, bodies and minds —which is to say, they produce producers. In the biopolitical sphere, life is made to work for production and production is made to work for life... (p. 32)

One site where we should locate the biopolitical production of order is in the immaterial nexuses of the production of language, communication, and the symbolic that are developed by the communications industries. The development of communications networks has an organic relationship to the emergence of the new world order—it is, in other words, effect and cause, product and producer. Communication not only expresses but also organizes the movement of globalization. It organizes the movement by multiplying and structuring interconnections through networks. It expresses the movement and controls the sense and direction of the imaginary that runs throughout these communicative connections...This is why the communications industries have assumed such a central position. They not only organize production on a new scale and impose a new structure adequate to global space, but also make its justification immanent. Power, as it produces, organizes; as it organizes, it speaks and expresses itself as authority. Language, as it communicates, produces commodities but moreover produces subjectivities, puts them in relation, and orders them. The communications industries integrate the imaginary and the symbolic within the biopolitical fabric, not merely putting them at the service of power but actually integrating them into its very functioning. (pp. 32–3).

This analysis reveals why it has been so important for the corporate world not only to dominate the media but also education, which is increasingly run to service the economy, and produce consumers rather than critical citizens (Monbiot 2000). In the teaching and marketing of 'communication skills', a shift from linguistic imperialism to communicative imperialism can be seen: 'Language becomes a global product available in different local flavours.... The dissemination of "global" communicative norms and genres, like the dissemination of international languages, involves a one-way flow of expert knowledge from dominant to subaltern cultures' (Cameron 2002, 70). The modern focus on communication skills, defined by 'experts,' entails the dissemination of American ways of speaking. Globalization is extending these worldwide, often without their ethnocentricity being perceived. The forms of communication, genres and styles of the dominant consumerist culture have the willing but possibly unwitting support of teachers of English and 'communication'.

Many continental Europeans appreciate that if shift to English and Anglo-American norms is allowed to continue unchecked, cultural vitality and diversity will suffer, as a result of contemporary linguistic imperialism. In government policy documents produced in Sweden in 2002 and Denmark in 2003 on how to strengthen the national language in view of the increasing importance of English, the declared goal is to cultivate 'parallel' linguistic competence.[6] This would mean that Swedes and Danes active in business, politics, higher education, science and the media are able to function equally well in the national language and in English. It would ensure that domain loss and linguistic hierarchization are counteracted, through ensuring resource allocation to the language that now risks marginalization, despite having had an unchallenged status nationally in recent centuries, and through fostering awareness of the need to provide conditions for languages other than English to thrive.

These proposed measures indicate clearly that states which traditionally have had a *laissez faire* approach to language policy are involved in status planning for national and international languages. France also promulgated a law in 1994 to counter an increasing use of English. What is problematical is that many of the pressures involved lie beyond the control of the nation-state, which may therefore be addressing symptoms rather than causes. It is likely that increasing European integration strengthens the forces of globalization, Americanization, and Englishization rather than constraining them.

The recognition of English as a threat to the languages and cultures of member states is beginning to influence the formulation and synchronization of language policy at the supranational level. During the 1990s EU policy-making has moved into the areas of education, language and culture. The Commission document *Promoting Language Learning and Linguistic Diversity: An Action Plan 2004-2006*, of August 2003,[7] is designed to curb an excessive focus on English in education systems and the wider society. It states (pp. 4 and 8): 'learning one lingua franca alone is not enough... English alone is not enough... In non-anglophone countries recent trends to provide teaching in English may have unforeseen consequences on the vitality of the national language.' The policy statement, which it is now up to member states to react to, advocates life-long foreign language learning, including two foreign languages in the primary school. It strives to bring language policy higher up on national agendas, and to raise awareness of linguistic diversity. It endorses the notion of an inclusive 'language-friendly environment'.

It is impossible to predict what impact, if any, this document will have. In a complex, evolving scene, with fuzzy dividing-lines between supranational and national interests and languages, it is difficult to gauge how significant the ritual support of multilingualism in many EU official texts is, and how far policies that can counteract Englishization will be pursued. There are sceptics: 'No-one is fooled by fiery declarations in favour of multilingualism, which is nothing but a smoke screen for the spread of English.' (Chaudenson 2003, 297). De Swaan regards English as 'the lingua franca' of the EU (an eminently falsifiable statement—there are several lingua francas), and claims that in the EU 'the more languages, the more English' (2001, 174, 144[8]).

To understand whether the EU can control, convert or resist the major pressures behind an increased use of English requires some historical analysis. The economic and political unification of Europe has followed two mutually reinforcing agendas: to establish forms of interdependence that would render military aggression impossible, and to position America as the pre-eminent force globally. The Marshall Plan was conditional on the integration of European economies. As Europeanisation intensifies (80 per cent of legislation in member states entails implementing decisions already made at the supranational EU level), communication between the citizens and representatives of European states and between national bureaucracies and the EU Commission increases, hence the focus in EU funding on strengthening foreign language learning, and the provision of language services in EU institutions. These are in principle committed to the equality of eleven official and working languages, buttressed by translation and interpretation services that employ literally thousands of translators and 750 interpreters per working day, at an average of

55 meetings. Official documents are promulgated in each language, with equal legal validity, and in theory there is no source text of which the others are translations. However, it is arguable that in some in-house EU activities, and in business, science, politics, the media, and education in European civil society, English is taking over to the point where other languages are on a fast track to second-class status. In the initial decades of the EU, French was *primus inter pares*, and since the accession of the UK, Ireland and Denmark in 1973, there has been a progressive shift to English. Two-thirds of EU drafts are now written in English, a figure that is rising by 2 per cent per annum. In negotiations with new member states, which will bring in at least ten additional languages over the coming decade, English has been in effect the sole language in use.[9]

The shift from French to English (that the French and Belgian governments are trying to counteract) signals a shift in power from French thought processes and influence to Anglo-American ones that reflect many of the contemporary trends in globalization. There is undoubtedly now linguicist favouring of competent users of English, whether as a first or second language. It is explicitly seen by some as symptomatic of linguistic imperialism.

The Germans have, because of the Nazi experience, been reluctant to be seen to promote their language energetically, despite the fact that a quarter of EU citizens have German as a mother tongue, and Germany foots a disproportionately large part of the EU bill. But bodies such as the *Verein Deutscher Sprache* (German Language Association) are concerned about whether German will retain its national pre-eminence. It accuses elites in Germany of facilitating Americanization and failing for decades to support German (Gawlitta and Vilmar 2002, a volume that begins with an article entitled 'Sprachimperialismus: Analyse; Widerstand' 'Linguistic imperialism, analysis, resistance').

By contrast, Germany was accused of linguistic imperialism during the Finnish presidency of the EU in 1999. Germany boycotted informal ministerial meetings in Finland because interpretation into and from German was not provided. The Finns accused the Germans of linguistic imperialism, because they insisted on the same rights as speakers of other 'big' European languages. The diplomatic crisis was solved by the Finns caving in to German pressure without matters of principle or language rights being clarified. The Finns failed to appreciate that French and German insistence on the equality of the official languages of the EU is in the interest of speakers of 'small' EU languages like Finnish (Kelletat 2001, 37). This study of the coverage of this crisis in the Finnish and German media concludes that the Americanization of Finland has reached the point where a Finnish Prime Minister, despite personal multilingualism, was in effect pressing for a single-language regime at EU meetings, an English-only solution, on the model of the European Central Bank in Frankfurt. Advocacy of this conflates globalization, Europeanization and Englishization under the guise of 'pragmatism'.[10] Such a change of policy would represent a volte-face in EU activities.

The equality of EU languages is a reality at meetings at the highest levels and in the massive output of legally binding documents from Brussels and Strasbourg. But the issue of linguistic hierarchies that exist *de facto* is so politically sensitive that it has never been squarely addressed. As the president of the group of French members of the European Parliament puts it, it is 'an explosive topic in Europe.'[11] The Spanish Foreign Secretary, Ana Palacio, implies this when writing in *El País* on 16 December 2002, after the Copenhagen EU summit that was primarily concerned with reaching an agreement on terms for the accession of new member states. At the concluding press conference with heads of state from the existing and potential states, the monolingual banner headline behind the politicians read 'One Europe'. Palacio wrote:

> The motto 'One Europe', solely in English, requires a reflection. Even though Copenhagen did not face the question of languages, this is one of the pending subjects that sooner rather than later must be debated for the very survival and viability of this project of Europe with a world vocation. Within it, Spanish, one of the official UN languages, spoken by more than 400 million people in more than 20 countries, must take on the place it is entitled to.

She did not write what that 'place' should be. This is not surprising, since little effort has gone into devising criteria that might guide more equitable language policies (but see Phillipson 2003, chapter

5). The EU is a novel political construction. Hitherto its language policies have represented those of the nation-state writ large at the supranational level, plus uncritical acceptance of a globalization agenda that has no overt language policy. Multilingualism is a EU mantra, but EU institutions reflect complex processes of reaching consensus among diverse national groups and the developments in the economic, political, military and cultural spheres that privilege English. Proactive language policy formation has yet to address how the changing communicative needs of European citizens and states can strengthen the cultural and linguistic diversity that has characterized Europe hitherto.

Conclusion

Even when the term 'linguistic imperialism' is used in a loose sense, as in the examples above, or not at all, as in the case of the Spanish minister, what is being referred to is inequality, absence of a level linguistic playing-field, unfair privileging of the use of one language and those who use it more easily, the uncritical acceptance of English having a 'natural' right to be the default language, a blind belief in English as a 'lingua franca' of Europe, as though this somehow detaches the language from Americanization and inequality.

Linguistic imperialism dovetails with communicative, cultural, educational, and scientific imperialism in a rapidly evolving world in which corporate-led globalization is seeking to impose or induce a neo-imperial world order. There are major unresolved tensions between national and international languages (English being both for some people), and in reconciling participation in the global economy with maintaining national sovereignty, linguistic diversity and personal freedoms. We may be moving in the direction of global linguistic apartheid of the kind that the first Prime Minister of independent India, Nehru, warned against, the emergence of an English-knowing caste at the summit of national or international society. But as Americanization is so pervasive, English is expanding in bottom-up processes as well as top-down ones, and in oppositional ways that seek the creation of a more just world order as an alternative to the current world disorder.

Notes

1   In Pennycook's Table 3.2, Frameworks for the Understanding of the Global Role of English (2001, 59), he states that a linguistic imperialism analysis entails that one should 'teach English sparingly'. Not so, one should teach English additively, as in Canagarajah's approach to resisting English linguistic imperialism. See also a range of views on linguistic imperialism and the global role of English in Seidlhofer 2003.

2   Skutnabb-Kangas 2000, 37–46 contrasts such figures.

3   For elaboration see Phillipson 2003, chapter 3.

4   See Brzezinski 1997, reported in The Wilderness Publications, <www. copvcia.com> accessed 1.9.2003. Condolezza Rice: 'The rest of the world is best served by the USA pursuing its own interests because American values are universal.', see also www.newamericancentury. org.

5   Biopower, following Foucault, is seen as 'a form of power that regulates social life from its interior, following it, interpreting it, absorbing it, and rearticulating it. Power can achieve an effective command over the entire life of the population only when it becomes an integral, vital function that every individual embraces and reactivates of his or her own accord… what is at stake in power is the production and reproduction of life itself.' (Hardt and Negri, 2000, 23-4).

6   Little is available on these policies in languages other than Swedish and Danish. Try internet searching under such key words as Denmark, Sweden, Ministry of Culture, language policy, sprogpolitik, språkpolitik.

7   Communication from the Commission to the Council, the European Parliament, the Economic and Social Committee and the Committee of the Regions, COM(2003) 449.

8   For a critical review of de Swaan's book, see Phillipson 2004.

9   For details of language in EU institutions, see Phillipson 2003, chapter 4.

10   The Finnish government is seen as convinced that Finnish membership of the EU is primarily a matter of Finland benefiting maximally from the economic dimension of globalization and europeanization. On

Finland as a success story economically while retaining strong cultural and linguistic traditions, see Phillipson 2003, 83.

11   Pierre Lequiller, Compte rendu no. 48, Délégation pour l'Union Européenne, 11 June 2003.

Annotated Bibliography

Canagarajah, Suresh 1999. *Resisting Linguistic Imperialism in English Teaching.* Oxford: Oxford University Press.

A theoretically subtle critique of Western analyses of language dominance and educational inappropriacy, which builds on a rich empirical grounding of critical pedagogy in Sri Lanka and documents how English can be appropriated.

Fishman, Joshua, Conrad, Andrew, and Alma Rubal-Lopez (eds.) 1996. *Post-imperial English. Status change in former British and American colonies, 1940-1990.* Berlin and New York: Mouton de Gruyter.

A compilation of empirical studies, with substantial sections on countries in the American and British spheres of influence and the EU, as well as general articles. There is some inconsistency in the way contributors analyse linguistic imperialism and the way the editors distance themselves from the concept and its application.

Jenkins, Jennifer 2003. *World Englishes. A Resource Book for Students.* London: Routledge.

A wide-ranging set of readings and questions bringing together analyses of the forms and functions of World Englishes, the historical development of English, current debates, and aspects of power, ownership, and norms for an international language.

Maurais, Jacques and Michael A. Morris (eds.) 2003. *Languages in a Globalising World.* Cambridge: Cambridge University Press.

An anthology of 21 articles, some dealing with general aspects of global linguistic ordering and language policy, some with the major regions of the world, others with specific widely used languages. Of particular relevance for the hegemony of English is Hamel on Mercosur countries in South America.

Mühlhäusler, Peter 1996. *Linguistic Ecology: Language Change and Linguistic Imperialism in the Pacific Region.* London: Routledge.

Covers the region with a great deal of linguistic and cultural detail from pre-colonial times, through europeanisation (the impact of literacy, creoles, language shift, policy) to future prospects for the maintenance of diversity.

Phillipson, Robert 2003. *English-only Europe? Challenging Language Policy.* London: Routledge.

A book for the general reader, with chapters on the risks of *laissez faire* language policies; European languages: families, nations, empires, states; global trends impacting on European language policy; languages in EU institutions; towards equitable communication; recommendations for action on language policies.

Discussion Questions

1. Can Englishization be seen as independent of globalization and Americanization? You might consider assessing whether the literature on World Englishes achieves this.

2. Are there ways of counteracting inequality in international communication that avoid privileging fluent users of English?

3. If it is possible that monolinguals will miss out in future, whereas multilinguals will thrive, is aiming at parallel linguistic competence a valid and realistic educational and social goal?

4. Consider whether the developments occurring in Europe are being experienced in other contexts, such as the Americas, Africa, or Asia.

5. If globalization is intrinsically neither good nor evil, just as no language is, what language policies should be adopted so as to maintain a balanced language ecology?

6. Can you think of a better term than 'linguistic imperialism' for the role that English plays in the current phase of globalization?

References

Block, David and Deborah Cameron (eds.) 2002. *Globalization and Language Teaching.* London: Routledge.

Bourdieu, Pierre 2001. *Pour un mouvement social européen* (Counter fire 2. For a European social movement). Paris: Raisons d'agir.

Brzezinski, Zbigniew 1997. *The Grand Chessboard – American primacy and its geostrategic imperatives.* New York: Basic Books.

Brutt-Griffler, Janina 2002. *World English: A Study of its Development.* Clevedon: Multilingual Matters.

Chaudenson, Robert 2003. 'Geolinguistics, geopolitics, geostrategy: The case for French,' in Maurais & Morris, 291–97.

de Swaan, Abram 2001. *Words of the World: The Global Language System.* Cambridge: Polity Press.

Gawlitta, Kurt and Fritz Vilmar (eds.) 2002. *'Deutsch nix wichtig?' Engagement für die deutsche Sprache* (German unimportant? Commitment for the German language), Paderborn: IFB Verlag.

Görlach, Manfred 1997. 'Review of Post-Imperial English. Status Change in Former British and American Colonies, 1940-1990. *Sociolinguistica* 11, 215-218.

Hardt, Michael and Antonio Negri 2000. *Empire.* Cambridge, MA: Harvard University Press.

Höglin, René 2002. *Engelska språket som hot och tillgång i Norden* (The English language as threat or opportunity in the Nordic countries). Copenhagen: Nordiska Ministerrådet.

Kelletat, Andreas F. 2001. *Deutschland:Finnland 6:0. Saksa:Suomi 6:0.* Tampere: University of Tampere, Deutsche Studien, volume 4.

Li, David 2002. 'Hong Kong parents' preference for English-medium education: passive victims of imperialism or active agents of pragmatism? In Andy Fitzpatrick (ed.), *Englishes in Asia. Communication, Identity, Power and Education.* Melbourne: Language Australia, 29-61.

Mair, Christian (ed.) 2003. *The Politics of English as a World Language: New horizons in postcolonial English studies.* Amsterdam and New York: Rodopi.

Monbiot, George 2000. *Captive State. The Corporate Takeover of Britain,* London: Macmillan.

Pennycook, Alastair 1998. *English and the Discourses of Colonialism.* London: Routledge.

Pennycook, Alastair 2001. *Critical Applied Linguistics, A Critical Introduction.* Mahwah, NJ: Lawrence Erlbaum.

Phillipson, Robert 1992. *Linguistic Imperialism*. Oxford: Oxford University Press.

Phillipson, Robert 2004. 'English in Globalization: three Approaches. Review article, books by de Swaan, Block and Cameron, and Brutt-Griffler.' *Journal of Language, Identity, and Education*, Vol. 3, No. 1, 73-84

Rothkopf, David 1997. 'In Praise of Cultural Imperialism.' *Foreign policy*, 38-53.

Seidlhofer, Barbara (ed.) 2003. *Controversies in Applied Linguistics*. Oxford: Oxford University Press.

Skutnabb-Kangas, Tove 2000. *Linguistic Genocide in Education – Or Worldwide Diversity and Human Rights?* Mahwah, NJ: Lawrence Erlbaum.

Stiglitz, Joseph 2002. *Globalization and its Discontents*. London: Penguin.

van Dijk, Teun 1977. 'Editorial: The Imperialism of English.' *Discourse and Society*, Vol. 8, No. 3, 291-2.

Yeung, Y-m. 2000. *Globalization and Networked societies. Urban–Regional Change in Pacific Asia*. Honolulu: University of Hawai'i Press.

Linguistic imperialism: a conspiracy, or a conspiracy of silence?

Chapter 4

ABSTRACT

The treatment of linguistic imperialism and the spread of English in Bernard Spolsky's book Language Policy (2004) is critiqued. Robert Phillipson's Linguistic Imperialism (1992) cannot be reduced to a conspiracy 'theory', a concept that is theoretically inadequate and often serves to deflect attention from underlying foreign policy goals and the realities of how dominance and inequality are maintained and legitimated. The interlocking of the promotion of English with wider political and economic activities is well documented: ignoring these, by detaching language from causative historical factors, amounts to a conspiracy of silence. The study of language policy and language 'management' requires more adequate theorisation, drawing on a wider range of social sciences than in Spolsky 2004, if it is to do justice to the complexity of how the power of English is constituted.

Man's mind cannot grasp the causes of events in their completeness, but the desire to find those causes is implanted in man's soul. And without considering the multiplicity and complexity of the conditions any one of which taken separately may seem to be the cause, he snatches at the first approximation to a cause that seems to him intelligible, and says: 'This is the cause!'

Leo Tolstóy, War and Peace, *1865-69*,

opening sentence of Book XIII

(Macmillan translation by Louise and Aylmer Maude, 1942, p. 1089).

This is a response to Bernard Spolsky's coverage of 'how English spread' in his book on language policy (2004) and his assertion that my book on linguistic imperialism (1992) subscribes to a conspiracy theory.

Branding scholarship as doing this implies that it lacks an account of the 'multiplicity and complexity' of the real world that Tolstoy portrays in his monumental analytical narrative of a society at war and peace. Tolstoy rejects simplistic understandings of historical events, and debunks the idea that great victories or policies were clinically executed top-down, an observation that tallies well with Spolsky's scepticism about whether language management actually succeeds. Tolstoy stresses human fallibility and multiple bottom-up influences, so that outcomes tend to be unpredictable and under the influence of forces beyond human control.

Accusing anyone of buying into conspiracy as an explanation is a serious allegation, since the concept implies activities that are covert and 'for an unlawful or reprehensible purpose' (*New Shorter Oxford English Dictionary*, 1993). The implication is that no sophisticated scholar would countenance such a simplistic diagnosis. Spolsky writes that my analysis of the global dominance of English does not see it as 'a complex result of a multitude of factors' (2004, 79) but as due to a conspiracy. However, a conspiracy theory is often:

> the standard invalidating predicate to block tracking of strategic decisions....

> As a philosopher, I am not interested in 'conspiracy theories', the favoured term to invalidate all questions about 9–11. I am interested in the deeper question of the life-and-death principles of regulating value systems which connect across and explain social orders (McMurtry 2002, 17, xiv).

It is false to suggest that the theoretical underpinning and empirical documentation of my book ignores complex political and social developments. In addition, the British and US governments have been open about their aims for global English and adopted policies to promote it. I report on policy statements that were in the public sphere as well as some of the more 'confidential' ones.

The imperialism theory that I elaborated tries to avoid reductionism by recognizing that what happens in the Periphery is not irrevocably determined by the Centre. The efforts of the Centre do not mesh in precisely with what the Periphery's needs are understood to be. Nor are the Periphery representatives passive spectators. They have a variety of motives, at the state and the personal level, as do the Centre inter-state actors. I state: 'A conspiracy theory is therefore inadequate as a means of grasping the role of the key actors in Centre or Periphery. The conspiracy explanation tends to be too vague and undifferentiated to merit being called a theory. It also ignores the structure within which the actors operate' (Phillipson 1992, 63).

Similar points are made by Stiglitz in his insider denunciation of how the World Bank operates:

> I have written this book because while I was at the World Bank, I saw firsthand the devastating effect that globalization can have on developing countries, and especially the poor within those countries ... decisions were often made because of ideology and politics. As a result many wrong-headed actions were taken, ones that did not solve the problem at hand but that fit with the interests and beliefs of the people in power... academics involved in making policy recommendations become politicized and start to bend the evidence to fit the ideas of those in charge...
>
> There are no smoking guns here. You won't find evidence here of a terrible conspiracy by Wall Street and the IMF to take over the world. I don't believe such a conspiracy exists. The truth is subtler. Often it's a tone of voice, or a meeting behind closed doors, or a memo that determines the outcome of discussions. (Stiglitz 2002, ix-x, xv)

Spolsky's 2004 book has a chapter on 'How English spread', with sub-sections entitled 'Causes of spread', 'Conspiracy theory', 'Imperialism, linguistic imperialism and globalization', 'English diffusion in the UK', 'English in the colonies', 'Empirical study of linguistic imperialism', 'The global language system', and a concluding sub-section entitled 'Was or did English spread?' The implicit structuring principle of the chapter, as the concluding section suggests, is a dichotomy between English as actively promoted so as to serve Anglo-American interests and the language merely spreading. He sees the vulnerability or demise of powerless languages as a 'natural' development, the alternative to which is implementation of 'some conscious policy on the part of governments, civil servants, English-teaching professionals and their elite collaborators and successors in the peripheral countries' (op.cit., 79), i.e. a conspiracy, in his terms.

In reality, it is inconceivable that any language can 'spread' without there being any causal factors or agents, meaning that both items in Spolsky's postulated binary pair—'did it happen or was it caused ?' (ibid.,79)—are invalid contentions. Spolsky detaches language from all the other factors involved in empire, military, economic, religious etc, whereas Phillipson (1992) integrates the role played by linguistic imperialism within a wider imperial, exploitative structure. In an earlier review of *Linguistic Imperialism*, Spolsky noted (1995, 233) that I conclude that there was no secret master-minded plan, but rather a hegemony, a concept that my book elaborates in some detail. The post-structuralist approach necessarily connects language to the wider interests it serves, and entails analysis of material, ideological and symbolic power, and the discourses that facilitate these.

Spolsky falsely states that Skutnabb-Kangas and Phillipson define linguicism as 'the intentional destruction of a powerless language by a dominant one' (2004, 79), which we have never written. The definition is 'ideologies, structures and practices which are used to legitimate, effectuate and reproduce an unequal division of power and resources (both material and non-material) between groups which are defined on the basis of language (on the basis of their mother tongues)' (Skutnabb-Kangas 1988, 13). Linguistic imperialism is a sub-type of linguicism—and manifestly not reducible to any conspiracy 'theory'.

Spolsky searches in his book for evidence of language management outcomes that are the 'direct and simple result of planned intervention by identifiable human agents, that they were the direct outcome of language management' (this reads like Tolstoy's 'first approximation to a cause'). After presenting evidence from a selective range of contexts, Spolsky concludes that the causal factor was imperialism rather than linguistic imperialism (ibid., 85). Drawing on work by Fishman and de Swaan, he concludes that the global pre-eminence of English is due to 'the changing nature of the world', English being widespread, and because 'the remaining superpower used it unselfconsciously' (ibid., 88), so that English was merely there for the taking (although he puzzlingly restricts this to 'international communication', this apparently not affecting what happens within countries).

Spolsky's analysis exonerates him from looking at the evidence of Anglo-American involvement in strengthening English either directly (see Phillipson 1992, Pennycook 1994), or through the World Bank and local partners (Mazrui 1997, Brock-Utne 2000), and at the interlocking of English with many forms of imperialism, educational (also ignored by de Swaan), scientific, cultural and economic (which involve, in Bourdieu's terms, cultural and linguistic capital). This is a conspiracy of silence, an ignoring of historical evidence.

The reluctance to countenance the interlocking of the multiple agendas of applied linguistics and the English teaching business (buttressed by the myth of these activities being apolitical) with geopolitical goals is symptomatic of a positivistic disconnection between identifiable activities and the wider picture of strategic political and economic interests. This paradigm is well entrenched in the academic world, not least in Britain, which has been heavily influenced by US scholarship at least since the 1920s. An unquestioning acceptance of hegemonic ideologies is also the case in the media world, which is now essentially integrated into few global corporations:

> In a resolutely empiricist culture like Britain's—where 'practical men' prefer to shun the bigger picture … it is hardly surprising perhaps that many people feel unhappy with any suggestion of behind-the-scenes collusion and manipulation of events … Among journalists in particular, it is an article of faith to insist on the 'cock-up theory' rather than the conspiracy theory of history. Real life is, of course, a mixture of the two. One side-effect of this dogmatic insistence that events are largely the product of an arbitrary and contingent muddle has been a chronic refusal by the mainstream media in Britain—and most opposition politicians—to probe or question the hidden agendas and unaccountable, secret power structures at the heart of government (Milne 2005, 311).

The secrecy and underlying agendas of British foreign policy—a parameter of paramount importance to the international promotion of English—are explored in a book that draws three conclusions

(Curtis 2004): 1) the culture of lying and misleading the electorate is deeply embedded in British policy-making; 2) by contrast the secret record of official files is quite open about goals that differ markedly from what is made public. Curtis regards this as evidence not of a conscious conspiracy, but rather that foreign-policy making is so 'secretive, elitist and unaccountable that policy-makers know they can get away with almost anything'; 3) humanitarian concerns do not figure at all in the rationale behind British foreign policy. Tony Blair's lying about the Iraq war provides a vivid example of these three, in tandem with similar behaviour by George W. Bush.

American goals have been explicit and consistent since World War II. In 1948, the State Department's senior imperial planner, George Kennan, wrote: 'We have 50 per cent of the world's wealth, but only 6.3 per cent of its population. In this situation, our real job in the coming period is to devise a pattern of relationships which permit us to maintain this position of disparity. To do so, we have to dispense with all sentimentality … we should cease thinking about human rights, the raising of living standards and democratisation' (quoted in Pilger 1998, 59). President George W. Bush is visibly cast in this mould.

The integration of European economies, along lines that the US dictates, has been US policy since 1945: 'The process of European integration might never have come about had it not been imposed on Europe by the Americans' (Holm 2001, 34). This policy implies adoption of the economic models and value systems that have been evolved in the USA over the past 200 years, this young country having arrogated to itself the 'manifest destiny' to determine policies in the Americas through the Monroe doctrine since the early nineteenth century, and policies globally in the twentieth century (see Harvey 2005a, 2005b, Smith 2003). The belief in the right of the US (i.e. its corporate and political leaders) to dominate the entire world was explicitly articulated during the election campaign that brought George W. Bush to the presidency in 2000:

> Our nation is chosen by God and commissioned by history to be a model to the world.

Condoleezza Rice, a Bush adviser who later became his Foreign Secretary, articulated this doctrine in 'Campaign 2000: Promoting the national interest' (cited in the Danish daily newspaper *Information*, 14 June 2001):

> The rest of the world is best served by the USA pursuing its own interests because American values are universal.

These are the explicit goals of the 'Project for the New American Century', the Cheney-Wolfowitz-Rumsfeld doctrine (D. Armstrong in *Harper's Magazine* 305, 2002, cited in Harvey 2005a, 80):

> The plan is for the United States to rule the world. The overt theme is unilateralism, but it is ultimately a story of domination. It calls for the United States to maintain its overwhelming military superiority and prevent new rivals from rising up to challenge it on the world stage. It calls for dominion over friends and enemies alike. It says not that the United States must be more powerful, or most powerful, but that it must be absolutely powerful.

Language policy is essential to this mission, as formulated in an article 'In praise of cultural imperialism' in *Foreign policy*, by David Rothkopf, Director of the Kissinger Institute, in 1997:

> It is in the economic and political interest of the United States to ensure that if the world is moving toward a common language, it be English; that if the world is moving toward common telecommunications, safety, and quality standards, they be American; and that if common values are being developed, they be values with which Americans are comfortable. These are not idle aspirations. English is linking the world.

I am not suggesting that Phillipson 1992 is a definitive statement, and indeed the closing pages suggest many ways in which study of this area could be refined and extended. Nor is this the place for more extended analysis (see Phillipson 2003, 2006a, b, c, in press). But the 1992 book, rather than being deterministic, as some claim, goes beyond traditional structuralist analysis, and fits better into what Giddens refers to as structuration theory, in which 'Structure is the medium and outcome of the conduct it recursively organizes' and 'Actors are knowledgeable and competent agents who reflexively monitor their action' (Bryant and Jary 2003, 254). In other words, speakers of languages that are subject to linguistic imperialism are not helpless victims, but in a more complex relationship with the forces propelling a language forward. This tallies with Bourdieu's approach to symbolic power, linguistic capital, and the relationship between dominant and dominated groups:

> To understand the nature of symbolic power, it is therefore crucial to see that it presupposes a kind of *active complicity* on the part of those subjected to it. Dominated individuals are not passive bodies to which symbolic power is applied, as it were, like a scalpel to a corpse. Rather, symbolic power requires, as a condition for its success, that those subjected to it believe in the legitimacy of power and the legitimacy of those who wield it. (Thompson 1991, 23)

We need research that can unmask some of this complicity, and active 'forces', such as a government's strategic goals and means, in order to reach a deeper understanding of how language policy fits into and constitutes the wider picture. One is then more likely to achieve what Spolsky recommends, namely studying the practices of language policy as well as official statements or regulations (op cit., 222).

Spolsky's concluding remarks classify people analysing language policy as falling into two groups, the optimists who regard language management as possible, and the pessimists who believe language is beyond control. He considers the evidence as favouring the latter, as shown by his assessment of the failures of French, Irish and Soviet language policy. In journalistic terms, Spolsky thus adheres to a 'cock-up theory', even if his choice of the technocratic term 'language management' presupposes that policies can be and are implemented. His position therefore represents a defence of the established order, an entrenchment of existing power structures (he describes himself as a liberal pragmatist, and draws on the CIA as a credible source of information, ibid., ix-x), and ultimately an acceptance of an American-dominated world order and the empire of English.

It is no mitigation to read in Spolsky's introduction that he is aware of the complexity of varying approaches in the social sciences, and the role of subjective choices—and that one can still be friends with those one sees the world differently from, like myself and Tove Skutnabb-Kangas, which I can only endorse. The problem is twofold, first, that one would like not to be misread or misrepresented, and second, that Spolsky's study of language policy essentially remains a sociolinguistic enterprise that fails to build on the extensive work on language in many other disciplines in the social sciences and humanities. Each of these seeks to engage with aspects of what Tolstoy refers to as 'the causes of events in their completeness'. The more multi-disciplinary that language policy is, the more chance it has of being theoretically and empirically well grounded, and of being significantly useful both for historical analysis and proactively. We need to avoid conspiracy theories and any conspiracy of silence.

References

Brock-Utne, Birgit 2000. *Whose Education for All? The Recolonization of the African Mind.* New York: Falmer Press.

Bryant, Christopher G.A. and David Jary 2003. Antony Giddens. In *The Blackwell Companion to Major Contemporary Social Theorists,* ed. George Ritzer. Malden, MA and Oxford: Blackwell, 247–74.

Curtis, Mark 2004. *Unpeople: Britain's Secret Human Rights Abuses.* London: Vintage.

Harvey, David 2005a. *The New Imperialism.* Oxford: Oxford University Press (first published in 2003).

Harvey, David 2005b. *Neoliberalism.* Oxford: Oxford University Press.

Holm, Erik 2001. *The European Anarchy. Europe's Hard Road into High Politics.* Copenhagen: Copenhagen Business School Press.

Mazrui, Alamin A. 1997. 'The World Bank, the language question and the future of African education.' *Race and Class,* Vol. 38, No. 3, 35–48.

McMurtry, John 2002. *Value Wars. The Global Market versus the Life Economy.* London: Pluto.

Milne, Seamus 2005. 'The secret war against the miners.' In Pilger (ed.) 2005, 284-331.

Pennycook, Alastair 1994. *The Cultural Politics of English as an International Language.* Harlow: Longman.

Phillipson, Robert 1992. *Linguistic Imperialism.* Oxford: Oxford University Press.

Phillipson, Robert 2003. *English-Only Europe? Challenging Language Policy.* London: Routledge.

Phillipson, Robert 2006a. English, a cuckoo in the European higher education nest of languages? *European Journal of English Studies*, Vol. 10, No. 1, 13–32.

Phillipson, Robert 2006b. 'Language policy and linguistic imperialism'. In Ricento, Thomas (ed.). *An Introduction to Language Policy. Theory and Method.* Oxford: Blackwell, 346–361.

Phillipson, Robert 2006c. 'Figuring out the Englishisation of Europe'. In Leung and Jenkins (eds). *Reconfiguring Europe: The Contribution of Applied Linguistics.* London: Equinox, and British Association for Applied Linguistics, 65–86.

Phillipson, Robert (2008). 'The linguistic imperialism of neoliberal empire'. *Critical Inquiry in Language Studies*, Vol. 5, No. 1.

Pilger, John 1998. *Hidden Agendas.* London: Vintage.

Pilger, John (ed.) 2005. *Tell me no lies. Investigative Journalism and its Triumphs.* London: Vintage.

Skutnabb-Kangas, Tove 1988. 'Multilingualism and the education of minority children'. In Skutnabb-Kangas, Tove and Jim Cummins (eds). *Minority Education: from Shame to Struggle,* Clevedon: Multilingual Matters, 9–44.

Smith, Neil 2003. *American Empire. Roosevelt's Geographer and the Prelude to Globalization.* Berkeley and Los Angeles, CA: University of California Press.

Spolsky, Bernard 1995. 'Review of Linguistic imperialism'. *Journal of Pragmatics*, Vol. 23, 231–233.

Spolsky, Bernard 2004. *Language Policy.* Cambridge: Cambridge University Press.

Stiglitz, Joseph 2002. *Globalization and its Discontents.* London; Penguin.

Thompson, John 1991. Editor's Introduction to Pierre Bourdieu, *Language and Symbolic Power.* Cambridge: Polity.

Chapter 5

English, no longer a foreign language in Europe?

Contemporary Europe is no exception to the worldwide trend of English being used and learned more widely. Europe is undergoing an intensive process of integration. Language, education and culture are no longer the exclusive prerogative of each state but are also policy concerns of the European Union (EU), which is constantly expanding its range of activities. In addition the enlargement process is bringing many more states into closer union, a total of 25 since May 2004. English figures prominently in these processes both within countries and as the dominant international language. In each country, English is intruding into domains in which other European languages have been unchallenged hitherto. There is a major challenge in the analysis of language policy in Europe to tease out the links between Englishization, Europeanization, globalization, and Americanization. The centrality of English learning in facilitating and constituting these ongoing processes requires language pedagogy and language policy to be situated within wider political, social and cultural contexts.

Why is there a problem if continental Europeans are able to function in English?

English is increasingly prominent in continental Europe in such key domains as business, education, and the media. Its privileged position has evolved quite differently from the way the primacy of English was established in Europeanized states to which English was transplanted in North America and Australasia (countries inaccurately referred to as 'English-speaking' when the United States, for instance, is 'one of the most linguistically and culturally diverse countries in the world', McCarty 2004, 74). Nor has the consolidation of English in Europe followed the same route as in former colonies of the US and the UK, such as the Philippines, India, or Nigeria, in which the language of colonisation was retained for elite formation and high-prestige functions internally and externally. In continental Europe, English has thus not been imposed through settlement by native speakers or through colonial dominance. Until recently English was a foreign language. Its increasing use in public, professional and private life, and in education means that for some it fulfils more the role of a second language.

In Europe, many languages have been consolidated as the key state language over the past two centuries. All domestic functions have been carried out in the key 'national' language, Danish, Estonian, French, Greek, etc. Foreign languages were learned for external communication purposes and familiarity with the cultural heritage associated with 'great' powers. Since 1945, and more intensively in recent years, there has been a gradual shift towards English becoming by far the most widely learned foreign language on the continent of Europe, taking over space, both in western and eastern Europe, occupied earlier by other foreign languages, French, German and Russian in particular.

There is massive exposure to Hollywood throughout Europe: '70-80% of all TV fiction shown on European TV is American... American movies, American TV and the American lifestyle for the populations of the world and Europe at large have become the *lingua franca* of globalization, the closest we get to a visual world culture' (Bondebjerg 2003, 79, 81). These US products are transmitted with the original soundtrack in the Nordic countries and the Netherlands, which strengthens the learning of English, and are generally dubbed elsewhere. By contrast in the USA the market share of films of foreign origin is 1 per cent.

The position of English is also strengthened by a proficiency requirement in many countries for access to higher education and for many kinds of employment. The triumphalist marketing of English is characteristically flagged on the cover page of *Business Week* (European edition) of 13 August 2001, which portrays twin executives, one communicating successfully, the English speaker, the other mouthless, speechless. The accompanying text 'Should everyone speak English?' flags the article 'The great English divide. In Europe, speaking the lingua franca separates the haves from the have-nots.' It deals with two symbiotically unified topics, English as a professional skill, and the mushrooming of English language schools. Such language schools, largely staffed by native speakers, are mostly a feature of countries in southern Europe in which the learning of English in state education tends to be less successful. In Scandinavia all university students are expected to be able to read texts in English; in Italy only 1 % are able to do so (information from Renato Corsetti, University of Rome).

English is increasingly the primary corporate language of transnational enterprises wherever they are based geographically. Top European executives tend to be multilingual, unless they come from the UK or the US (and it is arguable that monolingualism may in future be a liability, Graddol 1998, Nuffield Languages Inquiry 2000, Grin, 2001).

Academics and researchers in virtually all fields are expected to publish in English, either exclusively or as well as in the local language, depending on disciplinary pressures and the discourse communities that scholars contribute to (Petersen and Shaw 2002). They are also increasingly required to teach through the medium of English in higher education, since universities seek to recruit more foreign students. This development is a key feature of the 'internationalization' of higher education, and is obliging continental universities to address how best to function 'multilingually', which generally means in the national language and English. Conferences are being held to exchange experience (Wilkinson, 2004) and university administrators are being encouraged to address the language policy implications (for instance in policy statements in 2004 on internationalisation from the 'Danish Rectors' Conference', which is what the assembly of university Vice-Chancellors in Denmark call themselves, in a literal translation from Danish into words that are manifestly a sample of 'European English').

In 'English-speaking' countries, there is currently a boom market in foreign students, one that universities in many countries seek to benefit from. The British Council is worried about competition from other countries, and warned in 2004 that the UK economy is at risk if it doesn't invest more in international education. The UK economy benefits by £11 billion p.a. directly, and a further £12 billion indirectly, from international education. The goal is 8 per cent annual growth across the sector, and to double the present number of 35,000 research graduates contributing to the UK's knowledge economy by 2020. In addition over 500,000 attend language learning courses each year (www.britishcouncil.org/mediacentre/apr04/vision_2020_press_ notice.doc). Expansion has been so rapid (and commercially driven) that some language schools and universities that offer pre-sessional language proficiency courses appreciate that they are ill equipped to provide culturally and linguistically appropriate teaching for students from Asia, primarily China.

However what is at stake is not merely the local question of whether Chinese students are getting good value for money when opting for English-medium higher education, whether in the UK or a continental European country. An article in the British *The Guardian Weekly*, 13–19 August 2004, 9 (citing *The Observer*) claims that the 'Scramble for lucrative foreign students is corrupting universities' by dropping academic standards. This is perhaps not surprising if the content of teaching and its delivery have remained unchanged, even if students have a radically different cultural and linguistic starting-point. What is at stake globally is the role of the English as a Second/Foreign Language business and its practitioners, and higher education in general, as an integral dimension of the global economy. English learning and use are preconditions for the functioning and legitimating of the global system. They are not merely an epiphenomenon that can be evaluated on its own terms, divorced from its indispensable role in servicing the global economy, the financial circuit supporting it, and the educational institutions that validate credentials.

In authorizing and imprinting particular norms of use and discourse, English teachers function as professional midwives to the 'legitimate and illegitimate offspring of English', to use Mufwene's vivid image

(2001, chapter 4) when characterizing those forms of English that are considered authentic: maximal legitimacy for British English, despite its creole origins, and for English transported by native speakers to Europeanized states in America and Australasia; dubious status for 'new' English that only has local validity (Singapore, Malaysia, Nigeria), and complete illegitimacy for creoles which are beyond the linguistic pale (in the Caribbean or West Africa). Discourses, pedagogical practices and institutions maintain norms. As Alexander puts it (2003), 'policing the language of the world goes hand in hand with policing the world'. 'Global' English is a normative project, not a reality but a vision that powerful forces are keen to bring about.

There are major risks in considering that as English now functions outside many of its original sites, it is detached from social forces:

> English being disembedded from national cultures can never mean that it floats culture-free (... or) is culturally neutral. The point may be simple, but it is often elided; and this elision constitutes a politics of English as a global language which precisely conceals the cultural work which that model of language is in fact performing. (Kayman 2004, 17)

Kayman also makes the intriguing point that the prophets and proponents of English as a global language can be compared to the occupation by Europeans of other continents that were falsely seen as *terra nullius*. Contemporary linguists who proclaim the neutrality of English treat the language as a cultural *terra nullius* (ibid., 18)

This is an influential tradition in writings on Global English. Crystal (1997, 137, see Phillipson 1999), despite identifying many factors in the past that account for English being widely used, sees the language as 'independent of any form of social control'. Yet he foresees global diglossia, World Standard Spoken English functioning alongside national English dialects. Presumably such a 'standard' language will have guardians. Is it likely that a globally valid form of spoken English will be anything other than some sort of CNN/BBC hybrid?

Similarly Brutt-Griffler (2002, reviewed in Phillipson, 2004a) sees World English as doing away with hierarchy among speech communities, non-Western nations taking equal part in the creation of the world econocultural system and its linguistic expression. At the same time she acknowledges that the US and UK dominate the world market and that World English is the dominant socio-political language form. Her attempt to explain the growth of English worldwide is therefore internally inconsistent and based on argumentation that ignores the reality of the market forces that strengthen some languages at the expense of others locally and globally. It ignores the political, economic and military forces behind English in the current neo-imperial, US-dominated world 'order' (Phillipson 2005).

What is unclear in continental Europe is whether the learning and use of English remains an additive process, one that increases the repertoire of language competence of individuals and the society, or whether English threatens the viability of other languages through processes of domain loss and linguistic hierarchization. In theory there ought to be no problem, because of the strong position of national languages such as German, Italian and Polish, and because of the declared policies of the EU. Article 22 of The Charter of Fundamental Rights of the EU, which forms part of the constitutional treaty endorsed in 2004, and which represents principles that all member states are committed to, states: 'The Union shall respect cultural, religious and linguistic diversity'. In reality there are fundamental paradoxes:

- The first is that although the EU is essentially a Franco-German project, since France and Germany were founding member states and continue to occupy the political high ground in shaping the integration of Europe, English is expanding, and the French and German languages are on the defensive both at home and abroad. English is increasingly the dominant language both in EU affairs and in many societal domains in continental European countries.

- The second paradox is that EU rhetoric proclaims support for multilingualism and cultural and linguistic diversity in official texts, and the equality of all official and working languages in the EU, but in practice there is *laissez faire* in the linguistic marketplace (Phillipson, 2003). At the supranational level of EU institutions (the European Parliament, Commission, and Council), multilingualism is managed by the world's largest translation and interpretation services, but there is paralysis on broader language policy issues. The rhetoric of diversity and linguistic equality is pitted against the unfree market and the forces that strengthen English.

- The third paradox is that in the view of some scholars, multilingualism is synonymous with more English. Chaudenson (2003) from France concludes that 'No-one is fooled by fiery declarations in favour of multilingualism, which is nothing but a smoke screen for the spread of English.' In somewhat similar vein, de Swaan (2001) from the Netherlands asserts that in the European Union 'the more languages, the more English', which he is all in favour of, but his analysis of language policy is excessively selective (Phillipson 2004).

- The fourth paradox is that though we all live in a multilingual world, the monolingually-oriented English as a Second Language (ESL) profession thrives. However, the widespread faith in native-speaker teachers of English, and in expertise, teaching materials, postgraduate degrees, and theories of language learning deriving from the Anglo-American world, and in the mythology of 'Global' English is not widely influential in education systems in Europe. Here foreign language teaching presupposes deep familiarity with the linguistic and cultural background of the learners, and has never embraced a monolingual approach.

Many of the competing and conflicting trends in the analysis of English in the modern world, and norms for teaching the language, are brought together in two paradigms, a Global English paradigm and a World Englishes paradigm. The variables range from macro-level dimensions of economic and cultural globalization and language ecology to micro-level matters of equitable communication and target norms for language learners. The juxtaposition of a substantial number of variables serves to highlight the complexity of the tasks facing analysts of language policy and theorists of language pedagogy. Many of the dimensions are explored in the ongoing European context in the rest of this article.

Global English Paradigm	World Englishes Paradigm
assimilationist	celebrates and supports diversity
monolingual orientation	multilingual, multi-dialectal
'international' English assumes US/UK norms	'international' a cross-national linguistic common core
World Standard Spoken English	English as a Lingua Franca
Anglo-American linguistic norms	local linguistic norms, regional and national
exonormative English	endonormative Englishes
post-national, neo-imperial expansionist globalization	local appropriation, and resistance to linguistic imperialism
apparently *laissez faire* language policy strengthens market forces, hence English	proactive language policies serve to strengthen a variety of languages
English monopolizes prestige domains	local languages have high prestige
linguicist favouring of English	balanced language ecology
ideology stresses individual 'choice'	addresses the reality of linguistic hierarchies
no concern for languages other than English	a linguistic human rights approach
subtractive English learning	additive English learning
uni-directional intercultural communication	equitable bi-directional intercultural communication
standard language orientation	learning multiple forms of competence
target norm the 'native speaker'	target norm the good ESL user
reproductive curriculum	learner-created knowledge
external syllabus	learner-centred activities and discourses
teachers can be monolingual	bilingual and bicultural teachers
dovetails with the Diffusion of English paradigm (Tsuda 1994, Skutnabb-Kangas 2000)	dovetails with the Ecology of Languages paradigm (Tsuda 1994, Skutnabb-Kangas 2000)

The evolving hybridity of 'English'

The intensification of contacts between the citizens of EU states involves an ongoing process of 'building' and 'imagining' Europe, of strengthening European identity as a complement to national identity. This unification was impelled by two agendas, one European and one American. The visionary European founding fathers of the 1940s and 50s wished to create forms of economic integration that would make the blood-letting of the past an impossibility, a goal which has been largely achieved at least within the EU, even if Northern Ireland and the Basque territory provide tragic exceptions (which incidentally confirm the principle that linguistic unification through an imposed language does not guarantee peace or justice). The twin agenda has been the determination of the US to impose its vision of society and economy on the world. Funds under the Marshall plan were made conditional on the integration of European economies. The most significant achievements of the EU, the common market and the common currency, represent the implementation of plans formed by the European Round Table of Industrialists, which is intimately linked with the Transatlantic Business Dialogue, which aims at a Transatlantic Economic Partnership that would make the Americas and Europe a single market (Monbiot, 2000).

Condoleezza Rice is continuing a century-old tradition when proclaiming that 'The rest of the world is best served by the USA pursuing its own interests because American values are universal' (see also www.newamericancentury.org). Language, and the cultural universe and ways of thought it embodies, is a key dimension of this global mission. David Rothkopf, director of the Kissinger Associates, (wrote in the establishment journal *Foreign Policy* in 1997, (45): 'It is in the economic and political interest of the United States to ensure that if the world is moving toward a common language, it be English.' Englishization is manifestly a dimension of both Americanization and globalization. Americanization gradually gathered speed over the twentieth century, and has been marketed in recent years as globalization, from which it is indistinguishable (Bourdieu, 2001). Globalization is, however, not a uniform, uni-directional process: there are many supply and demand, push and pull factors. Cultural and linguistic products and processes undergo local transformation processes wherever they become embedded. Many factors, structural and ideological, contribute to the strengthening of English in Europe and to language policy paralysis (see chapter 3, 'Global trends impacting on European language policy', Phillipson, 2003).

In a recent article on 'The globalization of language. How the media contribute to the spread of English and the emergence of medialects', a Danish researcher invents the term medialect, by logical extension from dialect and sociolect, to refer to new variants of language and cultural form that generally originate in the Anglo-American world —computer games, email and internet interaction, SMSs, television programmes (whether transmitted in the original language or the local one), advertising for the younger generation, etc.—and are creatively adapted in continental European contexts and languages. In addition to English being the language in which these media products were evolved and marketed, 'English is the linguistic vehicle for meta-communication about mediated communication.' The medialects consolidate the position of English, while excluding other international languages, and open up for 'linguistic differentiation and innovation' in the way language is used (Hjarvad, 2004, 92). Englishization affects the form and content of other languages.

University degrees in 'English' at continental European universities typically include American Studies and British Studies. The teaching of English in schools has traditionally been connected to familiarization with the culture of Britain and other 'English-speaking' countries. The study of literature is still strong in many parts of Europe, just as a degree in 'English' at most British universities means a degree in English literature. The need of continental universities to cover the language, literature and cultures of the 'English-speaking world' has led to the addition of Postcolonial Studies, World Englishes, and a wide range of topics (see the electronic Annotated Bibliography of English Studies, ABES, and the website of the European Society for the Study of English, ESSE, www.essenglish.org).

In some countries English can be seen as a second rather than a foreign language because of its functions locally and the meshing of the use of English by second language speakers with the globalizing of commerce, finance, politics, military affairs, scholarship, education, and many grassroots networks. Some networks, particularly among the young, represent bottom-up sub-cultural influences that mesh with the more formal learning of English top-down in state education (Preisler 1999). The teaching of English should be adjusting to the changing nature of English use outside the classroom.

Referring to English as a 'second' language is perhaps terminologically unfortunate, because the position of ESL users and learners in continental Europe is radically different from that of learners of ESL in the US or the UK, just as it also significantly differs from English in postcolonial countries such as Singapore or Kenya, where the same label is sometimes used.

The fact that English is used for a wide range of intercultural communication that is unconnected to a British or US context may lead to English being seen as a *lingua franca*. However, this should not mislead one into believing that English is disconnected from the many 'special purposes' it serves in key societal domains, and where it might be more accurately described as a *lingua economica* (in business and advertising), a *lingua academica* (in research and higher education), or a *lingua cultura* (in entertainment and formal education). The ubiquitous function of English as a *lingua americana* is due to the massive economic and cultural impact of the USA, and English as a *lingua bellica* and empire is increasingly visible. There are clear ideological dangers in labelling English as a *lingua franca* if this is understood as a culturally neutral medium that puts everyone on an equal footing.

The risk in English teaching is that 'The dissemination of "global" communicative norms and genres, like the dissemination of international languages, involves a one-way flow of expert knowledge from dominant to subaltern cultures' (Cameron 2002, 70). In addition, '[M]uch intercultural communication itself is typical of a certain Anglo-Saxon culture, discourse and worldview...the concept of intercultural communication as it is currently used can be easily highjacked by a global ideology of 'effective communication' Anglo-Saxon style, which speaks an English discourse even as it expresses itself in many different languages'. (Kramsch 2002, 283–4).

Being at the receiving end of cultural forces and under the influence of Anglo-American norms, linguistic and pedagogic, is vividly expressed by Vassiliki Dendrinos of Greece, who bewails the monolingualism of British English Language Teaching (ELT) discourse (1999):

> There is a systematic construction of reality whereby, by not knowing English, one is excluded from anything of social importance... Greek ELT practitioners persistently evaluate their proficiency in English against the English of the native speaker... *This underlying contradiction of a 'culturally neutral' language used in a 'culturally appropriate way'*... the claim that the native speaker is the ideal ELT practitioner construes Greek ELT practitioners as 'knowledge deficient'.

Comparable worries are expressed in the post-communist world, by Miklós Kontra of Hungary (1997):

> Until 1989 there was little serious danger of English-American cultural and linguistic imperialism in Hungary but today there are unmistakable signs of such penetration and voices of concern are heard from a growing number of Hungarians ... Most ELT materials produced in and exported from the United Kingdom and the United States disregard the learners' L1, and in this respect we might question their professionalism ... business interests override a fundamental professional interest, or: business shapes our profession in ways that we know are unprofessional. This puts us, both native and nonnative teachers of English into quite a schizophrenic position. The challenge that we are faced with is to keep the professionalism and get rid of the embarrassment.

Others (e.g. House, 2003, drawing on some provisional empirical results in Germany) do not see the advance of English as problematical, but as merely the addition of a culturally neutral tool that has no impact on the German language, even if competence in English is spreading. Others from Germany stress the marginalization of German speakers in the scientific community (Ammon, 2000), and are seeking to persuade German policy-makers to be more proactive in strengthening German nationally and in the EU (Gawlitta and Vilmar, 2002).

At present there are many symptoms of diglossia. The rise of English has been of concern to many European states, leading to legislation to curb English in several. The effects of a switch to English in specific domains are generally considered to be more threatening than the borrowing of lexical items. Widespread or exclusive use of English may mean that expertise in the natural sciences, technology or medicine is no longer transmitted in the local language. Swedish research suggests that being obliged to operate extensively in a diglossic division of labour can lead to less efficiency and appropriacy in thought, expression, and communication; to dehumanization, and cold rationality, when operating in Anglo-American discourse norms; a loss of intertextuality when the local language is no longer used for certain purposes (e.g. fiction cannot draw on domains that operate in English); and ultimately to a loss of prestige for the local language (Melander, 2001). There is anecdotal evidence from several countries (Denmark, Greece, Serbia) that individual scholars who have used English successfully for decades experience a feeling of liberation when they shift to writing in the mother tongue.

The governments of the Nordic countries have commissioned research to assess whether domain loss is taking place, and whether Nordic languages run the risk of being downgraded into second-class languages (Höglin, 2002, which contains a 15-page summary in English of the Nordic findings). The studies are far from comprehensive, but they do indicate that there is a strong possibility of domain loss in technology and the natural sciences. There is definitely a need for language policy formation to counteract this. The Swedish government has gone a long way in undertaking a systematic analysis of the language policy issues, and consulting all relevant stake-holders. In government policy documents produced in Sweden in 2002 (and replicated on a much more modest scale in Denmark in 2003) on how to strengthen the national language in view of the increasing importance of English, the declared goal is to cultivate 'parallel' linguistic competence. This would mean that Swedes and Danes active in business, politics, higher education, science and the media should be able to function equally well in the national language and in English. This might mean that domain loss and linguistic hierarchization are counteracted, through ensuring resource allocation to the language that now risks marginalization, and through fostering awareness of the need to provide conditions for all languages to thrive as well as English. Whether an increased use of English will serve as a catalyst for biculturalism or monoculturalism is a completely open question. But at least the question is being asked today.

Some ongoing research and advocacy

Research that could represent a major contribution towards realizing a change of paradigm in English teaching includes analysis of the phonology of English as an International Language (Jenkins 2000). Work has also begun on clarifying the distinctive lexical and grammatical features of English when used by L2 speakers (Seidlhofer 2004 and this volume), in a project which labels this communication as English as a Lingua Franca (ELF), a term that is unfortunately open to many interpretations (see above), and is also often used to refer to communication between people speaking English as an L1 and as an L2. Quite apart from the potential of this research to make teaching more appropriate, it might, when combined with critical discourse analysis, help to unmask some of the spurious advocacy of English as a neutral *lingua franca* for the whole of Europe. It is impossible to reconcile the argument that English now belongs to everyone (a constant refrain from British government figures and British Council staff and which also occurs in writers like David Crystal and Tom McArthur, editor of *English Today*) with the major significance of the ELT business to the British economy, as stressed by the British establishment from the Prime Minister downwards. No British government has ever doubted that the privileged position of English also brought with it political and cultural influence. On the duplicity of some of the professional advocacy for ELT, see Pegrum 2004, and on the falsity of some scholarly marketing of 'global English', see Phillipson, 1999 and 2006.

A pioneer study of Englishisation such as House (2003) presents some empirical studies and reflections on the nature of English as a *lingua franca* (ELF) in Europe. I have major reservations about the validity of the three types of empirical ELF data presented in the study (see Phillipson forthcoming for details) and about the features that are seen as characteristic of this variant of English. In the table below I list the characteristics she attributes to ELF, alongside which are my reservations about each trait, which, in my view, demonstrates how difficult it is to make theoretical headway in this field.

Characteristics of ELF House 2003	Critique
functional flexibility, openness to integration of forms from other languages	it is false to claim that such traits are specific to ELF
not restricted or for special purposes	this conflicts with House referring to diglossic 'pockets of expertise'
negotiable norms	it is *use* of the code rather than the code itself that is negotiable
bereft of collective cultural capital	the global utility of English, often diglossically High, is significant linguistic capital
similar to English diversity in postcolonial countries	here English equals power, and there is no codification of local forms
non-identificational	English=cosmopolitanism, and House states that English in Germany has positive connotations of liberation from Nazi past
non-native ownership	a concern of the analyst, not the user

When House argues that English is a language for communication rather than a language for identification, the binary pair is tempting, as a way of separating English as a national language from English as an instrument for international communication that is less culturally shaped. The distinction is seen by Blommaert (2003, 620), commenting on House's use of the terms, as 'a metapragmatic dichotomisation that allocates specific indexicalities to particular speech varieties. ... matters are considerably more complex'. He sees them as deriving from a functionalist-referential ideology and an ideological perception that results in uses of language being seen as 'instrumental'.

Hüllen was earlier an advocate of the binary distinction in a far from simplistic way, his initial analysis addressing the social functions of English, the risk of a monoculture, and acknowledging that competence in foreign languages can lead to identification with them (1992, 313–5). Hüllen has explored some of these tensions in more recent work (2003), and to some extent distances himself from the dichotomy. He admits that seeing English as neutral, with 'nothing to do with the cultural identity of speakers', is problematical, since we are in an age

> with the United States as a kind of new empire. This makes it difficult to believe in the hypothesis that English as a national language and English as an international language are two separate systems, the latter being equidistant to all other languages and cultures. (Hüllen 2003, 121)

The advance of English in continental Europe is associated with particular functions of the language, in specific domains, some of them formal, others informal. This is why the language can be seen as a second, rather than a foreign language. Many of its uses can therefore not be detached from societal functioning. Indeed the widespread attraction of English as a learning goal, referred to by Kachru (1986) as its alchemy, the magic of which continues to enthral, is to a large extent explicable because of the significant linguistic and cultural capital that competence in English entails. The global system is seen by some as empire that transcends states and is dominated by corporate interests that create subjectivities as well as products (Hardt and Negri 2000). It functions through communication networks that can and do strengthen a lot of languages, but English most of all.

The recognition of English as a threat to the languages and cultures of EU member states is beginning to influence the formulation and synchronization of language policy at the supranational level. The Commission document *Promoting language learning and linguistic diversity: An Action Plan 2004–2006*, is designed to curb an excessive focus on English in continental education systems and the wider society. It states (4 and 8): 'learning one lingua franca alone is not enough… English alone is not enough… In non-anglophone countries recent trends to provide teaching in English may have unforeseen consequences on the vitality of the national language.' The policy statement advocates life-long foreign language learning, including two foreign languages in the primary school. It strives to bring language policy higher up on national agendas, and to raise awareness of linguistic diversity. It endorses the notion of an inclusive 'language-friendly environment', and states that this openness should include minority languages, those of both local regions and recent immigrants. Representatives of member states attend meetings in Brussels every three months, and are required to respond to questions on the implementation of the Action Plan and obstacles to it. Such activity takes place in the secrecy of the EU bureaucratic system, and may or may not influence national policy formation, but the very existence of international pressure of this kind can serve to force states to address language policy issues that they would prefer to ignore. The EU's position is in many respects similar to what the Council of Europe, which brings together nearly twice as many European states, has been advocating for decades. It has undertaken a great deal of activity to promote language learning (see the Common European Framework of Reference for Languages, and related documents, www.coe.int). The Council of Europe has also taken the lead in attempting to ensure respect for the rights of national minorities (see for instance the contributions of Duncan Wilson and Tove Skutnabb-Kangas on educational rights in Council of Europe 2004).

All these measures may have little impact when the reasons for young people to become competent in English, and perhaps ignore other languages, are so manifest in the present-day world, and when governments that may have reservations about English expanding are simultaneously attempting to ensure through the education system that their citizens are competent in English. English is such a chameleon in the modern world that it can serve countless purposes and be learned in countless ways. At the same time the interlocking of Englishization with globalization and europeanization processes makes it possible in many contexts to specify what particular purposes an increased use of English is serving. There is a manifest need for more energetic language policy formulation both in European states and in the EU (Phillipson 2003). If the advance of English is to strengthen and enrich the ecology of language in Europe, many of the dimensions of the Global English paradigm need to be challenged and resisted. When much of the use and learning of English no longer serves foreign language purposes, language pedagogy can advance in new dynamic ways, and language policy can strive to ensure that all languages thrive.

References

Alexander, Richard J. 2003. 'G.lobal L.anguages O.ppress B.ut A.re L.iberating, Too: The dialectic of English.' In Mair (ed.), 87–96.

Ammon, Ulrich (2000). 'Towards more fairness in international English: Linguistic rights of non-native speakers?' In Phillipson (ed.), 102–110.

Bex, Tony and Richard J. Watts (eds) 1999. *Standard English: The Widening Debate*. London: Routledge.

Block, David and Deborah Cameron (eds.) 2002. *Globalization and Language Teaching*. London: Routledge.

Bondebjerg, I. 2003. 'Culture, media and globalisation.' In *Humanities —Essential Research for Europe*. Copenhagen: Danish Research Council for the Humanities, 71–88.

Bourdieu, Pierre 2001. *Contre-feux 2. Pour un mouvement social européen.* Paris: Raisons d'agir.

Boyd, Sally and Leena Huss (eds.) 2001. *Managing Multilingualism in a European Nation-State. Challenges for Sweden,* Clevedon: Multilingual Matters.

Brutt-Griffler, Janina 2002. *World English: A Study of its Development.* Clevedon: Multilingual Matters.

Cameron, Deborah 2002. Globalization and the teaching of "communication" skills'. In Block and Cameron (eds.), 67–82.

Chaudenson, Robert 2003. 'Geolinguistics, geopolitics, geostrategy: The case for French.' In Maurais and Morris (eds.), 291–297.

Christidis, A.-F. (ed.) 1999. *'Strong' and 'weak' languages in the European Union. Aspects of linguistic hegemonism.* Proceedings of an international conference, Thessaloniki, 26-28 March 1997. Thessaloniki: Centre for the Greek Language, 2 volumes.

Council of Europe 2004. *Filling the frame. Five years of monitoring the Framework Convention for the Protection of National Minorities.* Strasbourg: Council of Europe.

Crystal, David 1997. *English as a Global Language*. Cambridge: Cambridge University Press.

de Swaan, Abram 2001. *Words of the World. The Global Language System*, Cambridge: Polity.

Dendrinos, Bessie 1999. 'The conflictual subjectivity of the periphery ELT practitioner'. In Christidis (ed.), 711–717.

Gawlitta, Kurt and Fritz Vilmar (eds.) 2002. *'Deutsch nix wichtig'? Engagement für die deutsche Sprache*. Paderborn: IBF Verlag.

Graddol, David 1998. *The Future of English?* London: The British Council.

Grin, François 2001. 'English as economic value: facts and fallacies'. *World Englishes* Vol. 20, No. 1, 65–78.

Hjarvad, Stig 2004. 'The globalization of language. How the media contribute to the spread of English and the emergence of medialects'. *Nordicom Information*, Gothenburg 2, 75–97 (original also published in Danish).

Höglin, Renée 2002. *Engelska språket som hot och tillgång i Norden*. Copenhagen: Nordiska Ministerrådet.

House, Juliane 2003. 'English as a lingua franca: a threat to multilingualism?' *Journal of Sociolinguistics*, Vol. 7, No. 4, 556–578.

Hüllen, Werner 1992. 'Identifikationssprache und Kommunikationssprache. Über Probleme der Mehrsprachigkeit', *Zeitschrift für germanistische Linguistik* Vol. 20, No. 3, 298–317.

Hüllen, Werner 2003. 'Global English–desired and dreaded.' In *Europäische Sprachenpolitik. European Language Policy*, ed. Rüdiger Ahrens 2003. Heidelberg: Universitätsverlag Winter, 113-122.

Jenkins, Jennifer 2000. *The Phonology of English as an International Language*. Oxford: Oxford University Press.

Hardt, Michael and Negri, Antonio 2000. *Empire*. Cambridge, MA: Harvard University Press.

Kachru, Braj B. 1986. *The Alchemy of English: The Spread, Functions and Models of Non-Native Englishes*. Oxford: Pergamon.

Kayman, Martin A. 2004. 'The state of English as a global language: communicating culture'. *Textual Practice*, Vol. 18, No. 1, 1–22.

Kontra, Miklós 1997. *English linguistic and cultural imperialism and teacher training in Hungary*. Report on the 2nd ELT Conference on Teacher Training in the Carpathian Euro-region, Debrecen, Hungary, 25–27 April 1997. Budapest: British Council, English Language Teaching Contacts Scheme, 83–88.

Kramsch, Claire 2002. 'In search of the intercultural'. Review article. *Journal of Sociolinguistics*, Vol. 6, No. 2, 275–285.

Mair, Christian (ed.) 2003. *The Politics of English as a World Language: New horizons in Postcolonial English Studies*. Amsterdam and New York: Rodopi.

Maurais, Jacques and Michael A. Morris (eds.) 2003. *Languages in a Globalising World*. Cambridge: Cambridge University Press.

McCarty, Teresa L. 2004. 'Dangerous difference: A critical-historical analysis of language education policies in the United States'. In Tollefson and Tsui (eds.), 71–93.

Melander, Björn 2001. 'Swedish, English and the European Union.' In Boyd and Huss (eds.), 13–31.

Monbiot, George 2000. *Captive State: The Corporate Take-Over of Britain*. Basingstoke: Macmillan.

Mufwene, Salikoko S. 1997. 'The legitimate and illegitimate offspring of English'. In Smith and Forman (eds.) 1997, 182–203.

Nuffield Languages Inquiry 2000. *Languages: The Next Generation. The Final Report and Recommendations of the Nuffield Languages Inquiry*, <www.nuffield.org>.

Pegrum, Mark 2004 'Selling English: advertising and the discourses of ELT'. *English Today* 77, Vol. 20, No. 1, 3–10.

Petersen, Margrethe and Philip Shaw 2002. 'Language and disciplinary differences in a biliterate context'. *World Englishes*, Vol. 21, No. 3, 357–374.

Phillipson, Robert 1999. 'Voice in global English: unheard chords in Crystal loud and clear'. *Applied Linguistics*, Vol. 20, No. 2, 265–276.

Phillipson, Robert (ed.) 2000. *Rights to Language. Equity, Power, and Education*. Mahwah, NJ: Lawrence Erlbaum.

Phillipson, Robert 2003. *English-Only Europe? Challenging Language Policy*, London: Routledge.

Phillipson, Robert 2004. 'English in globalization: three approaches. Review article on books by de Swaan, Block and Cameron, and Brutt-Griffler'. *Journal of Language, Identity and Education*, Vol. 3, No. 1, 73–84.

Phillipson, Robert 2006. 'Language policy and linguistic imperialism. In *An Introduction to Language Policy*, (ed.) Thomas Ricento. Oxford: Blackwell 346–361.

Phillipson, Robert forthcoming. Figuring out the Englishisation of Europe. Paper at the Annual Conference of the British Association of Applied Linguistics, September 2004, King's College, London, and to appear in the proceedings.

Preisler, Bent 1999. 'Functions and forms of English in a European EFL country'. In Bex and Watts (eds.), 239–267.

Seidlhofer, Barbara 2004. 'Research perspectives on teaching English as a lingua franca'. *Annual Review of Applied Linguistics* 24, 209–239.

Skutnabb-Kangas, Tove 2000. *Linguistic Genocide in Education—Or Worldwide Diversity and Human Rights?* Mahwah, NJ: Lawrence Erlbaum.

Smith, Larry E. and Michael L. Forman (eds.) 1997. *World Englishes 2000*. Honolulu: University of Hawai'i Press.

Tollefson, James W. and Amy B.M. Tsui (eds.), 2004. *Medium of Instruction Policies. Which Agenda? Whose Agenda?* Mahwah, NJ: Lawrence Erlbaum.

Tsuda, Yukio 1994. 'The diffusion of English: Its impact on culture and communication'. *Keio Communication Review* 16, 49–61.

Wilkinson, Robert 2004. *Integrating Content and Language. Meeting the Challenge of a Multilingual Higher Education*. Maastricht: Maastricht University Press.

Chapter **6**

The linguistic imperialism of neoliberal empire

ABSTRACT

The article explores the transition from the linguistic imperialism of the colonial and postcolonial ages to the increasingly dominant role of English as a neoimperial language. It analyses 'global' English as a key dimension of US empire. U.S. expansionism is a fundamental principle of the foreign policy of the United States that can be traced back over two centuries. Linguistic imperialism and neoimperialism are exemplified at the micro and macro levels, and some key defining traits explored, as are cultural and institutional links between the United Kingdom and the United States, and the role of foundations in promoting 'world' English. Whereas many parts of the world have experienced a longstanding engagement with English, the use of English in continental Europe has expanded markedly in recent years, as a result of many strands of globalization and European integration. Some ongoing tensions in language policy in Europe, and symptoms of complicity in accepting linguistic hegemony, are explored. Valid analysis of the role of language in corporate-driven globalization requires theory-building that situates discourses and cultural politics in the material realities of neoimperial market pressures. A plea is made for more active language policy formation to strengthen ongoing efforts to maintain linguistic diversity worldwide.

The whole world should adopt the American system. The American system can survive in America only if it becomes a world system.

President Harry Truman, 1947, cited in Pieterse 2004, 131.

We are experiencing massive changes in the world's economy, ecology, and communications. There is increasing inequality in our societies, and the military budget of the United States has doubled under President George Bush. In tandem with these momentous changes, the use of English is increasing. There is therefore a real challenge to explore how and why language use is changing, and how this relates to economic and political factors. In clarifying the linguistic dimensions of globalization, in relation to corporate power and what can be seen as the new imperialism (Harvey 2005) or neoliberal empire (Pieterse 2004), the challenge for macro-sociolinguistics is to identify factors influencing current and future language policy. These issues are addressed by documenting the expansion of 'global English', tracing its historical roots, and attempting to elaborate adequate theoretical principles for the study of neoimperial English. The progression in the article is from description, entailing global English being seen as product, process or project, through foundational influences and influential rhetoric advocating an intensification of English-speaking as a unifying factor globally, to theory-building that can capture and explain what we are experiencing.

Global English: Product, process and project

The English language has been taken worldwide by soldiers, traders, and settlers, the process being initiated in the British Isles (Wales, Ireland et al) and in the 'colonies' of North America. When these succeeded in detaching themselves from the British crown in the late eighteenth century, Noah Webster made a case for political independence being strengthened through linguistic independence from Britain so as to establish a specific 'national character': 'Let us then seize the present moment, and establish a national language as well as a national government.'[1]

There have been blueprints for US dominance of the two American continents since the Monroe Doctrine of 1823, and for global domination for more than a century. Edward Said's study of culture and imperialism notes (1993, 7) that 'The American experience, as Richard van Alstyne makes clear in *Rising American Empire*, was from the beginning founded upon an idea of 'an *imperium*—a dominion, state or territory, and increase in strength and power'. Throughout the 20th century, the American Century, as Henry Luce termed it in *Life* magazine in 1942, the need for new markets due to capital over-accumulation was a primary concern of US foreign policy. Said ruefully notes, when exploring the key role of ideas, of representations, and mental universes, that 'the rhetoric of power all too easily produces an illusion of benevolence when deployed in an imperial setting, ... used ... with deafeningly repetitive frequency in the modern period, by the British, the French, the Belgians, the Japanese, the Russians, and now the Americans' (Said 1993, xix). There is no clearer instance of the way political discourse corrupts than when the dominant economic system of capitalism has been conflated with 'democracy' and 'freedom', the rhetorical hubris of US occupation.

Opinions differ on the extent to which English remains a single language or has spawned independent offspring, the English languages (McArthur 2002). The outcome of any assessment depends on how the evidence is approached and the purpose of such sociolinguistic analysis, there being serious weaknesses in the existing research on English worldwide (Bruthiaux 2003). Webster certainly succeeded in promoting US linguistic autonomy, but Anglo-American linguistic and cultural unity survived US independence. It was axiomatic for Winston Churchill, whose mother was American. Churchill was awarded the Nobel Prize in Literature largely on the strength of his A *History of the English-Speaking Peoples* (four volumes, Cassell, 1954-56), a celebration of peoples united by English. In 1941 Prime Minister Churchill secretly met President Franklin Roosevelt to coordinate war strategy and plan for the ensuing peace. He declared in the House of Commons on 24 August 1941: '... the British Empire and the United States who, fortunately for the progress of mankind, happen to speak the same language and very largely think the same thoughts ...' (Morton 1943, p. 152).

This language was not to be confined to the territories of the United Kingdom and the United States. It was an instrument for disseminating 'the same thoughts' throughout the British Empire, encapsulated in Lord Macaulay's much quoted spin-doctoring text on the role of British education in India, 1835, namely to produce 'A class of persons, Indians in blood and colour, English in taste, in opinion, in morals and in intellect.' US President John Adams had earlier affirmed to Congress: 'English is destined to be in the next and succeeding centuries more generally the language of the world than Latin was in the last or French in the present age.'[2] As these examples suggest, efforts to globalize English are not a new phenomenon: the 'manifest destiny' that Americans have ascribed to themselves involves a linguistic component. The empires of the past two centuries have taken different forms as a result of wars and economic and financial changes, and to this day linguistic globalization remains a goal rather than a reality, an 'imagined community' akin to nationalist constructions (Anderson 1983), a project in the minds of those who celebrate the dissemination of English worldwide. Learners of English may well be motivated by a desire to become members of this imagined global community (Ryan 2006).

'Global English' can be seen as a *product* (the code, the forms used in a geographically and culturally diverse community of users), as a *process* (the means by which uses of the language are being expanded, by agents activating the underlying structures, ideologies, and uses), or as a *project* (the normative goal of English becoming the default language of international communication and the dominant language of intranational communication in an increasing number of countries worldwide). The processes and project are dependent on use of the product, and on ideological commitment to the project. There is a strong measure of wishful thinking in the projection of those who claim that English is 'the world's *lingua franca*', since maximally one-third of humanity have any competence in the language at all. Likewise, the notion that English is *the* language of science is contradicted by the fact that many other languages are used in higher education and research. But such discourse serves both to constitute and confirm English dominance and American empire, and the interlocking structures and ideologies that underpin 'global' English and corporate interests. Investing in the linguistic capital of English (to use Bourdieu's term, 1992) is a project that transcends national borders, with the product and processes privileging users of the language in the current world 'order'. This is profoundly influenced by those who wield economic and finance capital (Harvey 2005) and military might (Pieterse 2004). The power of English as a symbolic system in the global linguistic market is such that its legitimacy tends to be uncritically accepted. Bourdieu's analysis of the consolidation of the power of the national (official) language can be upgraded to account for the ways in which English is being promoted and accepted globally:

All symbolic domination presupposes, on the part of those who submit to it, a form of complicity which is neither passive submission to external constraint nor a free adherence to values. The recognition of the legitimacy of the official language … is inscribed, in a practical state, in dispositions which are impalpably inculcated, through a long and slow process of acquisition, by the sanctions of the linguistic market, and which are therefore adjusted, without any cynical calculation or consciously experienced constraint, to the chances of material and symbolic profit which the laws of price formation characteristic of a given market objectively offer to the holders of a given linguistic capital. (Bourdieu 1992, 50–51).

Attempting to develop adequate theory for exploring the nature and forms of the global linguistic market will be reverted to in the final section of this article. We first need some idea of how the linguistic market is being shaped and legitimated.

The project and its cheerleaders

The neoliberal project for the New American Century that was hatched by the likes of Cheney, Wolfowitz, and Rumsfeld in the late twentieth century is quite explicit about its goals (www.newamericancentury.org). These were assessed by D. Armstrong in *Harper's Magazine* 305, 2002 (cited in Harvey 2005, 80).

The plan is for the United States to rule the world. The overt theme is unilateralism, but it is ultimately a story of domination. It calls for the United States to maintain its military superiority and prevent new rivals from rising up to challenge it on the world stage. It calls for dominion over friends and enemies alike. It says not that the United States must be more powerful, or most powerful, but that it must be absolutely powerful.

English has been essential to this mission, the project being explicitly endorsed in an article 'In praise of cultural imperialism' in *Foreign Policy*, by David Rothkopf, Director of the Kissinger Institute (1997, 45):

It is in the economic and political interest of the United States to ensure that if the world is moving toward a common language, it be English; that if the world is moving toward common telecommunications, safety, and quality standards, they be American; and that if common values are being developed, they be values with which Americans are comfortable. These are not idle aspirations. English is linking the world.

The role of scholars in facilitating this empire in the twentieth century is explored in Neil Smith's *American Empire. Roosevelt's Geographer and the*

Prelude to Globalization (2003). Geography served a similar function in legitimating and servicing French empire (Said 1993, 205), as did linguistics (Calvet 1974). Smith's study traces the shift through territorial, colonial dominance (the invasion of the Philippines in 1898) to the attempt to dominate globally through economic means: 'The American Empire, which grasped for global power at the beginning, middle, and end of the twentieth century, was built on a strategic recalibration of geography with economics, a new orchestration of world geography in the pursuit of economic accumulation' (Smith 2003, xvii–xviii). The narrative thread of the book is the biography of one geographer, Isaiah Bowman, who played a key role in the politics of negotiating the treaties that concluded the First World War and the institutional arrangements (Bretton Woods, UN, etc.) concluding the Second World War. The book is thus 'a history of geography, but even more, it is a geography of history' (op.cit., p. xvii). The study reveals how academia serves to legitimate the thrust for global dominance, in particular the interlocking of the discipline of geography with economics, politics and international affairs. Academia services the 'global' needs of the political project: 'In the 1980s the Defense Mapping Agency alone employed nine thousand people, far outstripping any civilian counterpart, and was the major single employer of geography majors' (op.cit., 3). Academia perpetuates a system in which '... global power is disproportionately wielded by a ruling class that remains tied to the national interests of the United States' (op.cit., xix). This class uses English, probably to the exclusion of all other languages, unlike the captains of industry and finance in continental Europe, who tend to be multilingual.

Political discourse is an important constituent of the empire project, with English energetically marketed. Thus after the fall of communism in eastern Europe, the panaceas marketed for the solution of the post-communist world were 'liberal democracy, the free market, and above all, the English language' (British Council Annual Report 1991–92). The British Council was established in 1935 to promote British interests and English, partly in response to the success of the fascist governments of Italy and Germany in using language teaching and higher education scholarships to promote their national interest. The British Council is a para-statal body that promotes British cultural, educational and linguistic interests worldwide. 'English should become the first foreign language throughout Europe, the *lingua franca* of the changed economic and political circumstances', according to Douglas Hurd, British Foreign Secretary in 1991. 'Britain is a global power with worldwide interests thanks to the Commonwealth, the Atlantic relationship, and the English language', according to Malcolm Rifkind, British Foreign Secretary in 1995.[3] English is marketed for seemingly altruistic purposes, 'English skills have been identified as a major factor in the process of reconstruction and transition to democracy' (British Council recruitment ad., 1993), but self-interest never lags far behind. The English language is promoted in order 'to exploit the position of English to further British interests' as one aspect of maintaining and expanding the 'role of English as the world language into the next century' (British Council press pack launching 'English 2000' in March 1995).

English is not merely an instrument for communication, it is a value one identifies with for the social functions the language is seen as serving, its utility in the linguistic market. Its use is spreading worldwide. Thus in *continental Europe*, English is by far the most widely taught foreign language, and proficiency in English is increasingly required in key societal domains, such as business and higher education (Phillipson 2006) and in European Union institutions (Phillipson 2003). In *Singapore*, English has played a key role in nation-building and is increasingly used not only in commerce and the public sphere but also in the home: the proportion of children starting school who come from English-speaking homes has increased from 35% in 1996 to 50% in 2006, the figures varying considerably between the key ethnically-defined groups (Pakir 2008).[4] In *India*, in schools in Karnataka, the heartland of the Indian information technology industry, English is increasingly being adopted as the sole medium of education, but the state is in principle committed to enforcing Kannada-medium education —while 71% of the state government's ministers send their children to English-medium schools.[5] There are proposals to make *Chile* bilingual in Spanish and English, advocates of adopting English as a second official language in *Japan*, etc. etc. In all these instances, processes are in force that involve implementing greater use of the English language product. The declared goals are primarily economic but also cultural and political, with considerable uncertainty about where the project will lead.

The scholarly cheer-leaders of global English are complicit in legitimating this dominance. The tone is set by Kaplan, an influential US language policy scholar, in an article that asks 'English—the accidental language of science?', to which he replies: 'The ascendancy of English is merely the outcome of the coincidence of accidental forces' (2001, 21, see Phillipson 2002). Kaplan detaches the current role of English from its historical causal determinants, and conflates *process* and *project*. In similar vein, Crystal (1999, 110), the prolific British linguist, explains that the current dominance of English is due to the language being 'in the right place at the right time'. It is baffling that any linguist, writing in a standard, normative form of the language, can claim that 'The English language has already grown to be independent of any form of social control' (op.cit., 139). His description of both the *product* and the *process* serves to legitimate the *project* in an uncritical way.

Some political scientists (of the relatively few who are concerned with language issues) have embraced the project eagerly. Van Parijs (2004) sees the move towards English as a global *lingua franca* as inevitable, and also desirable, provided certain conditions of fairness are met. He envisages English as the language of a global *demos* without there being a single *ethnos*: 'a forum can be shared thanks to a common language without the culture' (ibid., 118). Both van Parijs and de Swaan (2001) are adherents of rational choice theory, which stresses individual choice but ignores many of the societal factors, including education, that constrain choice. This detaches present-day English from its historical roots, its current role being due to 'No conspiracy by the Brits, let alone the Americans, but the spontaneous outcome of a huge set of decentralized decisions, mainly by non-anglophones, about which language to learn and which language to use' (van Parijs 2004, 124). Both scholars focus on language as communication and fail to integrate it with issues of identity and power, in effect detaching language from politics. This is a weakness that Gramsci's work on language hegemony would remedy, so as to ensure that the study of 'global' English does not concentrate falsely on purely instrumental functions and draws on a rich tradition in earlier political theory (Ives 2006, which contains a detailed analysis of the weaknesses of van Parijs' and de Swaan's approaches). De Swaan's book on 'the global language system' (2001, reviewed in Phillipson 2004) has little on globalization or linguistically defined social stratification, linguicism (Skutnabb-Kangas 1988). There is no analysis of the cultural dimensions of North–South relations or global cultural flows, or how English serves to integrate particular communities (states, or professions) and interest groups (finance capital, corporations, media and educational products). His layered language 'constellation' is essentially a simple model of triglossia, wrapped in algebraic game theory. Like most work in diglossia, it is loosely anchored in (neo)liberal social theory.

One example of how English Language Teaching specialists service empire can be seen in a report in November 1995 in *TESOL Matters* by Sandra McKay, an 'Academic Specialist in a United Nations sponsored program to develop the use of Latvian among Latvian residents in all domains of society.' The efforts were to be directed towards building up Latvian learning among those with Russian as a mother tongue. (Latvian has in fact recovered its pre-1939 role as the sole unifying language for all its citizens, Druviete 1999, and is one of the European Union's 23 official languages). But McKay reports that the language to unite the two communities ought to be English. 'English will provide a natural medium in which Latvians and Russians ... can work to establish a new independent Latvia' (McKay 1995, 17). She also notes that 'English is opening Latvia to trade and commerce with the West', and names McDonald's and TV films as showing the way. Corporate consumerism and US lifestyle are thus wedded to the learning of English.

It is also important to recall that TESOL (the Teaching of English to Speakers of Other Languages) itself is a significant export item—teaching materials, examinations, know-how, teachers et al.—for the British and Americans, and a vital dimension of English linguistic neoimperialism. The asymmetrical relationship between 'natives' and 'non-natives' is confirmed in the naming of the profession. 'The naming "TESOL" already assigns dichotomous *Self-Other* subject positions to teacher and learner. It interactionally and officially positions the Anglo-teacher as *Self*, and positions the learner in a life trajectory of forever being *Other*—continuing the colonial storyline ...' (Lin and Luke 2006, 67). Language is a central dimension of ideological control, perpetuating the subordination of colonial times into the present: '...colonization's legacy has become invisible ideological hegemony—domination with consent; that is, the previously colonized peoples still worship the languages, cultures, music, arts, knowledges, pedagogies, or most aspects of Western life as more advanced, progressive and superior—as lying closer towards the end point of modernity' (ibid., 69). Discrimination against immigrants to the United States, for whom English is a foreign language, is integral to public education, ESOL being construed as deficit and inferior, with all Other languages having low status (Motha 2006). The ambivalence of the TESOL enterprise is explored insightfully in a number of the contributions to Edge 2006.

Some of the key players are disarmingly frank about their global ambitions. The Website of Educational Testing Services of Princeton, NJ, which is responsible for the TOEFL test of English language proficiency, states:[6]

- As ETS's wholly-owned subsidiary, ETS Global BV is structured to bring ETS's expertise and experience with tests, assessments, and related services to educational and business communities around the world. ETS Global BV now has subsidiaries in Europe and Canada, and it will be expanding into other countries and regions as well.

- Our subsidiaries offer a full range of ETS products, services and learning solutions, including English language learning products and services training and technical assistance design, development and delivery of large-scale assessments, test design and delivery.

- Our global mission goes far beyond testing. Our products and services enable opportunity worldwide by measuring knowledge and skills, promoting learning and performance, and supporting education and professional development for all people worldwide.

US interests and services are thus in symbiosis with the evaluation of proficiency in English, with the assessment of linguistic capital. Those wishing for credentials in this linguistic market must invest in the form of 'global' English that ETS (and its UK equivalent, www.cambridgeesol. org) profitably dispense. They administer what Bourdieu refers to as the sanctions of the (global) linguistic market. We need to trace its origins.

Foundational influences on 'world' English

US foundations were active in funding research in Europe in the inter-war period, and influencing the way that many academic disciplines such as anthropology, medicine, and sociology were fashioned. In the natural sciences, US funding and influence facilitated the shift from German to English as the dominant language. In October 1934 the Carnegie Foundation sponsored a conference on *The use of English as a World Language* (Smith 2003a and 2003b). This brought to New York British and American teachers of English with extensive Asian experience, people who were a major influence on textbook production, dictionaries, and the theorization of language teaching. They included Harold Palmer (Japan), Michael West (Bengal) and Lawrence Faucett (China/Japan). Key Americans who were working on the statistical analysis of vocabulary also participated. The conference 'marked a significant turning-point in... establishing a consciousness that English as a foreign language teaching was a serious pedagogical enterprise with its own separate identity' (Smith 2003a, xxxi).

Some earlier seeds had been sown at University College, London, by Daniel Jones in phonetics and by Palmer in grammar. What was new about this professional identity was the involvement of native speakers in disseminating their language worldwide, in fixing the language and how it should be approached. In continental Europe, the professionalism of the teaching of English as a foreign language had developed along quite different lines, resulting in pedagogical reform from the end of the nineteenth century and influential books on English and its learning by scholars like Otto Jespersen of Denmark. Of greater influence on the Anglo-American approach to English as a Foreign Language was the practical Berlitz approach first elaborated in the United States. Howatt (2004, 133) sees these influences coalescing in the 'emergence of English language teaching (ELT) in its modern sense after the First World War'.

A multi-volume history of the development of English as a Foreign Language (EFL) concludes that 'The Carnegie Conference of October 1934 was the first ever international (UK–US) conference to bring together experts on English as a Foreign Language teaching. It involved a deliberate attempt to set the agenda with regard to the lexical contents of EFL materials worldwide, with an explicit intention of spreading *English* '*as a world language*' *on a basis of UK–US collaboration*' (Smith 2003b, xx, italics added). Among the participants were scholars from Teachers College Columbia University, which 'was to serve as a model for the Institute of Education in London' (ibid., xxi).[7]

A follow-up conference was held in London in June 1935 at the Colonial Office, one of whose representatives had attended the New York conference. There were Carnegie subsidies for the second conference, for several appointments at the Institute of Education, and for the preparation and ultimate publication of the Longman 'General Service List of English Words' (West 1953). The first year-long training course for English as a foreign language (EFL) was established at the Institute of Education in 1935, in a Department of Colonial Education, also with financial support from the Carnegie Corporation. The Institute has played a decisive role in the development of EFL/ELT ever since.

The language specialists attending these conferences had pedagogic concerns at heart. A second goal of the world language conferences was to counteract the influence of Basic English, which was seen as both educationally ill-conceived and contaminated by an imperialist agenda, a mission to create a world language at the expense of other languages. 'What the World needs most is about 1000 more dead languages—and one more alive', wrote the inventor of Basic English, the Cambridge semanticist, Charles Ogden. Basic (British American Scientific International Commercial) was invented to serve as an international auxiliary language and a route to English proper (Bailey 1992, 208–211; Howatt 2004, 283–288).[8] Winston Churchill was interested in promoting it (and insisted that the British Council should take it on board, a task which they chose to ignore). He is reported as saying in 1943: 'I am very much interested in the question of Basic English. The widespread use of this would be a gain to us far more durable and fruitful than the annexation of great provinces.' This anticipates the transformation of a colonial world into one where language plays an increasingly important role. Developments since that time have shown that rather than an artificially skeletal (Basic) variant of English proving of 'durable and fruitful' value to the Anglo-American world, it is English in all its variants, Global Englishes, that has attained this economic and cultural role. Churchill would doubtless have approved.

President Roosevelt was equally taken by the idea of Basic English (Richards 1968, 244). Although interest in it died out rapidly, I. A. Richards, an influential scholar[9] who combined appointments at Cambridge and Harvard, went to some lengths to promote it. A book entitled *So much nearer. Essays toward a World English* (1968) both provides a rationale for taking Basic seriously as an international auxiliary language, and lays out a case for 'successors to Basic English' (ibid., 241). When English is approached appropriately, its acquisition is not merely for 'wealth and prestige', but because 'new levels of mental capacity are induced ... the development of those concepts and sentiments: methodic, economic, moral, political, on which the continuance of man's venture depends. We of the West have somehow, out of a strangely unself-regardful, indeed a regardless impulse of benevolence, committed ourselves to universal education as well as to universal participation in government, nominal though this last can be' (ibid., 240). Richards considered the study of English (primarily literature) as the ultimate qualification for global leadership. His book ends with the words:

> There is an analogy between the conception of a world order and the design of a language which may serve man best. The choice of words for that language and the assignment of priorities among their duties can parallel the statesman's true tasks. And it is through what language can offer him that every man has to consider what should concern him most. If rightly ordered, and developed through a due sequence, the study of English can become truly a humane education. May not such a language justly be named 'EVERY MAN'S ENGLISH'?

This is the Anglo-American civilizing mission of the 20th century, to ensure that all citizens of the world (presumably females were not deliberately excluded, even if they represented fewer than 10% of the student body in Cambridge at that time) are not confined to English for merely instrumental purposes. Its users will also adopt worldviews that will make them understand that the West, out of sheer benevolence, has taken upon itself the right to decide how world affairs should be run. The final sentence has an artfully erudite association to the medieval English morality play Everyman, in which the eponymous character, representing humanity, must justify a Christian approach to life and destiny in an encounter with Death. When Kindred Knowledge, Beauty and the Five Wits (Senses) are of no avail, what is decisive is Good Deeds.[10]

Richards' text is uncannily like the neoconservative agenda that was elaborated in the United States in the 1990s, and implemented as soon as George W. Bush became President. 'Our' values are universal, and we reserve the right to enforce them globally by all available means. Literature takes over the role of religion in concealing the special interests of privileged classes or states, and the hegemony of speakers of privileged languages.

The subordination of humane values to political forces is explored in *Who Paid the Piper? The CIA and the Cultural Cold War* (Saunders 1999), which focuses on how the Americans influenced intellectuals and cultural elites in western Europe, through subsidies for conferences, publications (such as *Encounter*) and other activities. Many were co-opted. The key channel for these covert activities was foundations of dubious pedigree, and CIA-funded. As one of the key players reports: 'The joke of the cold war is that each of the rivals is aware that the other's idea would be irresistible if it were actually put into practice… The West wants freedom to the extent that freedom is compatible with private ownership and with profits; the Soviets want socialism to the extent that socialism is compatible with the dictatorship of the Communist bureaucracy' (cited ibid., 414). But loyalty to the system meant that ends justified indefensible means, including lying: 'ethics were subject to politics' (ibid., 415). An insider in the murky universe of CIA 'intelligence' over several decades wrote in 1998 that there was an underlying:

> devastating truth: the same people who read Dante and went to Yale and were educated in civic virtue recruited Nazis, manipulated the outcome of democratic elections, gave LSD to unwitting subjects, opened the mail of thousands of American citizens, overthrew governments, supported dictatorships, plotted assassinations, and engineered the Bay of Pigs disaster. 'In the name of what?' asked one critic. 'Not civic virtue, but empire.' (ibid.)

This is in fact what a 'liberal education' can easily lead to, not least when fired by a sense of national duty and some of the trappings of global leadership. It is not a uniquely US phenomenon. 'Britain's role remains essentially an imperial one: to act as a junior partner to US global power; to help organise the global economy to benefit Western corporations; and to maximise Britain's (i.e. British elites') independent political standing in the world and thus remain a great power' (Curtis 2003, 5). The ideological system underpinning this prevents the public from seeing this reality, but 'It is not a conspiracy; rather the system works by journalists and academics internalising sets of values, generally accepted wisdom and styles of reporting.' (ibid., 4)

Anglo-American collaboration on strengthening the teaching of English worldwide, and some key conferences in the 1950s and 1960s, have been summarized (Phillipson 1992, 164–172). Richards was a key contributor to the 1961 conference in Cambridge, at which he made an apologia for English at all costs (op.cit., 167), along similar lines to his 1968 book. It provides a pseudo-intellectual rationale for a career service of native speakers to disseminate their language globally in the firm conviction that their professionalism is apolitical but can make the world a better place.

To claim that the Americans have not deliberately promoted their language worldwide (as Spolsky 2004 does[11]) is simply false.[12] The consolidation of English globally to further American interests was 'greatly abetted by the expenditure of large amounts of government and private foundation funds in the period 1950–1970, perhaps the most ever spent in history in support of the propagation of a language' (Troike 1977, 2, at the time Director of the Center for Applied Linguistics (CAL), Washington, DC).

There was extensive involvement of corporate foundations in shaping postcolonial education and in funding sociolinguistic studies of multilingual former colonies (Phillipson 1992, 160–163, 226–230, 235–238). Specifically in relation to the role that English was increasingly playing in countries where it was not the first language, the Ford Foundation played a seminal role, both in a large range of countries and through the activities of CAL, which it funded. A retrospective study of the quality of Ford projects assesses that Western agenda-setting was of paramount importance:

> The World Second Language Survey was undertaken as the first major task by the CAL (with separate Ford Foundation support) in cooperation with the British Council, and the then Bureau de l'Étude et de Liaison pour l'Enseignement du Français dans le Monde (BEL) … This program produced the first body of data on the worldwide role of English and French as second languages and significantly increased international contacts and co-operation and exchange of information and scholars. *It set the pattern for collaboration on the language problems of developing countries* that CAL sparked for almost a decade through co-operative establishment with the British and the French of annual meetings of the International Conferences on Second Language Problems. (Fox 1975, 37, emphasis added)

A wartime book on *The Diffusion of English Culture Outside England* (Routh 1941) by an adviser to the British Council articulated the need for a new career service, for gentlemen teachers of English with equivalent status to 'the Civil Service, Army, Bar, or Church', an 'army of linguistic missionaries' generated by a 'training centre for post-graduate studies and research', and a 'central office in London, from which teachers radiate all over the world'. The new service must 'lay the foundations of a world-language and culture *based on our own*' (emphasis added). This culture was a joint Anglo-American one. 'Teaching the world English may appear not unlike an extension of the task which America faced in establishing English as a common national language among its own immigrant population.' (Annual Report of the British Council 1960–61, cited in Phillipson 1992). This global English project which in predictable fashion has 'forgotten' the North American indigenous population, implicitly endorses English replacing other languages.

Anglo-American community of purpose and language

Churchill and Roosevelt, at their secret meeting in August 1941, agreed on the text of a joint Atlantic Charter. It was then made public in London and Washington. It elaborates the 'common principles in the national policies of their respective countries on which they base their hopes for a better future for the world'. Ten additional countries, among them the Soviet Union, endorsed the text at a meeting in London on 29 September 1941. The Atlantic Charter (in what reads like a forerunner of Orwellian Newspeak, language devised to accomplish changed ideological needs and impose novel ways of understanding the world[13]) states:

> FIRST, their countries seek no aggrandisement, territorial or other.
>
> SECOND, they desire to see no territorial changes that do not accord with the freely expressed wishes of the people concerned.
>
> THIRD, they respect the rights of all peoples to choose the form of government under which they will live; and they wish to see sovereign rights and self-government restored to those who have been forcibly deprived of them. (Appendix to Morton 1943)

The remaining principles relate to free access to trade and raw materials, increased economic collaboration, unhindered use of the high seas, the creation of a post-Nazi peace, freedom from want, a commitment to abandonment of the use of force, the disarmament of aggressive nations, and ultimately the 'establishment of a wider permanent system of general security.'

Churchill, in a broadcast describing this commitment, refers to the 'two major groupings of the human family, the British Empire and the United States' and refers to the 'deep underlying unities which stir and, at decisive moments, rule the English-speaking peoples throughout the world' (cited in Morton 1943, 152).

The Atlantic Charter was seized on by colonial subjects in the British and French empires, from southern Africa to Algeria, who naturally wished the principle of freedom from oppressive rule to apply to them as well. They tried to argue that due to the Charter, 'recognition of the right of peoples to liberty and self-determination gave to nationalism the sanction of the great powers' (cited in Davidson 1978, 202). But Churchill declared in the House of Commons that the Charter was only supposed to apply to countries occupied by the Germans and Italians. Churchill had no wish to preside over the dissolution of the British Empire. Roosevelt, by contrast, said the Charter applied to 'all of humanity' (ibid.).

There are many instruments that bind Anglo-American elites together and consolidate linguistic hegemony. A major link is the Rhodes scholarships at the University of Oxford (www.rhodesscholar.org). Cecil Rhodes, the ultimate British imperialist, was convinced that 'the Anglo-Saxon race was the highest to be evolved in a divine plan... hence his preoccupation with British expansion, particularly in Africa, and with making money for the power to carry out his ideas' (*Encyclopedia Britannica*, 1971 edition). The Rhodes scholarships, established in his will, aim at educating future world leaders and at instilling 'the advantage of the colonies as well as to the United Kingdom of the retention of the unity of the empire'. Through collaboration with the United States, the scholarships are intended to lead to 'the union of the English-speaking people throughout the world' (ibid.). More than 7000 Rhodes scholars have been selected since 1904, mostly from the USA but also from a wide range of Commonwealth countries and Germany, making them the 'oldest international fellowships' awarded not so much on academic merit as their 'promise of effective service in the world in the decades ahead'.

A primarily Anglo-American body with similar goals and means is the English-Speaking Union, which aims at 'creating global understanding through English.' Its publication *English—a world language* (1991) declares on the rear cover that it was 'originally founded to foster good relations between Britain and the United States, later extended its orbit to the Commonwealth. It now operates on a worldwide scale.'[14] Its website declares that it is an international educational charity founded in 1918 to promote 'international understanding and friendship through the use of the English language. That has never been so important and never so possible... With almost 40 branches in the UK, and over 50 international branches in countries in every part of the world, the ESU's mission to bring people together and share their experiences has never been more relevant.' It organizes competitions, lectures and educational activities, enjoys royal patronage, and is funded by corporate sponsors on both sides of the Atlantic. These include, not surprisingly, educational institutions and publishers of English-learning materials. I am not familiar with any research on this institution and its contribution to the maintenance of English linguistic hegemony.

Right-wing US think tanks are also busy promoting the idea of a single cultural English-speaking universe. For instance, Bennett's *The Anglosphere challenge. Why the English-speaking nations will lead the way in the twenty-first century* (2004) defines the Anglosphere as implying 'the sharing of fundamental customs and values at the core of English-speaking cultures: individualism; rule of law; honouring of covenants; in general the high-trust characteristics described by Francis Fukujama in *Trust: The Social Virtues and the Creation of Prosperity*; and the emphasis on freedom as a political and cultural value.'[15] (ibid., 79–80). Bennett et al. have formed a 'non-profit organization,' the Anglosphere Institute, to conduct policy research and further the concepts of the Anglosphere and the Network Commonwealth (www.anglosphereinstitute.org). The underlying conviction is that 'Increasingly during the past few centuries, the English-speaking world has been the pathfinder for all of humanity' through the 'first modern nation-state, the first liberal democratic state,...' (ibid., 67). He argues that the North American Free Trade Association and the EU are 'of limited value at best, and at worst do harm when they attempt to homogenize nations with substantially different characteristics.' (ibid., 68). In other words, British people have more in common with Americans, and the media and internet are intensifying this convergence, rather than variants of English signifying fragmentation (ibid., 75). Bennett advocates the merging of the United Kingdom with NAFTA and its detachment from Europe so that the British defence industry can merge with the US defence industry and, as in finance, function as a 'seamless market' (ibid., 167). This would fit snugly with the massive and increasing influence of military expenditure in a USA committed to permanent war. Bennett is convinced that 'The past thirty years of British history have encompassed a period of political and cultural schizophrenia that has created ongoing unresolved tensions in its national life and identity' (ibid., 236), the solution to which is an Anglosphere Network Commonwealth.

Rotary International is another good example of the way English and Anglo-American interests go hand in hand. Rotary has existed since 1905. Half of its 1.3 million members are native speakers of English, but the organization has nine official languages (see www.rotary.org). At its annual conference in Barcelona in 2002, neither Spanish (one of the nine) nor Catalan was used at the opening ceremony, and English was virtually the exclusive conference language. The proceedings of Rotary's centenary conference in Chicago in 2005 were published only in English.[16] In this way, Rotary operates in a similar way to many 'international' conferences, at which English dominates, even when the organization in theory operates in other languages as well. 'International' events tend to be conducted in English without thought being given to the advantages that this gives native speakers or the way this practice marginalizes other languages and their speakers.

The attempt to impose American empire on friends as well as enemies alike is clearly exemplified in the way Europeans have been treated since World War II. The 'special relationship' linking the UK and the USA has always been asymmetrical, as a top British conservative leader concedes: 'Where substance is important to America, the most that Britain can do is to affect process' (Patten 2005, 96). Tony Blair notably failed to affect either substance or process over Iraq. During World War II the Lend-Lease scheme was vital for propping up the British economy but consolidated US power over the UK economy.

The extent of US involvement in determining European integration needs reporting in some detail, since few are aware of it. Pascaline Winand's *Eisenhower, Kennedy, and the United States of Europe* (1991) traces the involvement of key people in US government circles in planning how Europe could be integrated after World War II. Many were close friends and allies of Jean Monnet, the Frenchman who planned many of the institutional developments and headed the first European institutions. The planning process started in the Council on Foreign Relations, founded in 1921, which drew on 'the elite of the American business, academic, law, media and government communities' (ibid., 2). The COFR, together with the editor of *Foreign Affairs,* saw the need in September 1939 for policy papers: 682 memoranda were transmitted to the Department of State, mainly funded by the Rockefeller Foundation (ibid., 3). John Foster Dulles, a Republican who later became Eisenhower's Foreign Secretary, proposed western Europe as a single economic unit in 1947. This agenda underpinned the Marshall Plan, which was made conditional on the economies of European countries being opened up. Sixteen European nations formed the Committee for European Economic Cooperation on 15 July 1947. The Schuman Plan, 9 May 1950, was essentially written by Monnet, with assistance from American diplomats based in France (ibid., 22). General Eisenhower, when Supreme Allied Commander, Europe, 'made a strong plea for European economic and political integration before the English-Speaking Union in the great ballroom of Grosvenor Place, Park Lane, on 3 July 1951' (ibid., 28). There were many competing views on both sides of the Atlantic (Atlanticists, internationalists, Europeanists, Gaullists, the British), but those in favour of a unification that would be economic, political and military were able to influence matters decisively. Increasingly the Americans saw the need to work behind the scenes, so that it could appear that it was Europeans deciding matters. The free flow of goods, services, capital and people was a founding principle of European integration from 1957, and ultimately achieved in the 1990s with the common market (ibid., 129). European Union (EU) policies implement the plans of the corporate world, as documented in George Monbiot's *Captive State. The Corporate Takeover of Britain* (2000), the neoliberal agenda that Reagan and Thatcher embraced. Tony Blair's support for Bush II confirms President de Gaulle's analysis that the UK was (and remains) a Trojan horse for US interests.

Denmark has been a less visible Trojan horse, but its existence has been verifiable in recent years. A covert agreement in 1951 allowed the United States to use a base in Greenland for aircraft with nuclear warheads, although this was illegal under Danish law.[17] When a right-wing Danish government came to power in 2001, Danish Prime Minister Anders Fog Rasmussen informed the Danish Foreign Ministry that Denmark's relationship with the United States now had the highest priority, higher than both NATO and the EU,[18] such a commitment being logically incompatible with EU membership. Denmark committed troops to a war of aggression in Iraq with the votes of roughly one-third of the Parliament, since which the government has permitted no parliamentary debate on or enquiry into the legality of the operation, which is being challenged in court. The government admitted 45 covert CIA flights in Denmark between 2001 and 2006, but has chosen not to ask questions about their legality or purpose. This abject acceptance of the increasing militarization that the imposition of US empire entails is worthy only of a vassal state, a colonized subservience, passively accepting structural and mental occupation. American military interests, from the Cold War to proposed anti-ballistic missile shields, explain why Denmark is more deeply committed to US empire than all the other Nordic states. This poodle behaviour is disastrous for Denmark (earlier regarded as an enlightened Nordic country), for the European Union (which in theory has a common security and foreign policy), for the United Nations, and for international law.

In parallel with this political subordination, the Danish government naively believes that English is the only important foreign language. It is neglecting the learning of other languages in the education system. Linguistic neoimperialism dovetails with political and military subordination. The global English project has already been established, the product merging with many of the overt and covert processes which consolidate the power of users of the language.

The neoimperial language system in function in Europe

Neoliberalism was marketed by Margaret Thatcher with the dogmatic claim that There Is No Alternative. Neoliberalism requires that the forces of global corporate restructuring are seen as all-powerful, lawless, unaccountable, and absolutist (McMurtry 2002, 19). As expressed by one of its devotees in Churchillian terms: 'These forces of change driving the future don't stop at national boundaries. Don't respect tradition. They wait for no-one and no tradition. They are universal.' (ibid., 15) The author is none other than Tony Blair, whose discourse is analysed by McMurtry as follows:

Their structure deletes the subject of every sentence as nameless, inhuman 'forces' without definition, accountable to nothing beyond themselves. They affirm with no qualifier an occupation of societies everywhere by 'forces' which will stop at no line of national jurisdiction or cultural identity. All that was once secure in historical time and place is here declared powerless against 'the universal forces' that are presumed without meaning as the Good ... the economic theology of the Market is the soul of its absolutist world order. (op.cit., 13, 21)

This theology has been adopted by many governments worldwide, including those of the European Union. A 'single market where competition is free and undistorted' is enshrined in the draft Constitutional Treaty that was endorsed by 25 heads of state in 2003. It was rejected by the voters of France and the Netherlands, subjected to a minor revision in 2007 and re-named a Reform Treaty.

Even though this draft treaty also included a substantial section of human rights provisions, the clauses on language rights are extremely weak (Creech 2005). There is currently a great deal of fluidity in language policy in Europe, with unresolved tensions between linguistic nationalism, EU institutional multilingualism, and English becoming dominant nationally and internationally (Phillipson 2003). There are competing agendas at the European, state (national), and sub-state levels; there is increasing grassroots and elite bi- and multilingualism, except in the United Kingdom and among the older generation in demographically large EU countries; there is a largely uncritical adoption of English as the *lingua economica* and *lingua Americana*; the EU advocates linguistic diversity, and achieves this inconsistently in its management of the largest translation and interpretation system in the world. Some language rights are in force nationally and supranationally, but EU financial support for linguistic diversity is in fact diminishing.[19]

How language policy and diversity will evolve is unpredictable, but there are plenty of voices seeking to influence matters. The unfree linguistic market is underpinned by hegemonic discourse, such as when the ambassador of the USA to Denmark states that 'the most serious problem for the European Union is that it has so many languages, this preventing real integration and development of the Union,' and the Director of the British Council in Germany suggests that 'English should be the sole official language of the European Union'.[20] These are monstrous ideas when the vast body of EU law takes effect in all member states, overriding national law, and must therefore be promulgated in the 23 official languages (of the 27 member states). In any case, the EU is founded on a principle of respect for linguistic and cultural diversity.

This principle is, however, under massive pressure because of the impact of globalization (Phillipson 2003, chapter 3). 'Discipliner l'économie globale, c'est aussi discipliner le local' (Mattelart 2005, 61) applies not only to the economy but also to culture, the media, and language. Communications scholars refer to the phase since 1980 as electronic colonization, which can be combined theoretically with the World-System of core, periphery and semi-periphery countries (McPhail 2006). Cultural globalization is a reality: '70-80% of all TV fiction shown on European TV is American … American movies, American TV and the American lifestyle for the populations of the world and Europe at large have become the lingua franca of globalization, the closest we get to a visual world culture' (Bondebjerg 2003, 79). (By contrast in the United States the market share of films of foreign origin is dropping and now a mere 1%.) '… marketing strategies, research, advertising, and economic savvy permit core-zone businesses to influence consumer behaviour by creating appropriate global mindsets toward their cultural products and services. Core nations thrive on market-based activities since they make the rules' (McPhail 2006, 32). The Americanization of mindsets and consumer practices is deeply established in Europe. For Bourdieu, probably the most influential sociologist in Europe, globalization means Americanization (2001). The interlocking of neoliberal capital, empire, and US power is insightfully explored in Pieterse 2004.

Cultural imperialism has been an important weapon in the struggle to assert overall hegemony (Harvey 2005, 56). Changes in forms of consciousness accompany the forces of economic and technological change, and are embodied in linguistic forms of expression both in the original language English and by transfer into other languages: 'The vocabulary of the market has spread from English to the entire world's languages, without citizens having the time to interrogate its conditions and place of production. … Terminology crosses the frontiers of the geo-economy and geofinance so as to irradiate society,' entailing the adoption of 'the concepts, a standardisation of ways of thinking and of understanding the destiny of the world' (Mattelart 2005, 62; translation, RP). This cultural imperialism is carefully packaged 'in a mantle of the apolitical' (ibid.), as is global English Language Teaching.

There is currently a penetration of the vocabulary of the 'knowledge society', benchmarking, public relations, branding, coaching, networking, and suchlike business-world technocratic jargon into more and more domains. When universities find themselves entrapped in such logic, how can they preserve academic freedom and live up to their traditional role of training students to think independently and critically? Granted the origins of such concepts in a specific cultural universe, what happens to the worldviews embedded in other languages when the terms are transplanted, whether in translation or in the original language, to other conceptual territories?

New variants of language and cultural form that generally originate in the Anglo-American world, such as computer games, email and internet interaction, SMSs, television programmes (whether transmitted in the original language or the local one), and advertising for the younger generation, all are creatively adapted in continental European contexts and languages. New medialects are emerging (akin to dialects and sociolects) as technological innovation and 'Englishization' affect the form and content of other languages, opening up for 'linguistic differentiation and innovation' in the way language is used (Hjarvad 2004). In addition to English being the language in which these media products are evolved and marketed, 'English is the linguistic vehicle for meta-communication about mediated communication' (ibid.). The medialects consolidate the position of English, while excluding other international languages, such as French and Russian.

The many symptoms of glocalization and hybridity should not obscure the fact that even if a great deal of local creativity is in force, the innovation primarily emanates from the United States, which invests far more than most countries in research. European intellectuals cling to the belief that "English, in fact, *is not* and will not be the 'language of Europe'" (Balibar 2004, 177). But for this scenario not to materialize presupposes strong measures in European states to maintain linguistic diversity. Such continental European luminaries as George Steiner, Umberto Eco, and

Zygmunt Bauman remain convinced, in the tradition of Goethe and Victor Hugo, that translation is the 'idiom of Europe'. However this presupposes multilingual competence across a range of European languages, which is a totally different heritage from the current position of English as the default language of globalization, from which translation into other languages occurs, translation thus constituting globalisation (Cronin 2003).[21] Some Nordic countries and the Netherlands are addressing some language policy challenges, and the EU is advocating the learning of two foreign languages in education, but language policy tends not to have a high priority.

Building on research in Switzerland and worldwide, François Grin (2005) was commissioned by a French educational research institution to investigate the impact of the current dominance of English in education. He calculates quantifiable privileged market effects, communication savings effects, language learning savings effects (i.e. not needing to invest so much in foreign language learning), alternative human capital investment effects (e.g. school time being used for other purposes), and legitimacy and rhetorical effects. The research led Grin to conclude that continental countries are transferring to the United Kingdom and Ireland at least €10 billion *per annum*, and more probably about €16–17 billion a year. The amounts involved completely dwarf the British EU budget rebate of €5 billion annually that has been a source of friction between the United Kingdom and its partners. The finding is likely to be politically explosive, as this covert British financial benefit is at the expense of its partners. It is also incompatible with the EU commitment to all European children acquiring competence in two foreign languages. It shows that European education is skewed in fundamentally inequitable ways. It indicates that *laissez faire* in the international linguistic marketplace gives unfair advantages to native speakers of English not only in cross-cultural interaction but also in the workings of the market. The commodification of English has massive implications. Grin (2004) has also calculated that the US economy saves $19 billion p.a. by not needing to spend time and effort in formal schooling on learning foreign languages.

Even the declared commitment of France to maintaining French as a dominant language nationally and internationally is open to question, as the reality of the internalization of linguistic hegemony takes effect (Charles Durand, private communication):

> Like a cuckolded husband who is the last person to learn that his wife is deceiving him, continental Europeans seem to be the last ones to discover or to recognize that they are part of an empire, and that the learning of English, along with the use of the dollar in the international arena, are only necessary because they are respectively the language and the currency of the empire, with all the advantages and inconveniences that this can entail. 'Above all English' is the equivalent of saying 'Above all Russian' in what used to be the Soviet empire.

This internalization process in the relationship between dominant and dominated groups and languages entails what Bourdieu refers to as symbolic power:

> To understand the nature of symbolic power, it is therefore crucial to see that it presupposes a kind of *active complicity* on the part of those subjected to it. Dominated individuals are not passive bodies to which symbolic power is applied, as it were, like a scalpel to a corpse. Rather, symbolic power requires, as a condition for its success, that those subjected to it believe in the legitimacy of power and the legitimacy of those who wield it. (Thompson 1991, 23)

Linguistic capital, its acquisition and investment, is a prime example of symbolic power in use. The active complicity can be seen in the way continental European countries are increasingly, and willingly, using English in key societal domains: in commerce (English as the corporate language, at least at senior management level), research publication (a trend towards publication exclusively in English in the natural sciences, technology, medicine etc), in higher education (English as a medium of instruction in some graduate-level courses, especially those intended to attract 'international' students), in popular entertainment, and in EU affairs. Although there has been some analysis of whether English represents a boon or a threat to national languages,[22] the extent of the impact of English is unknown.

In addition the terminology used to review the phenomenon is deceptive. There is now much talk, at least in Sweden and Denmark, of 'domain loss,' which is a seemingly innocuous term, but like 'language spread' and 'language death' (Skutnabb-Kangas 2000, 365–374), it appears to signify a natural, agent-less process. What is under way is a much more actively driven process of linguistic capital accumulation by dispossession (to adapt terms from Harvey 2005, where he is referring to the commercial world in its global pursuit of markets and profit). Linguistic capital accumulation entails, as in commerce, some combination of internal motivation and external pressure, push and pull factors. There are agents both among locals and in the Anglo-American world that are only too keen to see a consolidation of English, irrespective of the implications for other languages. In reality the amount of any domain loss, or rather domain dispossession, in European languages, is unknown. The governments of both Sweden and Denmark are acting to ensure the maintenance of the role of the national, unifying language as well as the promotion of proficiency in English, ideally to the level of 'parallel competence'. One Danish political party has suggested that English should be given the same position as Danish in public services, ostensibly as a way of tackling globalization. The implications of this totally unrealistic suggestion have clearly not been thought through.

Whether national measures of this kind, and policies in school and the media, will prove adequate in the face of internationalization pressures that derive from globalization remains to be seen. The Bologna process seeks to integrate the research and higher education systems of 45 European countries (with Australia and the United States as observers, since higher education is big business for them) into a single, unified 'area'. This 'internationalization' is in theory committed, by the original Bologna declaration of 1999 'within the framework of our institutional competences and taking full respect of the diversity of cultures, languages, national education systems and of University autonomy—to consolidate a European Higher Education Area at the latest by 2010.' At the bi-annual ministerial meetings (most recently in Bergen in 2005 and London in 2007), the main focus has been on structural uniformity (a single BA, MA and PhD system), on quality control (nationally and internationally), student mobility, recognition of qualifications, and joint degrees—all of which are demanding tasks for most countries—and making European universities attractive enough to compete with the United States and Australia. What is striking and shocking is that in the long communiqué from the Bergen meeting, there is not one word on bilingual degrees or multilingualism in higher education. On the contrary, the impression is created that what internationalization means is English-medium higher education (see Phillipson 2006 on whether English is a cuckoo in the European higher education nest of languages).

If this outcome emerges, it will strengthen the position of higher education in the Anglo-American world, including Ireland. It will also mean that the rhetoric of maintaining Europe's linguistic diversity and cultural heritage will remain empty words on paper. Prior to the 2007 London meeting, EU Commissioner Figel stated (press release IP/07/656):

> Bologna reforms are important but Europe should now go beyond them, as universities should also modernize the content of their curricula, create virtual campuses and reform their governance. They should also professionalize their management, diversify their funding and open up to new types of learners, businesses and society at large, in Europe and beyond. ... The Commission supports the global strategy in concrete terms through its policies and programmes.

In other words, universities should no longer be seen as a public good but should be run like businesses, should privatize, and let industry set the agenda. This is precisely what the right-wing Danish government that has been in power since 2001 is implementing. The latest Bologna buzzwords are that degrees must be 'certified' in terms of the 'employability' of graduates. 'Accountability' no longer refers to intellectual quality or truth-seeking but means acceptability to corporate imperatives. Before *European* integration has taken on viable forms, universities are being told to think and act *globally*—through the medium of English of course—rather than remain narrowly national or European. This is insulting to universities, most of which have been internationally oriented for decades, if not centuries.

That the process of internalizing linguistic hegemony progressively and insidiously is underway is clear from many sorts of data. Much of it is inevitably anecdotal, but can be brought into the open, as in a review of David Crystal's *English as a Global Language*, by Ranko Bugarski (1998, 90), a professor of English and linguistics at the University of Belgrade. He comments that 'many readers may feel that he has underestimated some of the dangers' as well as the implications of 'the advantage mother tongue speakers of a global language automatically have over those who have to acquire it as an official or second language—in scientific research and publication, in trade negotiations or political debate, and so on.' This assertion confirms the impression of EU interpreters, who are convinced that people for whom English is not their first language do themselves and their states less than justice when they 'choose' to function at EU meetings in English, rather than using interpretation.

Distinguished European scholars, such as Bessie Dendrinos of Athens and Peter Harder of Copenhagen, have commented (in personal communications), on the sensation of freedom they experienced when, after decades of professional functioning in English, they had occasion to write something in their first language. Ulrich Ammon of Duisburg, who is not an Anglicist, makes a plea (2000) for more tolerance of non-native English, and cites evidence of the evaluation of medical research in the Netherlands and Scandinavia to the effect that an identical text is ranked as being of better content when written in English rather than in the local language (see also Phillipson 2002). Gate-keeping in scholarly journals tends to be firmly in the hands of native speakers of English, and affects content as well as form.

In the 'information society' and the 'global' village, the languages used for information are hierarchically ordered and the communication is often asymmetrical. The entire internationalization process is skewed in favour of native speakers of English and their cultures. The role of English in European and global integration raises key challenges for the maintenance of other languages in the geopolitics of knowledge creation (see Mendieta, Phillipson and Skutnabb-Kangas 2006).

Theorising linguistic neoimperialism

Stephen Howe begins his stimulating *Empire: A Very Short Introduction* (2002) by asserting that 'The very word empire ... has had a complicated history and many different, fiercely contested meanings', and he ends a chapter of historical and terminological clarification by concluding that reaching agreement on definitions is elusive because 'the subject is so highly charged with political passions and emotion' (ibid., 34).

Harvey (2005) stresses the need to define the concept imperialism if it is to be used analytically rather than merely polemically. This principle also guided my definition of linguistic imperialism as a variant of linguicism, operating through structures and ideologies, and entailing unequal treatment for groups identified by language (Phillipson 1992). For Harvey, capitalist imperialism 'is a contradictory fusion of *"the politics of state and empire*" (imperialism as a distinctively political project on the part of the actors whose power is based in command of a territory and a capacity to mobilize its human and natural resources towards political, economic, and military ends) and "*the molecular processes of capital accumulation in space and time*" (imperialism as a diffuse political-economic process in space and time in which command over and use of capital takes primacy)' (Harvey 2005, 26, italics added). The first is the top-down process of what a state, or combination of states, or an institution such as a corporation or a university, does to achieve its goals, which includes the way it manages linguistic capital. The second is the way 'economic power flows across and through continuous space, towards or away from territorial entities (such as states or regional power blocs) through the daily practices of production, trade, commerce, capital flows, money transfers, labour migration, technology transfer, currency speculation, flows of information, cultural impulses, and the like' (ibid.). Most of these are crucially dependent on language, and constituted by language.

Building on this diagnosis of American empire, we can see global English as the *capitalist neoimperial language* that serves the interests of the corporate world and the governments that it influences so as to consolidate state and empire worldwide. This dovetails with the language being activated through *molecular processes of linguistic capital accumulation in space and time*. As Harvey explains for the new imperialism, 'the relation between these two logics should be seen, therefore, as problematic and often contradictory (that is, dialectical) rather than as functional or one-sided.' The challenge for the analyst is to 'keep the two sides of this dialectic simultaneously in motion and not to lapse into either a solely political or a predominantly economic mode of argumentation' (ibid., 30). So far as linguistic neoimperialism is concerned, the 'political mode of argumentation' refers to decision-making, policy formation of a general kind (corresponding to status, corpus and acquisition planning, both overt and covert, to which a fourth type can be added, language technology planning)[23], whereas the 'economic mode of argumentation' refers to the working through of such decisions at all levels, the implementation of language planning decisions, actual use of English in myriad contexts.

To revert to the examples of earlier sections of this paper, when English increasingly occupies territory that earlier was the preserve of national languages in Europe or Asia, what is occurring is *linguistic capital accumulation* over a period of time and in particular territories in favour of English, the capitalist neoimperial language. When Singaporean parents gradually shift from an Asian language to the use of English in the home, this also represents linguistic capital accumulation. If users of German or Swedish as languages of scholarship shift to using English, similar forces and processes are at work. Demographically small languages have the additional problem that investment in language technology is vastly greater in larger, more economically powerful languages.

When considering agency in each of these examples, the individuals concerned opt for the neoimperial language because it is felt that this linguistic capital will serve their personal interests best. In relation to each example, what has not been explored is whether this language shift is additive or subtractive (Skutnabb-Kangas 2000, 72). Individual agency and decision-making reflect a range of societal forces and ideologies (see the typology of fifteen factors contributing to the increased use of English in Europe, grouped as structural and ideological, Phillipson, 2003, 64–65). When language shift is subtractive, and if this affects a group and not merely individuals, there are serious implications for other languages. If domains such as business, the home, or scholarship are 'lost', what has occurred is in fact *linguistic capital dispossession*. There are agentive forces behind the language shift, causal factors that lead to an increased use of English. If Cantonese is dropped in Singapore, and if German and Swedish are no longer used for particular functions within the German- or Swedish-speaking areas, this is a consequence of 'daily practices' that do not respect national borders or languages.

Analysis of the interlocking of language policy with the two constituents of the 'contradictory fusion' can serve to highlight both corporate agendas, which serve political, economic and military purposes, and the multiple flows that make use of English for a range of what ELT experts refer to as 'special purposes'. New discourses and technologies are adopted and creatively adapted, new medialects evolved, but in an unfree global and local market. Thus it is false to project English as though it is 'neutral', English as a mere tool that serves all equally well, in whatever society they live. Much of the celebratory literature on 'global' English analyses it exclusively in such instrumental terms. However, as a recent work on the semantics and culture embedded in the grammar and words of English stresses, publications on 'global English,' 'international English,' 'world English', 'standard English', and 'English as a *lingua franca*' neglect the distinctive heritage embedded in the language, in its core semantic and grammatical structures, since ultimately 'in the present-day world it is Anglo English that remains the touchstone and guarantor of English-based global communication' (Wierzbicka 2006, 13–14). She also refers to the ethnocentricity of many theorists from the Anglo-American world who mistakenly take Anglo English for the human norm (ibid., 12).

Teaching materials that falsely build on such analyses can compound the error: '[M]uch intercultural communication itself is typical of a certain Anglo-Saxon culture, discourse and worldview…the concept of intercultural communication as it is currently used can be easily highjacked by a global ideology of "effective communication' Anglo-Saxon style, which speaks an English discourse even as it expresses itself in many different languages" (Kramsch 2002, 283–84). In much intercultural communication, it is the native speakers who are the problem rather than the non-natives (for an example, see Phillipson 2003, 167–68).

Linguistic imperialism (which continued under neo-colonialism) is transmorphing into linguistic neoimperialism during the transition from neoliberalism into empire:

> The rapid succession from a neoliberal to an imperial project yields a combine of American economic and political-military unilateralism and a novel formation of neoliberal empire. *Neoliberal empire* twins practices of empire with those of neoliberalism. The core of empire is the national security state and the military-industrial complex; neoliberalism is about business, financial operations, and marketing (including marketing neoliberalism itself). … Neoliberal empire is a marriage of convenience with neoliberalism, indicated by inconsistent use of neoliberal policies, with the attempt to merge the America whose business is business with the America whose business is war, at a time when business is not doing so great. … The grand strategy of permanent war signals the beginning of the end of American power (Pieterse 2004, 45, 159).

Hardt and Negri's controversial book on empire sees power in deterritorialized networks, and stresses (2000, 32–33) that

> Language, as it communicates, produces commodities but moreover produces subjectivities, puts them in relation, and orders them. The

communications industries integrate the imaginary and the symbolic within the biopolitical fabric, not merely putting them at the service of power but actually integrating them into its very functioning.

Their analysis reveals why it has been so important for the corporate world to dominate not only the media but also education, which is increasingly run to service the economy, and produce consumers rather than critical citizens. English contributes to the imperial production of subjectivities, through communicative networks, creating a synergy that integrates structural and ideological elements in the new world 'order'. The key networks are identifiable, and their language policies can be empirically verified. This 'order' is upheld through English at the global level, and through other languages in hierarchical structures. This symbolic violence is invariably contested but is widely, uncritically internalized. The dominance of English and its differential impact on other languages is applauded by scholars who see the rise of 'world' English as unproblematical (on de Swaan and Brutt-Griffler, see Phillipson 2004), but they fail to capture how English functions in the new imperialism.

It is a weakness if the use of English is looked at purely empirically without engaging with the fundamentally political roles that use of the language performs (Ives 2006). Even studies which question whether the dominance of English is secure in the foreseeable future (Graddol 2006), and which rightly point out the strength of Asian economies, seem to ignore the significance of the corporate world and the role of the guardians of the norms of the standard Anglo-American language. The invasions of Afghanistan and Iraq have done massive damage to the image that the 'English-speaking' world would like to create of the values that they claim to subscribe to, as well as to international law, but one can scarcely claim that viable alternatives to neoliberalism and corporate-driven English-using globalization and empire are emerging, with the exception of unpredictable and inscrutable China. *The Guardian Weekly* reported in 2007[24] that China is massively expanding the dissemination of its language and culture worldwide in 150 Confucius Institutes, and offering tuition to vastly more foreign students at over 500 universities, using English, Chinese and other Asian and European languages.

Global insecurity, political polarization, ecological and climatic threats, and the untenable lifestyles of the minority of the world's privileged make prediction uncertain. Fundamental changes in the global economy make US dominance via the dollar and control of the oil trade precarious: fewer goods are produced in the United States and parts of Europe, which are therefore dependent on goods and investment from Asia and elsewhere, creating an untenable US budget deficit, an unequal society where 30% of the workforce do not earn a living wage, and a dollar that is volatile, operating in a finance capital market that is rigged in favour of the rich (Hatlen 2006). US military dominance globally (350 bases and 800 military facilities in 130 countries, Pieterse 2004, 58) is symptomatic of unilateralism based on force that both 'friends and enemies' may choose to accept no longer. It is therefore perfectly possible that the global linguistic map may change violently in the coming decades, and that in the intervening period, monolingualism in English may be a serious liability in the job market. It is therefore an issue that the British are being encouraged to address (Nuffied Languages Inquiry, www.nuffield.org, Graddol 2006). If postcolonial elites in Asia or Africa confirm a trend towards monolingualism in English, this is likely to intensify the gaps between haves and have-nots locally and globally and consolidate states that are untenable socially, culturally and ecologically.

For the present I concur with the diagnosis of a survey of 'Language empires, linguistic imperialism, and the future of global languages' (Hamel 2003), which concludes as follows:

> Neither the number of speakers, nor the number of countries, nor the density of its population makes the difference. Rather, we have to consider economic power, military strength, the ranking in scientific and technological development, the role in international organizations and the cultural industries of those countries and international corporations that back a given language and are determined to operate through it in order to establish the real power and ranking of a language as international (Pennycook 1994), global (Crystal 1997) or imperialist (Phillipson 1992).

> Certainly agency is relevant, but we will have to extend our view of agency to include all activities propelled by a given habitus, in Bourdieu's sense, not only planned and conscious action. And second, we need to consider the agency of all those who, from subaltern positions and a second language status, help to strengthen the dominant role of a language which in turn contributes to maintain and increase imperial and imperialist power

relations. … the forces that maintain control over English are clearly rooted in a small number of sovereign states.

These ideas are endorsed in an analysis in *Globalization and language in the Spanish-Speaking World* that relates specifically to the way Spanish is being promoted and adopted internationally (Mar-Molinero 2006).[25] There is competition among the most dominant 'international' languages, though currently it is only English that is a constituent part of a neoliberal empire.

Linguistic neoimperialism entails the maintenance of inequalities between speakers of English and other languages, within a framework of exploitative dominance. As in earlier linguistic imperialism, this is achieved through penetration, fragmentation, marginalization, and supremacist ideologies in discourse. Changes in communication technology have revolutionized the impact of English globally, in tandem with the expansion of the information society of corporate globalization (especially in commerce, finance and the media) and multiple networks. Acceptance of the status of English, and its assumed neutrality implies uncritical adherence to the dominant world disorder, unless policies to counteract neolinguistic imperialism and to resist linguistic capital dispossession are in force.

US expansionism is no longer territorial, except in the sense that military bases, military occupation, and sales of military hardware to client regimes (e.g. Turkey, Skutnabb-Kangas and Fernandes, in press) all serve to ensure the economic structure that perpetuates corporate dominance. Occupation is by economic, technological and material means, and is increasingly ensured through mental and electronic control, through the barrage of advertising and Hollywood products, and the networks of political and scholarly collaboration that uphold an exploitative economic structure. The salience of each of the three dimensions of English as product, process and project will vary according to local circumstances, dovetailing with multilingualism when this maintains the neoliberal world 'order' that constitutes empire.

There is a need for explicit language policies based on ethical human rights principles. Language policy formation and implementation at the supranational, national and subnational levels is needed if linguistic diversity is to be sustainable, and if speakers of all languages are to enjoy linguistic human rights (Skutnabb-Kangas 2000)—and to resist mental and economic occupation. Regarding linguistics, the social sciences and humanities as apolitical, is a deeply political act. Language professionals should

- formulate policies for maintaining linguistic diversity
- help to create conditions for equality between speakers of different languages
- counteract the linguistic dispossession currently threatening minorised languages
- educate politicians, journalists, translators, and the general public
- use all languages to decolonise minds, so as to facilitate equitable dialogue and to counteract occupation, physical or mental.

Notes

1   Cited in Graddol, Swann and Leith (eds.), 1996, pp. 93–94. See also Phillipson, 2003, pp. 30–31.

2   Cited in Bailey 1992, p. 103.

3   Cited in *The Observer*, 24.9.1995.

4   Data in 'Report of the English Language Curriculum and Pedagogy Review', Executive Summary, Singapore 2006 (19 pp.)

5   *The Guardian Weekly*, Learning English Supplement, 16.02.2007, citing Henry Chu in the *Los Angeles Times*.

6   See Templer 2004.

7   The Institute of Education is a graduate college of the University of London. It has been involved in teacher training since its creation in 1902. Teachers College dates from 1892 and has been attached to Columbia University since 1898.

8   The latest form of simplified English is globish, which claims to be based on experience in the commercial world, seems to be commercially driven, and is being marketed in the 'global' press, http://www.ipn-globish. com.

9   See Williams 1961, pp. 239–46, analysing Richards' key role in literary criticism in Britain and the United States from 1920–60. Williams approves of the requirement of the close reading of texts (New Criticism), but is critical of what he sees as a naïve faith in literary criticism being a preparation for the wider world (while demonstrating 'servility to the

literary establishment') and politically unaware (which Williams phrases as innocence of process and innocence of company). This is especially worrying to a committed Marxist when Richards asserts that his approach to communication can solve 'global problems', since essentially his programme remains one for Aesthetic Man. The equally powerful influence on literary criticism in the same period was F.R. Leavis, also at the University of Cambridge (as was Williams). Both scholars had a massive influence on British cultural life and education. Williams (1961, 246–257) sees Leavis' approach as potentially constituting a training in democracy and direct judgement, whereas in fact it led 'at worst to a pseudo-aristocratic authoritarianism, at best to a habitual scepticism which has shown itself very intolerant of any contemporary social commitment.' Both scholars have contributed to the anti-intellectualism of British higher education and public life, and to generations of 'educated' Britons who saw themselves as apolitical. This was a fertile breeding ground for the profession of English teaching worldwide to see itself as apolitical while convinced that they could contribute to the solution of problems of 'global communication'. See also the references to Richards in Collini, 2006.

[11] Medieval Christianity was European: *Everyman* probably has Flemish origins in 1495, and exists in many adaptations, e.g. by Hugo von Hoffmanstahl.

[12] After selectively presenting evidence from a range of contexts, Spolsky concludes that the causal factor in the expansion of English was imperialism rather than linguistic imperialism (2004, 85). Drawing on work by Fishman and de Swaan, he concludes that the global pre-eminence of English is due to 'the changing nature of the world' (a curiously amorphous catch-all term that is detached from causal influences), English being widespread, and because 'the remaining superpower used it unselfconsciously. English was there to be grabbed as the most valuable hyper-collective goods…available for international communication' (ibid., p. 88). Spolsky's 'unselfconsciously' reads like a re-run of the 'benevolence' that Richards ascribes to the Anglo-Americans. It is equally false to focus on 'international' communication as though it somehow exists in detachment from what happens nationally, whether as a first or second language.

[13] It is false to suggest that my work on linguistic imperialism represents a conspiracy theory (Spolsky, 2004) a position I explicitly reject (Phillipson

1992, 63; Phillipson 2007). A conspiracy accusation entails an allegation of an unsophisticated, simplistic explanation for historical events. The charge tends to be simply a put-down, a diversion, 'the standard invalidating predicate to block tracking of strategic decisions' (McMurtry 2002, 17).

[14]   See Appendix 'The principles of Newspeak' in *Nineteen eighty-four*, George Orwell, 1949.

[15]   The Journal of the English-Speaking Union, Year One Number 1, January 1991, www.esu.org.

[16]   Bennett's first thanks go to Baroness Thatcher, evidently an eminent representative of Anglosphere thinking. He cites the quip that NATO was a 'device for keeping the Americans in, the Russians out, and the Germans down.' (ibid., 237).

[17]   Information from Eskil Svane, president of the Esperanto Friends of Rotary organisation in France.

[18]   A plane carrying hydrogen bombs crash-landed in 1986, causing serious contamination to those sent from Denmark to 'clean up', with mortal medical consequences which have only recently come to light.

[19]   Information from Niels Bjerre Hansen, head of American Studies at Copenhagen Business School.

[20]   A New Framework Strategy for Multilingualism was published by the Commission on 22.11.2005 (www.ec.europa.eu/education). The follow-up report by the Committee on Culture and Education (23.10.2006, A6-0372/2006) of the European Parliament (www.europarl.europa.eu) recommended many measures to strengthen language policy and minority languages, virtually all of which were rejected by the Parliament.

[21]   Cited in *Frankfurter Allgemeine Zeitung*, 26 February 2002. See Phillipson, 2003.

[22]   See my comprehensive review of the book in *Language policy* 2006/5, 227–32.

[23]   The pilot studies of English in relation to Nordic languages are summarised, in Swedish, in Höglin, 2002, with a somewhat imprecise summary in English.

[24]   I am grateful to Mart Rannut for this suggestion, at a conference in Lithuania in 2006.

25 'One plausible interpretation of globalization and its effects is indeed that it is a form of dominance brought about by a kind of imperialism – albeit a different kind of postmodern imperialism, no longer characterized only by military victory or nation-state political power. The agents of imperialism, and therefore many globalization processes, are no longer only armies and national governments, but multinational companies, transnational cultural and leisure organisations, global media corporations, or international political elites. This may entail a different, more subtle form of imposition and dominance, but nonetheless seems to me to be a kind of imperialism in a postcolonial world, a twenty-first century form of hegemony.' (Mar-Molinero 2006, 14).

References

Ammon, Ulrich 2000. 'Towards more fairness in international English: Linguistic rights of non-native seakers?' In Phillipson (ed.), *Rights to Language: Equity, Power and Education*, New York: Lawrence Erlbaum Associates, 111–116.

Anderson, B. 1983. *Imagined Communities. Reflections on the Origin and Spread of Nationalism*. London: Verso.

Bailey, R. W. 1992. *Images of English*. Cambridge: Cambridge University Press.

Balibar, Étienne 2004. *We, the People of Europe, Reflections on Transnational Citizenship*. Princeton: Princeton University Press.

Bennett, J. C. 2004. *The Anglosphere challenge. Why the English-speaking nations will lead the way in the twenty-first century*. Lanham, MD: Rowman and Littlefield.

Bourdieu, Pierre 1992. *Language and Symbolic Power*. Cambridge: Polity

Bourdieu, Pierre 2001. *Contre-feux 2. Pour un mouvement social européen*. Paris: Raisons d'agir.

Bondebjerg, Ib 2003. 'Culture, media and globalisation'. In *Humanities —essential research for Europe*. Copenhagen: Danish Research Council for the Humanities, 71–88.

Bruthiaux, Paul 2003. 'Squaring the circle: issues in modelling English worldwide'. *International Journal of Applied Linguistics*, Vol. 13, No. 2, 159–178.

Bugarski, R. 1998. Review of David Crystal 'English as a global language'. *Journal of Multilingual and Multicultural Development*, Vol. 19, No. 1, 90–92.

Calvet, L.-J. 1974. *Linguistique et colonialisme: Petit traité de glottophagie.* Paris: Payot.

Collini, S. 2006. *Absent Minds: Intellectuals in Britain.* Oxford: Oxford University Press.

Creech, Robert L. 2005. *Law and Language in the European Union. The Paradox of a Babel 'United in diversity'.* Groningen: Europa Law Publishing.

Cronin, Michael 2003. *Translation and Globalization.* London: Routledge.

Crystal, David 1997. *English as a Global Language.* Cambridge: Cambridge University Press.

Curtis, M. 2003. *Web of deceit. Britain's real role in the world.* London: Vintage.

Davidson, B. 1978. *Africa in Modern History. The Search for a New Society.* Harmondsworth: Penguin.

de Swaan, Abram 2001. *Words of the World: The Global Language System.* Cambridge: Polity Press.

Druviete, I. 1999. 'Language policy in a changing society: Problematic issues in the implementation of international linguistic human rights standards'. In Kontra, Phillipson, Skutnabb-Kangas and Várady (eds.), *Language: A right and a resource. Approaching linguistic human rights.* Budapest: Central European University Press, 263–276.

Edge, Julian (ed.) 2006. *(Re-)locating TESOL in an age of empire.* Basingstoke: Palgrave Macmillan.

Fairclough, N. 2006. *Language and Globalization.* Abingdon and New York: Routledge.

Fox, M. 1975. *Language and development. A retrospective survey of Ford Foundation Language Projects, 1952-1974,* New York: Ford Foundation.

Graddol, David 2006. *English Next. Why global English may mean the end of 'English as a Foreign Language'.* London: British Council.

Graddol, D., J. Swann and D. Leith (eds.) 1996. *English. History, Diversity and Change.* London: Routledge, for the Open University.

Grin, François 2004. 'On the costs of cultural diversity'. In *Cultural diversity versus economic solidarity,* P. van Parijs (ed.), Bruxelles: de boeck, 189–202.

Grin, François 2005. L'enseignement des langues étrangères comme politique publique. *Rapport au Haut Conseil de l'évaluation de l'école* 19 (2005). 3 Jan. 2006 <http://cisad.adc.education.fr/hcee/documents/rapport_Grin.pdf>

Hatlen, B. 2006. 'The eroding foundations of American imperialism'. *Public Resistance*, Vol. 2, No. 1. <www.publicresistance.org>

Hamel, R. E. 2003. Language empires, linguistic imperialism, and the future of global languages. Universidad Autónoma Metropolitana, México, unpublished.

Hardt, Michael and Antonio Negri 2000. *Empire*. Cambridge, MA: Harvard University Press.

Harvey, D. 2005. *The New Imperialism*. Oxford: Oxford University Press.

Hjarvad, S. 2004. 'The globalization of language. How the media contribute to the spread of English and the emergence of medialects'. *Nordicom Information*, Gothenburg 2: 75-97.

Höglin, R. 2002. *Engelska språket som hot och tillgång i Norden*. Copenhagen: Nordiska Ministerrådet.

Holborrow, M. 2006. 'Ideology and language'. In Edge, *(Re-)locating TESOL in an age of empire*. Basingstoke: Palgrave Macmillan, 84–103.

Howatt, A.P.R. with H.G. Widdowson 2004. *A History of English Language Teaching*, second edition. Oxford: Oxford University Press.

Howe, S. 2002. *Empire: A Very Short Introduction*. Oxford: Oxford University Press.

Ives, P. 2006. '"Global English": linguistic imperialism or practical lingua franca'. *Studies in Language and Capitalism* 1, 121–142; <http://www.languageandcapitalism.info/>.

Kaplan, Robert B. 2001. 'English—the accidental language of science?' In Ammon, (ed.) *The Dominance of English as a Language of Science. Effects on other Languages and Language Communities*. Berlin and New York: Mouton de Gruyter, 3–26.

Kramsch, C. 2002. 'In search of the intercultural'. Review article, *Journal of Sociolinguistics*, Vol. 6, No. 2, 275–285.

Lin, A. and A. Luke 2006. Special Issue Introduction: 'Coloniality, postcoloniality, and TESOL… Can a spider weave its way out of the web that it is being woven into just as it weaves?' *Critical Inquiry in Language Studies* Vol. 2, Nos. 2 and 3, 65–73.

Mar-Molinero, C. 2006. Forces of globalization in the Spanish-speaking world: Linguistic imperialism or grassroots adaptation. In Mar-Molinero, and Stewart (eds.) *Globalization and Language in the Spanish-Speaking world. Macro and Micro Perspectives.* Basingstoke: Palgrave Macmillan, 8–26.

Mattelart, A. 2005. *Diversité culturelle et mondialisation.* Paris: La Découverte.

McArthur, Tom 2002. *The Oxford Guide to World English.* Oxford: Oxford University Press.

McMurtry, J. 2002. *Value Wars. The Global Market versus the Life Economy.* London: Pluto.

McPhail, T. L. 2006. *Global Communication. Theories, Stakeholders, and Trends.* Malden, MA and Oxford: Blackwell.

Mendieta, E., R. Phillipson and T. Skutnabb-Kangas 2006. English in the geopolitics of knowledge. *Revista Canaria de Estudios Ingleses,* 53, 15-26.

Monbiot, George. 2000. *Captive State. The Corporate Takeover of Britain.* London: Macmillan.

Morton, H.V. 1943. *Atlantic Meeting.* London: Methuen.

Motha, S. 2006. 'Decolonizing ESOL: Negotiating linguistic power in U.S. public school classrooms'. *Critical Inquiry in Language Studies,* Vol. 3, No. 2 and 3, 75–100.

Pakir, Anne 2008. 'Bilingual education in Singapore'. In *Bilingual Education,* volume 5 of *Encyclopedia of Language and Education,* second edition, ed. Jim Cummins and Nancy H. Hornberger. New York: Springer, 191–203.

Patten, C. 2005. *Not Quite the Diplomat. Home Truths about World Affairs.* London: Penguin, Allen Lane.

Pieterse, J. N. 2004. *Globalization or Empire.* New York and London: Routledge.

Phillipson, Robert 1992. *Linguistic Imperialism.* Oxford: Oxford University Press.

Phillipson, Robert 2002. Review of Ammon (ed.) 2001 'The dominance of English as a language of science. Effects on other languages and language communities'. *Journal of Language, Identity, and Education,* Vol. 1, No. 2, 163–169.

Phillipson, Robert 2003. *English-Only Europe? Challenging Language Policy.* London: Routledge.

Phillipson, Robert 2004. Review article, English in globalization: three approaches (books by de Swaan, Block and Cameron, and Brutt-Griffler). *Journal of Language, Identity, and Education*, Vol. 3, No. 1, 73–84.

Phillipson Robert 2006. English—a cuckoo in the European higher education nest of languages? *European Journal of English Studies*, Vol. 10, No. 1, 13–32.

Phillipson, Robert 2007. Linguistic imperialism: a conspiracy, or a conspiracy of silence? *Language Policy*, Vol. 6, No. 3–4, 377–383.

Richards, I. A. 1968. *So much nearer. Essays toward a world English*. New York: Harcourt, Brace & World.

Rothkopf, D. 1997. In praise of cultural imperialism. *Foreign Policy*, 38–53.

Routh, R.V. 1941. *The diffusion of British culture outside England. A problem of post-war reconstruction*. Cambridge: Cambridge University Press.

Ryan, S. 2006. 'Language learning motivation within the context of globalisation: An L2 self within an imagined global community'. *Critical Inquiry in Language Studies*, Vol. 3, No. 1, 23–45.

Said, Edward 1993. *Culture and Imperialism*. London: Chatto & Windus.

Saunders, F. S. 1999. *Who Paid the Piper? The CIA and the Cultural Cold War*. London: Granta.

Skutnabb-Kangas, Tove 1988. 'Multilingualism and the education of minority children'. In Skutnabb-Kangas and Cummins (eds.), *Minority Education: from Shame to Struggle*. Clevedon: Multilingual Matters, 9–44.

Skutnabb-Kangas, Tove 2000. *Linguistic Genocide in Education—Or Worldwide Diversity and Human Rights?* Mahwah, NJ: Lawrence Erlbaum.

Skutnabb-Kangas, T. and D. Fernandes (in press). Kurds in Turkey and in (Iraqi) Kurdistan – a comparison of Kurdish educational language policy in two situations of occupation. *Genocide Studies and Prevention*, Vol. 3, No. 1.

Smith, N. 2003. *American empire. Roosevelt's geographer and the prelude to globalization*. Berkeley and Los Angeles, CA: University of California Press.

Smith, R. C. 2003a. 'General Introduction' to Smith, R.C. (ed.), *Teaching English as a Foreign Language, 1912–36: Pioneers of ELT*, Volume 1. London: Routledge, xi–xxxix.

Smith, R. C. 2003b. Introduction to *Volume 5, Towards Carnegie of Teaching English as a Foreign Language, 1912–36: Pioneers of ELT*, ed. R.C. Smith. London: Routledge, xi–xxix.

Spolsky, Bernard 2004. *Language Policy*. Cambridge: Cambridge University Press.

Templer, Bernard 2004. 'High-stakes testing at high fees: Notes and queries on the international English proficiency assessment market'. *Journal for Critical Education Policy Studies*, Vol. 2, No. 1, March 2004 www.jceps.com.

Thompson, J. B. 1992. Editor's Introduction to *Language and Symbolic Power*, Bourdieu. Cambridge: Polity, 1–31.

Troike, R.C. 1977. Editorial: The future of English. *The Linguistic Reporter* 19/8, 2.

van Parijs, P. 2004. Europe's linguistic challenge. *Archives Européennes de Sociologie* XLV/1, 113-154.

West, Michael 1953. *A General Service List of English Words*: Harlow: Longman.

Wierzbicka, Anna 2006. *English: Meaning and Culture*. New York: Oxford University Press.

Williams, Raymond 1961. *Culture and Society 1780–1950*. Harmondsworth: Penguin.

Winand, P. 1993. *Eisenhower, Kennedy, and the United States of Europe*. New York: St. Martin's Press. The Franklin and Eleanor Roosevelt Institute Series on Diplomatic and Economic History, volume 6.

Lingua franca or lingua frankensteinia? English in European integration and globalization[1]

Chapter 7

ABSTRACT

The paper explores how we think of English and 'English Studies' in present-day Europe. It questions the apparent neutrality of the term lingua franca by suggesting a more differentiated set of terms. It relates the current consolidation and expansion of English to processes of global Americanization and Europeanization. The European Union (EU) member states are increasingly integrating their economies and cultures in a US-dominated world. The history and many divergent uses of the term lingua franca are explored, and related to discourses and policies that tend to reinforce English linguistic hegemony uncritically. The paper explores the policies of the EU for maintaining multilingualism, and contemporary constraints and pressures in European academia. It analyses the promotion of 'global' English in terms of the project, the product, and the processes, and considers criteria for assessing whether its advance is as a lingua franca or rather as a lingua frankensteinia.

English: *Lingua divina or diabolica?*

Reference to English as a *lingua franca* generally seems to imply that the language is a neutral instrument for 'international' communication between speakers who do not share a mother tongue. The fact that English is used for a wide range of purposes, nationally and internationally, may mislead one into believing that *lingua franca*

English is disconnected from the many 'special purposes' it serves in key societal domains. English might be more accurately described as a *lingua economica* (in business and advertising, the language of corporate neoliberalism), a *lingua emotiva* (the imaginary of Hollywood, popular music, consumerism and hedonism), a *lingua academica* (in research publications, at international conferences, and as a medium for content learning in higher education), or a *lingua cultura* (rooted in the literary texts of English-speaking nations that school foreign language education traditionally aims at, and integrates with language learning as one element of general education). English is definitely the *lingua bellica* of wars between states (aggression by the US and its loyal acolytes in Afghanistan and Iraq, building on the presence of US bases in hundreds of countries worldwide). The worldwide presence of English as a *lingua americana* is due to the massive economic, cultural and military impact of the USA. Labelling English as a *lingua franca,* if this is understood as a culturally neutral medium that puts everyone on an equal footing, does not merely entail ideological dangers—it is simply false. The history, etiology and misuse of the concept will be explored below.

While English manifestly opens doors for many worldwide, it also closes them for others, as recounted by an Indian with experience of the language being seen as a *lingua divina* (Chamaar, 2007), for which he had rather more empirical justification than the hopefully apocryphal story of the American head teacher informing immigrants that if English was good enough for Jesus, it was good enough for them.

> It wasn't until he was 18 that Kanchedia Chamaar realized that God spoke and understood English and nothing else. Because unfamiliarity with the *lingua divina* was a matter of intense shame at Delhi School of Economics in the 1970s, he started learning English on the sly, and continues to be consumed by the process to this day. Over a period of three years after his master's degree, no fewer than one hundred and eight Indian firms found him unfit for gainful employment. While doing his Ph.D. in the 1980s, he found that at Universities in the US, even those not fluent in English were treated as human beings, a dignity that not everybody seemed willing to accord him in Delhi. He has been hiding in the US ever since.

In India, as in many former colonies, English is the language of elite formation, social inclusion and exclusion. Are there then grounds for referring to English as a *lingua frankensteinia?* We need to recall that Frankenstein in Mary Shelley's novel is the person who created the monster rather than the monster itself. This is a useful reminder of the role of agency, particularly in relation to language use, and of the truism that any language can serve good or evil purposes, whether humane or monstrous ones. English tends to be marketed as though it serves exclusively laudable purposes (a language of international understanding, human rights, development, progress etc.: Phillipson 1992, 271–88). Since languages have never been co-terminous with state boundaries, and granted the current pre-eminence of English as the most extreme case of a language with international impact, we need to consider which agents promote or constrain English and for what purposes.

The elimination of linguistic diversity has been an explicit goal of states attempting to impose monolingualism within their borders: linguicist policies favour the *lingua frankensteinia* and lead to linguicide. This was the case in the internal colonization of the British Isles, with the attempted extermination of Welsh and Gaelic, and in North America and Hawai' at the expense of First Nations languages. Skutnabb-Kangas (2000) avoids seemingly innocuous terms like 'language death' and 'language spread', concepts that obscure agency, by referring to 'killer languages', language murder, and linguistic genocide, basing this term on definitions in international human rights law and the historical evidence of government policies. Swales (1996), after a lifetime of work on scientific English, is so concerned about other languages of scholarship being on the way to extinction that he labels English a *lingua tyrannosaura*. The widespread concern in political and academic circles in Scandinavian countries with domain loss signifies a perception that segments of the national language are at risk from the English monster, hence the national policy to ensure that Danish, Norwegian and Swedish remain fully operational in all domains.

How far domain loss is a reality in Scandinavia has yet to be researched adequately, and preliminary surveys are of limited theoretical and empirical validity. Existing efforts are hampered by loose terminology: domains are not 'lost' but are subjected to linguistic capital accumulation by dispossession when the forces behind an increased use of English marginalize other languages (Phillipson 2008). This is a gradual, long-term process, and generally unobtrusive, but sometimes the underlying agenda can be seen in operation. Thus the language policies connected to the Bologna Process, the creation of a single European higher education and research 'area', are largely covert, but policy statements imply that 'internationalization' means 'English-medium higher education' (Phillipson 2006a). This is also the way government ministers understand the process (e.g. in Norway: Ljosland, 2005).

Prior to the bi-annual ministerial meeting to take stock of the Bologna Process in London, 17–18 May 2007, EU Commissioner Figel stated:[2]

> Bologna reforms are important but Europe should now go beyond them, as universities should also modernize the content of their curricula, create virtual campuses and reform their governance. They should also professionalize their management, diversify their funding and open up to new types of learners, businesses and society at large, in Europe and beyond. … The Commission supports the global strategy in concrete terms through its policies and programmes.

In other words, universities should no longer be seen as a public good but should be run like businesses, should privatize, and should let industry set the agenda. The new buzzwords are that degrees must be 'certified' in terms of the 'employability' of graduates. 'Accountability' no longer refers to intellectual quality or truth-seeking but means acceptability to corporate-driven neoliberalism. The recommendation that there should be more 'student-centred learning' probably implies more e-learning rather than a more dialogic, open-ended syllabus. Before *European* integration has taken on any viable forms, universities are being told to think and act *globally* rather than remain narrowly European. This is insulting to higher education in general and to all universities that have been internationally oriented for decades.

What therefore needs further analysis is whether English is a cuckoo in the European higher education nest of languages, a *lingua cucula*. Cuckoos substitute their own eggs for those in place, and induce other species to take on the feeding and teaching processes. Higher education authorities in the Nordic countries are increasingly addressing the question of cohabitation between the local language and English. The current strategy is to aim at 'parallel competence' in the two languages.[3] The Nordic Declaration of Language Policy, signed by ministers from five countries, endorses this goal. Quite what parallel competence[4] means in practice, for an individual or for institutions, remains obscure.

The elimination of a language from certain domains can threaten social cohesion and the vitality of a language. The experience of ethnocide and linguicide is traumatic—a fact of which people of First Nations origins in North America are only too aware. The importance of the issue is explained in a recent Canadian report:

> Language and culture cannot be separate from each other—if they are, the language only becomes a tool, a thing … Our language and culture are our identity and tell us who we are, where we came from and where we are going.…We came from the land—this land, our land. We belong to it, are part of it and find our identities in it. Our languages return us again and again to this truth. This must be grasped to understand why the retention, strengthening and expansion of our First Nation, Inuit and Métis languages and cultures is of such importance to us and, indeed, to all Canadians. (Task Force ... 2005, 58, 24)

Amos Key, of the Six Nations of the Grand River, Ontario, is committed to the languages being revived, even if few in the younger generation speak anything other than English or French. Amos tells the story of encountering scepticism when expressing a wish for the First Nations to recover their languages. What's the point? To which he replies: well, when I die and go to heaven, I shall want to communicate with my ancestors, my grandfathers and grandmothers. To which the sceptic replies: but what happens if you have been evil and end up in the other place? No problem, because I know English. For Amos Key, English has been a *lingua diabolica* rather than a *lingua divina*, even if, like Caliban in Shakespeare's *The Tempest*, he has become proficient in the language. English, like other colonizing languages, has functioned as a *lingua frankensteinia* throughout the history of the occupation by Europeans of North and South America, Australia and New Zealand.

Europeanization as a variant of global Americanization

What is the relevance of this for Europe? Surely the languages that have been consolidated in independent states over the past two centuries cannot be at risk? Isn't the commitment of the EU to maintaining and respecting linguistic diversity a guarantee of equality and fair treatment for European languages? In fact, the position is far from clear, not least because language policy tends to be left to nationalist and market forces, and there is a fuzzy dividing-line between language policy as the prerogative of each member state and language as an EU concern (Phillipson 2003).

The French have been aware of the threat from cultural and linguistic imperialism for several decades. In the Nordic countries, recent concern about domain loss suggests that English is now perceived as a threat, albeit a relatively diffuse one, since so many factors and influences, push and pull forces, are involved. One of the most visible causal factors is cultural globalisation in the media, which utilize the original language in the north of Europe:

> Seventy to eighty per cent of all TV fiction shown on European TV is American. ... American movies, American TV and the American lifestyle for the populations of the world and Europe at large have become the *lingua franca* of globalization, the closest we get to a visual world culture. (Bondebjerg 2003 79, 81)

By contrast in the USA the market share of films of foreign origin is 1 per cent. The cultural insularity of the US and the UK is also clear from the figures for translation: 2% of books published in the UK and 3% in the USA are translations from other languages, whereas the corresponding figures for Italy are 27%, for Denmark 41%, and Slovenia 70% (from a survey for International PEN). There is therefore a massive asymmetry in how globalization impacts on national cultures. There is no doubt that this is a direct result of US policies, which have become more visibly aggressive as the neoconservatives behind the Project for the New American Century, the Cheney-Wolfowitz-Rumsfeld doctrine, have been in power under Bush II. The overall strategy was analyzed in *Harper's Magazine* in 2002 (cited in Harvey, 2005, 80):

The plan is for the United States to rule the world. The overt theme is unilateralism, but it is ultimately a story of domination. It calls for the United States to maintain its overwhelming military superiority and prevent new rivals from rising up to challenge it on the world stage. It calls for dominion over friends and enemies alike. It says not that the United States must be more powerful, or most powerful, but that it must be absolutely powerful.

Condoleezza Rice regularly articulates this vision. The rhetoric of global 'leadership' is warmly embraced by Tony Blair:

> Globalization begets interdependence, and interdependence begets the necessity of a common value system. History ... the age-old battle between progress and reaction, between those who embrace the modern world and those who reject its existence. Century upon century it has been the destiny of Britain to lead other nations. That should not be a destiny that is part of our history. It should be part of our future. We are a leader of nations or nothing.

The first sentence is from an article in the US establishment journal *Foreign Affairs* in January/February 2007, which argues for common values being imposed, if need be, by force. The remainder from a speech in 1997 (cited in Labour's love's lost', by David Keen, *Le Monde Diplomatique*, May 2007, 16.)

The British government under Blair was blindly supportive of the US, in the analysis of the eminent British playwright David Hare, whose play *Stuff Happens* dramatised the political intrigues behind the Iraq war:

> They [US leaders] know we have voluntarily surrendered our wish for an independent voice in foreign affairs. Worse, we have surrendered it to a country which is actively seeking to undermine international organizations and international law. Lacking the gun, we are to be only the mouth. The deal is this: America provides the firepower. We provide the bullshit. (Hare 2005, 207–8)

Blair's belief system is based on a vision of progress that religious belief entitles him and US neoconservatives to impose worldwide (Gray 2007). Creative writers have a crucial role to play in sensitising the general public to this kind of abuse. The Kenyan writer Ngũgĩ wa Thiong'o is exemplary in both his fiction and critical analysis:

> It is obligatory for writers ... the world over to keep on fighting with the rest of the population to strengthen civil society ... against encroachment by the state, ... where democratic freedoms are equated with the freedom of finance capital. ... there should be no ambiguity about the necessity to abolish the economic and social conditions which bring about the need for charity and begging within any nation and between nations, and language should sensitize human beings to that necessity. (1998: 131)

The project of establishing English as the language of power, globally and locally, is central to this empire. The manifest destiny that colonial Americans arrogated to themselves has been explicitly linked since the early 19th century to English being established globally: 'English is destined to be in the next and succeeding centuries more generally the language of the world than Latin was in the last or French in the present age' (John Adams to Congress, 1780, cited in Bailey 1992, 103). 'The whole world should adopt the American system. The American system can survive in America only if it becomes a world system.' (President Harry Truman, 1947, cited in Pieterse 2004, 131). The Webster dictionaries reflect the transition from a language being forged to form American national identity, to a language accompanying territorial expansion (invariably by violent means, as in other colonial empires) and economic expansion, spurred by capital over-accumulation and an ever-increasing demand for raw materials and new markets. The *American Dictionary of the English Language* of 1828 became in 1890 *Webster's International Dictionary*, while *Webster's Third New International Dictionary of the English Language*, 1981, aims at meeting the needs of the 'whole modern English-speaking world'.

This entails ensuring that English serves the 'needs' of the entire world, as Rothkopf (1997):

> It is in the economic and political interest of the United States to ensure that if the world is moving toward a common language, it be English; that if the world is moving toward common telecommunications, safety, and quality standards, they be American; and that if common values are being developed, they be values with which Americans are comfortable. These are not idle aspirations. English is linking the world.

Anglo-American cooperation in promoting English worldwide has been government policy since the 1950s (Phillipson 1992, 164–9). The Annual Report of the British Council for 1960-61 proclaims: 'Teaching the world English may appear not unlike an extension of the task which America faced in establishing English as a common national language among its own immigrant population.' The means for achieving this domestically in the USA involved transforming a diverse immigrant and indigenous population into monolingual English users, as articulated by President Theodore Roosevelt in 1919, reportedly in a letter to the next President:[5]

> In the first place, we should insist that if the immigrant who comes here in good faith becomes an American and assimilates himself to us, he shall be treated on an exact equality with everyone else, for it is an outrage to discriminate against any such man because of creed, or birthplace, or origin. But this is predicated upon the person's becoming in every facet an American, and nothing but an American ... There can be no divided allegiance here. Any man who says he is an American, but something else also, isn't an American at all. We have room for but one flag, the American flag ... *We have room for but one language here, and that is the English language* ... and we have room for but one sole loyalty and that is a loyalty to the American people. (Emphasis added)

US colonization policies externally were comparable to practices in European colonial empires. The policies were not as actively linguicidal as in the home country, but rather installed a hierarchy of languages, a diglossic division of linguistic labour. According to British India's spin doctor, Thomas Babington Macaulay, in 1835, in territories that were climatically unsuitable for Europeans to settle in permanently but which were subjected to political colonization and economic exploitation, the purpose of education was to produce 'a class of persons, Indians in blood and colour, English in taste, in opinion, in morals and in intellect'. In like fashion 'it was largely through the English language and the introduction of a free public school system during the Philippine American war (1899–1902) and the succeeding decades of colonial rule that the Filipino elite were co-opted to help the United States pacify the rest of the Filipino people' (Constantino 1975, cited in Ruanni Tupas 2001, 85).

Language policy in former colonies is well documented. What is not so well known is that the urge to establish English was not limited to parts of the world that were under European or American control. There is a very topical ring to the following text on reasons for becoming familiar with English:

> Science cannot be advanced without the English language and textbooks and students will make better progress in the sciences by taking the English textbooks and learning the English to boot than they will by giving exclusive attention to their own language and textbooks in our field and the same is true of any field where the Gospel is preached to intelligent beings. We need disciplined and educated men.
> (Greenwood 2003, 65)

This rationale was written in 1847 by Cyrus Hamlyn, an American missionary who spent a lifetime in Istanbul and founded a school, Robert College, named after an American 'philanthropist'. By 1857 the mission had become 'Westernization rather than Christianization'. The school has functioned uninterruptedly since that time. It taught multilingually in the early years, later switched to English-medium, and ultimately became a prestige English-medium university, Boğaziçi University.

The role of Christian missionary activity worldwide since the 16th century has been extensively documented (Etherington, 2005). The termination of colonial empires did not eliminate the symbiosis of English teaching with Christianity. In recent years the issue has been hotly debated at the annual conferences of TESOL (Teachers of English to Speakers of Other Languages), not least since much of this activity is engaged in covertly by US citizens, while otherwise employed as teachers of English in the Middle East, China and the former Soviet Union. A British website reports: 'as missionaries are still banned from China, it represents one of the most effective ways to support Christians in China through the sending of teachers of English from overseas.' This dual role raises profound ethical issues for the profession (Canagarajah and Wong, forthcoming), while highlighting the interlocking of language learning with cultural and political agendas.

While it is more obviously the 'great' powers that have been involved in the slave trade, empire building, and the Europeanization of the world, Nordic citizens were also involved. The fictional characters from Sweden and Denmark in Conrad's *Heart of Darkness* (1902), staffing the army, Christian missions, and river boats, were grounded in historical fact. The dire need to find employment entailed the sacrifice of feelings for our fellow mortals. Education delivered the goods, as explained in 1926 by Bertrand Russell (1960, 31):

> The aim was to train men for positions of authority and power, whether at home or in distant parts of the empire.... The product was to be energetic, stoical, physically fit, possessed of certain unalterable beliefs, with high standards of rectitude, and convinced that it had an important mission in the world. To a surprising extent, the results were achieved. Intellect was sacrificed to them, because intellect might produce doubt. Sympathy was sacrificed, because it might interfere with governing 'inferior' races or classes. Kindliness was sacrificed for the sake of toughness; imagination, for the sake of firmness.

Isn't this precisely what globalization expects of us in the privileged world? That we should not be concerned about what happens in the Asian sweatshops that produce our cotton and electronic goods, nor about unfair, unsustainable trade policies which mean that food subsidies to producers in the rich world undermine the livelihood of growers in poor countries? Are these the values that unite the Americans and the EU, the 'deep ties of kinship' stressed by José Manuel Barroso, President of the European Commission, when endorsing the 'Transatlantic Economic Integration Plan' agreed on at the 2007 EU–US summit.[7] The transatlantic policy statement indicates that neoliberal economic policy and foreign policy are being progressively and intensively integrated. There is a shift away from an attempt to find global solutions to world trade (WTO, Doha), towards protection in the face of the expanding economies of Brazil, China and India, alongside 'Free Trade Areas' with 'new emerging markets'. These defensive, egoistic measures are cloaked in a rhetorical smokescreen in the summit declaration that proclaims that our 'common values ... peace, prosperity and human development depend on the protection of individual liberty, human rights, the rule of law, economic freedom, energy security, environmental protection and the growth of strong, democratic societies'. US actions in recent years have undermined all these causes, both domestically and internationally. EU involvement indicates complicity, while it pursues similar goals for 'Global Europe —competing in the world,' the agenda of the EU Commissioner for Trade and External Competitiveness, the British ex-New Labour guru and twice-sacked minister, Peter Mandelson.

It is well known that politicians lie, and that Bush and Blair did so when making a case for war against Iraq. Whistle-blowers in the employ of a state run the risk of criminal prosecution. David Keogh, a British civil servant was convicted of disclosing the minutes of a meeting between Bush and Blair about Iraq. In court Sir Nigel Scheinwald, Tony Blair's 'top foreign policy adviser, said private talks between world leaders must remain confidential, however illegal or morally abhorrent aspects of their discussions might be' (*Guardian Weekly*, 18 May 2007). This is a brazen revelation of how morally bankrupt our leaders are, the men who believe they have the right to impose their values worldwide.

In EU–US negotiations, English is the sole language involved. This is in conflict with the declared policy that in the EU's international relations, the multilingualism that characterizes its internal affairs should also apply. This is a clear case of English as the *lingua cucula*. Externally the EU has become monolingual.

European agendas and Englishization

Transatlantic partnership builds on the cultural origins of millions of Europeans who emigrated to the USA, and the 'special relationship' with Britain as the successful colonising power, replacing the Dutch and French, until the Declaration of Independence. The strong links between the US and the UK were articulated by Churchill and Roosevelt in 1941 in the 'Atlantic Charter' (Brinkley and Facey-Crowther 1994), Churchill stressing in the House of Commons on 24 August 1941: 'the British Empire and the United States who, fortunately for the progress of mankind, happen to speak the same language and very largely think the same thoughts' (Morton 1943, 152).

European integration is the local variant of a global trend. Marshall Aid was made conditional on the integration of European economies. European political and economic unification also represented a decisive, laudable break with the warfare of centuries. The need for this was foreseen by thinkers who sought to transcend national and dynastic conflict, such as Immanuel Kant, in *Theory and practice* (1792), when pleading for an international rule of law (2004, 91, 92):

> Nowhere does human nature appear less admirable than in the relationships which exist between peoples ... I put my trust in the theory of what the relationships between men and states *ought to be* according to the principle of right ... a universal federal state ... a permanent universal peace by means of a so-called *European balance of power* is a pure illusion.

The role of the USA in defeating fascism and in setting the agenda for the postwar world (the creation of the United Nations Organisation, the Bretton Woods agreements, the World Bank, the IMF, NATO) is well known. What is less well known is that European integration was imposed on Europe by the Americans. The close links between the US political elite and the pioneer European architects of what has become the EU are detailed in Winand (1993). Jean Monnet and many of the key Europeans were quite open about their wish to create a federal Europe on the model of the USA. Churchill also called for the creation of 'a kind of United States of Europe.'

The 'Europe' of the EU can be seen as a *project*, a *product* and a *process*. The *project*, referred to in French as the 'construction' of Europe, is the moving target of the creation of joint policies in the economy, legal process, the environment, and foreign affairs, including military affairs. There is a deep uncertainty about whether increased integration means the abolition of the nation-state or its maintenance, evolution towards a federal United States of Europe or a continuation of the present pooling of sovereignty between member states and EU institutions. The project faltered significantly when Dutch and French voters defeated the proposed draft Constitution in 2005, and was salvaged in the form of a 'Reform Treaty' signed in December 2007, which virtually all EU governments were unwilling to subject to a popular referendum.

The *products* are the buildings, the people working for the Commission, the Parliament, and many other bodies, as well as budgets for programmes, the activities that the EU funds. The *processes* are essentially the ongoing interaction between the Commission, which proposes activities, and the representatives of member states, including governments that meet in the Council of Ministers to decide on policy.

The low turnout of voters in elections for the European Parliament is symptomatic of the cleavage between the EU as an elite/corporate project and the aspirations of citizens Europe-wide. The lack of clarity about what 'Europe' is for, the absence of a clear vision of what it can achieve, the manifest democratic deficit, and fundamental scepticism all reflect serious problems in how 'Europe' is communicated and experienced. The language policies of the EU permeate all these processes, the European project itself and its products.

The complexity of the European Union can be seen in the huge range of topics now covered by EU programmes. The largest translation and interpretation in the world (provided for 50–60 meetings per working day) service the institutions. However, it is impracticable for all documents to be available in all of the 23 official EU languages, other than those with legislative effect in each member state. The Commission website, its link with citizens, confirms a hierarchy of languages: virtually everything is available in English, much in French, and little in other languages.

When the current Commissioners took office they declared that the central policies that they would concentrate on by 2010, in 'A partnership for European renewal' were:

- the 'Lisbon agenda' and the 'knowledge economy' (a neoliberal project for strengthening the European economy, in part by improving education, and with member states committed to introducing two foreign languages in the primary school);

- a Europe of freedom (which has the ring of Bush II: for detailed exemplification of misuse of the concept, see Poole 2007, Chapter 8);

- creating a European public space (through European citizenship programmes);

- establishing a European Justice Space (a tall order—EU law, the 80,000-page 'acquis communautaire,' has legal validity in each state, but to merge judicial systems and integrate common law, Napoleonic law, post-fascist and post-communist legal systems is extremely ambitious: Creech 2005);

- a single European education and research area (for which joint research projects, student and staff exchanges, and the Bologna process are key instruments).

Multilingualism has a higher profile since 2007, when it became the portfolio of the new Commissioner from Romania, Leonard Orban.[8] The most important policy statement is the 2005 Framework Strategy for Multilingualism which stresses:

* the learning of 'mother tongue' plus two languages;

* the formation of national plans to give coherence and direction to actions to promote multilingualism, including the teaching of migrant languages;

* improving teacher training, strengthening early language learning, and Content and Language Integrated Learning;

* the promotion in higher education of more scholarship on multilingualism;

* strengthening diversity in foreign language learning in higher education;

* implementing a European Indicator of Language Competence, a Europe-wide testing system;

* promoting Information Society technologies in language learning and translation;

* facilitating the multilingual economy.

It is up to individual states to decide whether or not to undertake activity in such policy areas, but they are under an obligation to report back on what they are doing. Reports on achievements in this area, such as the implementation of the Action Plan 2004–2006 for Language Learning and Linguistic Diversity have been provided by nearly all EU states. Norway is also very active in exchanging experience on innovation and best practice, even though it is not a member of the EU. Denmark, by contrast, is inactive both in implementing EU proposals and in reporting to the EU on what is currently happening in foreign language education. The UK is not implementing the proposals, even if some excellent work in foreign language learning and related research and planning does take place. These varying responses to this area of EU activity reflect a deep-rooted ambivalence, in this as in many other fields, about what the EU represents.

The rhetoric of maintaining linguistic diversity is pitted against the unfree market. EU treaties and proclamations decree support for multilingualism, and cultural and linguistic diversity, but in practice EU treaties are weak on language rights, there is *laissez faire* in the linguistic market, and political paralysis afflicts language policy analysis and formation at the supranational level (Phillipson 2003). There is formal equality between 23 official languages, but in the internal affairs of the EU institutions, French was earlier *primus inter pares* and English is the current *lingua cucula*.

The advance of English can be seen clearly in the figures for the language used in the initial drafting of EU texts, which show a significant and accelerating shift from French to English over time (see table below).

Table 1. EU texts: Initial drafting language, 1970–2006, percentages.

	French	German	Other	English
1970	60	40	0	n.a.
1996	38	5	12	46
2004	26	3	9	62
2006	14	3	11	72

When English is used so extensively, confirming its dominance in many domains, this serves to make the learning of English more attractive than learning other languages. The UK has a vested interest in promoting this trend, and the increased influence that follows with it, as well as economic benefits. 'The English language teaching sector directly earns nearly £1.3 billion for the UK in invisible exports and our other education related exports earn up to £10 billion a year more', writes Lord Kinnock in a Foreword to David Graddol's book *English Next* (2006), commissioned by the British Council. This declares itself on www.britishcouncil.org as '[t]he United Kingdom's international organization for cultural relations and educational opportunities.' Though it is largely government-funded, the British Council relies on the teaching and examining of English worldwide as a major source of revenue. It is also a pillar of the British government's cultural diplomacy strategy worldwide. It ought, according to a policy survey conducted by a pro-government NGO (Leonard, Stead and Smewing 2002, 81) to be more energetic: the students it teaches and 'the 800,000 people who take exams administered by the Council every year ... would make good targets for public diplomacy activity', as part of 'Diplomacy by Stealth: Working with others to achieve our goals....The general lesson is ... make sure it appears to be coming from a foreign government as little as possible. Increasingly...it must work through organizations and networks that are separate from, independent of, and even culturally suspicious toward government itself.' Thus the activities of English teachers, some of whom may be suspicious of the motives of their own government, can stealthily serve whatever the government sees as a national cause, global English for the local purposes of Britain.

Global English is not a reality, however much it may be described as 'the world's *lingua franca*', or 'the *lingua franca* of the European Union'—claims that are eminently falsifiable, but which serve to substantiate the *processes* of language hierarchisation. Global English, like globalisation, and like the European Union, is a normative project. 'English' can also be seen *as project, process and product*. The *project* involves establishing it as the default language of international communication, and ensuring its increasing use intranationally in business, the media, education, and EU affairs.

English is frequently legitimated in this way by its native speakers. Morgan (2005, 57) writes:

> The spread of English as the European lingua franca, the emergence of a common transnational youth culture, the convergence of business practices, and—most important of all—widespread adoption of European constitutional practices (and perhaps even a Constitution) can be seen as steps along the road to a European nation-state.

He seems unaware that his possible scenario builds on biased presuppositions:

* It assumes that English is a neutral *lingua franca*, serving all equally well, which is manifestly not true, there being many *lingua francas* and many languages in Europe.

- It fails to reveal that 'a common transnational youth culture' is essentially American, promoting a Hollywood consumerist ideology.

- It ignores the fact that 'business practices' derive from the US corporate world, and the conceptual universe it embodies, and which is taught at business schools worldwide, in asymmetrical symbiosis with national traditions.

- EU constitutional practices and legislation have hybrid origins, and equal force in 23 languages, so that even if English is increasingly the language in which EU texts, including Eurolaw, are drafted in, a monolingual EU is not imminent.

Morgan (of Welsh origin, now at Harvard) exemplifies the 'tendency to mistake Anglo English for the human norm' (Wierzbicka 2006), a myopia that some linguists are accused of adopting: 'Publications on "global English", "international English", "world English", "standard English" and "English as a lingua franca" ... neglect the Anglo cultural heritage ... the semantics embedded in the words and grammar.... In the present-day world it is Anglo English that remains the touchstone and guarantor of English-based global communication' (Wierzbicka 2000b, 13, 14). It is this variant of English at which English learning in general education in Europe aims, even if receptive competence may be built up in relation to the diversity of ways in which English is used worldwide: the weighting is more towards Quirkian standard English than Kachruvian liberation linguistics (see Seidlhofer 2003, 7–33).

In international communication there are modifications in 'world Englishes' of a minor type in lexis, syntax, and discourse patterns, and more major ones in pronunciation. There is substantial variation in the use of English within and across countries; but, especially in writing, there is a standardised *product* that ensures intelligibility (Rajadurai 2007). There are serious theoretical and empirical weaknesses in the way 'world' Englishes are classified and analyzed, since the reification involved in any standardization is not faithful to the variety and complexity of sociolinguistic realities (Bruthiaux 2003). Analyses of 'postcolonial' Englishes tend to ignore the constraints that affect the way languages are experienced and used: decolonization 'has become another convenient term used to legitimise world Englishes without problematising its political, economic, educational and ideological significations ... world Englishes are played out across such structures and determinations of inequality' (Ruanni Tupas 2001, 87, 93). In the European context, the parameters determining hierarchies of language are multiple and mobile: there is an unresolved tension between the maintenance of the autonomy of national languages and the hegemonic consolidation of English both in the supranational institutions and within each state. How the linguistic mosaic of Europe will evolve in the coming decades is unpredictable, but manifestly there is a need for explicit language policy formation and implementation to maintain diversity.

There are plenty of distinguished Europeans expressing resistance to the advance of 'global' English. For Bourdieu (2001), globalization means simply Americanization. Balibar (2004) affirms that English cannot be the language of Europe, and for Eco (1997), translation is the language of Europe. This presupposes proficiency in more than one language. Whether the expansion of English will be as a *lingua frankensteinia* remains to be seen, but clarification of the issue requires addressing the origins and uses of the term *lingua franca*.

The history and evolution of *lingua franca*

Mackey (2003) reports that the Germanic Franks moved into the territory of Gaul, later France, as early as in the 5th century, and that large numbers adopted the local language, a form of low Romance or early French, which became known as the language of the Franks, *lingua franca*. Ostler's magisterial *Empires of the Word* (2005) covers the many functions of languages serving widely as instruments of international communication, from Akkadian and Aramaic to Quechua and Swahili. He and Barotchi (2001, 503–4) relate the use of the term *lingua franca* to the way speakers of Arabic, at the time of the crusades, referred to the language of Western Europeans whom the Franks were assumed to represent as *lisan alfiranj*. The language that the Crusaders evolved derived from a vernacular Romance tongue, to which elements of many Mediterranean languages were added. Barotchi quotes a UNESCO Conference on Vernacular Languages in 1953 for a definition of *lingua franca* as 'a language which is used habitually by people whose mother tongues are different in order to facilitate communication between them', and concludes that the term therefore applies to auxiliary languages, including pidgins, and should also apply to planned languages such as Esperanto. In fact until the 1970s the term 'international language' generally referred to planned languages rather than dominant national languages. As examples of 'natural' *lingua francas*, Barotchi cites Greek and Latin in the ancient world, and Latin thereafter. His coverage avoids addressing the issue of the term *lingua franca* often being used to refer to dominant international languages, as in 'English as the *lingua franca* of international scientific contact', or to other languages that are used in a number of countries, such as Swahili or Arabic, which also function as mother tongues.

In colonial Africa, European languages were placed at the apex of a linguistic hierarchy and the vernaculars at the bottom, while *lingua franca* was restricted to dominant African languages. Thus French was not considered a *lingua franca* in the Belgian Congo, and also ceased being designated as a 'vehicular language' when four local languages emerged as the key languages of interethnic communication, education, and labour relations, these languages ultimately radiating as mother tongues (Fabian 1986).

In the Report on the Conference on the Teaching of English as a Second Language, held at Makerere, Uganda, in 1961 (one which decisively influenced the formation of the new profession of teaching English worldwide: Phillipson 1992, chapter 7), a *lingua franca* is defined as 'any non-English language which is widely used, or taught in schools for use, between nationals of the same country, but which is not the mother tongue of all'. This definition does not clarify whether the *lingua franca* can be the mother tongue of some; but the placing of English in a category of its own, superior to all languages, which are merely *lingua francas* or vernaculars, is a clear example of colonialist discourse.

Seidlhofer (2004) and Jenkins (2007) have been at the forefront of exploring English in use as a second language, which they label 'English as a Lingua Franca', ELF (see also the *Annual Review of Applied Linguistics* 2006, and Rubdy and Saraceni 2006).[11] This is an expanding research field, a search for a new foundation for more appropriate language pedagogy, linked to language function and identity. Such work hopes to trigger a paradigm change, a decoupling from the norms that currently determine the power of English. While sympathizing with the goal of contributing to criteria for more equality in communication, I consider that any empirical re-standardization of English is at several removes from the forces that currently propel English forward. Its protagonists readily admit that they are in for the long haul. I suspect that they may be doing themselves a disservice by using ELF for what they see as a distinct new variant of English, since the term *lingua franca* has so much cultural baggage and is open to so many interpretations.

Hamel (2003: 134) comments on the misuse of the term *lingua franca* in an Argentine government educational policy document:

> English is the language of international communication which unites a universal community in brotherhood with no geographic or political frontiers. English has become the natural lingua franca and has thus gained distance from its cultural roots.

Hamel comments: 'This is a good example of the ideology of "many Englishes", of a de-territorialized and neutralized language that belongs to nobody and therefore to everybody; as if English were not backed any longer by the world's most powerful army and navy.'

Clearly the term *lingua franca* has been used in widely different senses in the past and is so still. I would claim that *lingua franca* is a pernicious, invidious term if the language in question is a first language for some people but for others a foreign language, such communication typically being asymmetrical. I would claim that it is a misleading term if the language is supposed to be neutral and disconnected from culture. And that it is a false term for a language that is taught as a subject in general education. There is an ironic historical continuity in *lingua franca* being used as the term for the language of the medieval Crusaders battling with Islam, for the language of the Franks, and currently for English as the language of the crusade of global corporatization, marketed as 'freedom' and 'democracy'.

English studies and 'global' English

One of the most influential figures in English Studies in the 20th century was I. A. Richards. He wrote (1968, 241) that the study of English had unique qualities; the ultimate qualification for global leadership:

> [its] acquisition is not merely for 'wealth and prestige', but because 'new levels of mental capacity are induced...the development of those concepts and sentiments: methodic, economic, moral, political, on which the continuance of man's venture depends. We of the West have somehow—out of a strangely unself-regardful, indeed a regardless impulse of benevolence–committed ourselves to universal education as well as to universal participation in government, nominal though this last can be. There is an analogy between the conception of a world order and the design of a language which may serve man best. The choice of words for that language and the assignment of priorities among their duties can parallel the statesman's true tasks. And it is through what language can offer him that every man has to consider what should concern him most. If rightly ordered, and developed through a due sequence, the study of English can become truly a humane education. May not such a language justly be named "EVERY MAN'S ENGLISH"?

This is the Anglo-American civilizing mission of the twentieth century, to ensure that all citizens of the world (presumably females too) are not confined to English for merely instrumental purposes. Its users will also adopt world views that will make them understand that the West, out of sheer benevolence, has taken upon itself the right to decide how world affairs should be run. Literature takes over the role of religion in concealing the special interests of privileged classes or states, and the hegemony of speakers of a privileged language. Richards' text is uncannily like the neoconservative agenda that was elaborated in the US in the 1990s, and implemented as soon as George W. Bush became president. 'Our' values are universal, and we reserve the right to enforce them globally by all available means. The white man's burden of the modern world is the English teacher's burden.

Since the 1970s, English Studies has expanded in countless directions, but can we be sure that we are not still tarred with a nationalist, anglocentric brush? Greek critical scholars suspect that foreign language departments remain within a nationalist paradigm:

> the very purpose of these departments is to cultivate culturally defined knowledge and to promote the particular language, literature

and culture of the metropolis…they themselves are based on, and reproduce, practices which seek to develop native-like users of the target language who are cultural subjects,…'culturally assimilated' (Dendrinos and Mitsikopoulou, 2004, 37)

They see the influence of English native speaker norms and ideologies —with a strong British ELT and Eng.Lit. tradition—as constituting a language-pedagogical *lingua frankensteinia.*

Is English Studies still underpinned by the same implicit agenda, however much radical rethinking is currently taking place (Kayman, Locatelli and Nünning 2006)? Syllabuses, publications, and conference papers reveal few efforts to integrate the study of 'literature', 'society' and 'language'. Absence of a holistic perspective is aggravated by scholarly specialization, the 'subdivision of knowledge into an ever-multiplying profusion of mutually incomprehensible and inward-looking academic disciplines', to quote Collini's study of intellectuals in Britain (2006, 461). Sub-specializations (e.g. on the language side, between theoretical and applied linguistics, language pedagogy, sociolinguistics, grammar, phonetics, translation, 'composition', etc.) run the risk of failing to form a coherent whole. Simultaneously, external pressures, accountability to the 'knowledge society', marketization, and competition for research funding are transforming communities of learning, independent scholarship and truth-seeking. We run the risk of English Studies not living up the ideals of the intellectual:

> Academic intellectuals will have to continue to foster the rigour, the respect for evidence, the disinterestedness, and the wider perspective which are among the animating ideals of academic scholarship while at the same time managing to break out from its increasingly self-referring hermeticism to bring these qualities to bear in wider public debate. (Collini 2006, 504)

There is a tension between academic freedom and a legitimate requirement that our research time can be shown to produce results. This presupposes no undue influence from funding bodies. Bertrand Russell (1960, 166–8) expressed concern eighty years ago about the academic being limited by utilitarian constraints and an excessive influence on universities by business. New knowledge, theorization and creativity can only be achieved by 'disinterested investigation'.

Taking the analysis of English in European integration forward

I shall attempt to bring together some of the many threads drawn on in this paper.

Project

- The *lingua franca/frankensteinia* project can be seen as entailing the imagining of a community, in the same way as polities are imagined (Anderson 1983), an English-using community without territorial or national boundaries.

- The invention of traditions (in the sense of Hobsbawm and Ranger, 1983), customs, rituals and discourses that connect people through a merging of the language with hybrid agendas uniting the national, the European, the universal and the global.

- Ultimately the project reflects metaphysical choices and philosophical principles that underpin the type of community we wish to live in, the beliefs, values, and ethical principles that guide us, in a world that is currently dominated by neoliberalism, unsustainable consumerism, violence, and linguistic neoimperialism.

- Our choices can either serve to maintain diversity, biological, cultural and linguistic or to eliminate it, and current trends are alarming.[12]

- All these influences lead to visions of and for English, in Europe and elsewhere; and if these do not define *lingua franca* in such a way as to ensure equality and symmetry in intercultural communication, but are essentially the one-sided promotion of English, the project tends to be more that of a *lingua frankensteinia*.

Process

The *lingua franca/frankensteinia* process can be seen as entailing:

- in contexts of use, discourses, and domains;
- which conform to norms of linguistic behaviour that are institutionally (re-) inforced, legitimated and rationalized;
- in societies that hierarchize by means of race, class, gender, and language;

- leading to English being perceived as prestigious and 'normal', hence the feeling of native speakers that the language is universally relevant and usable, and the need for others to learn and use the language, in some cases additively, in others subtractively.

Product

The *lingua franca/frankensteinia* product:

- interlocks with economic/material systems, structures, institutions, and US empire;

- is supported ideologically in cultural (re-)production and consumption;

- is asserted in political, economic, military, media, academic and educational discourses;

- is marketed in narratives of the 'story', the 'spread' of English, and language 'death';

- is branded through metaphors of English as 'international', global, God-given, rich;

- uses the prestige code, that of elites in the dominant English-speaking countries, and embedded in the lexis and syntax of the language.

Heuristic ways of clarifying whether the advance of English represents *lingua franca* rather than *lingua frankensteinia* trends would entail asking a series of questions, and relating each of them to English as project, process and product:

- Is the expansion and/or learning of English in any given context additive or subtractive?

- Is linguistic capital dispossession of national languages taking place?

- Is there a strengthening or a weakening of a balanced local language ecology?

- Where are our political and corporate leaders taking us in language policy?

- How can academics in English Studies contribute to public awareness and political change?

- If dominant norms are global, is English serving local needs or merely subordinating its users to the American empire project? Empirical studies of such questions are needed before firmer conclusions can be drawn, in tandem with a refinement of the theoretical framework for understanding these changes in the global and local language ecology.

Notes

1   This is a modified version of a plenary lecture given at the Nordic Association for English Studies Conference, Bergen, Norway, 24–6 May 2007.

2   For the ongoing EU involvement in the Bologna Process, see http://ec.europa.eu/education/policies/educ/bologna/bologna_en.html

3   For Norway, see *Framlegg til ein språkpolitikk for universitet og høgskolar i Noreg*, 2006. http://www.uhr.no/documents/Framlegg_til_ein_spr_kpolitikk_for_UHsektoren_1.pdf

4   http://www.norden.org/sprak/sk/Sprogdeklarationen per cent20per cent20endelig per cent20version.pdf

5   http://urbanlegends.about.com/library/bl_roosevelt_on_immigrants.htm, accessed 7.9.2007.

6   Amity Foundation, www.uspg.org.uk

7   http://ec.europa.eu/commission_barroso/president/focus/eu_us_042007_en.htm

8   For EU initiatives see http://ec.europa.eu/commission_barroso/orban/index_en.htm

9   http://ec.europa.eu/commission_barroso/orban/keydoc/keydoc_en.htm

10   http://ec.europa.eu/education/policies/2010/doc/lang2004.pdf

11   For a critique of empirical studies of this variant of *lingua franca* English in Germany, see Phillipson (2006b).

12   See www.terralingua.org

References

Anderson, Benedict 1983. *Imagined Communities: Reflections on the Origin and Spread of Nationalism*. London: Verso.

Bailey, Richard W. 1992. *Images of English*. Cambridge: Cambridge University Press.

Balibar, Étienne 2004. *We, the People of Europe? Reflections on Transnational Citizenship*. Princeton: Princeton University Press.

Barotchi, M. 2001. 'Lingua franca'. In Rajend Mesthrie (ed.) *Concise Encyclopedia of Sociolinguistics*. Oxford: Elsevier, 503–04.

Bondebjerg, Ib 2003. 'Culture, media and globalisation'. In *Humanities: Essential Research for Europe*. Copenhagen: Danish Research Council for the Humanities, 71–88.

Bourdieu, Pierre 2001. *Contre-feux 2. Pour un mouvement social européen*. Paris: Raisons d'agir.

Brinkley, Douglas and Facey-Crowther, David R. (eds.) (1994). *The Atlantic Charter*. New York: St. Martin's Press.

Bruthiaux, Paul 2003. 'Squaring the circles: issues in modeling English worldwide'. *International Journal of Applied Linguistics,* Vol. 13, 159–78.

Canagarajah, Suresh A. and Wong (eds.) forthcoming. *Spiritual Dimensions and Dilemmas in English Language Teaching*.

Chamaar, Kanchediar 2007. 'A resolutely uncivilised colonial bumps into postcolonialism'. *Studies in Language and Capitalism,* Vol. 2, 145–54.

Collini, Stefan 2006. *Absent Minds: Intellectuals in Britain*. Oxford: Oxford University Press.

Creech, Richard L. 2005. *Law and Language in the European Union. The Paradox of a Babel 'United in Diversity'*. Groningen: Europa Law.

Dendrinos, Bessie and Mitsikopoulou, Bessie (eds.) 2004. Introduction, in *Policies of Linguistic Pluralism and the Teaching of Languages in Europe*. Athens: Metaixmio/National and Kapodistrian University of Athens, 31–40.

Eco, Umberto 1997. *The Search for the Perfect Language*. London: Fontana.

Etherington, Norman (ed.) 2005. *Missions and Empire*. Oxford: Oxford University Press.

Fabian, Johannes 1986. *Language and Colonial Power: The Appropriation of Swahili in the former Belgian Congo 1880–1938*. Cambridge: Cambridge University Press.

Graddol, David 2006. *English Next: Why Global English May Mean the End of 'English as a Foreign Language'*. London: British Council.

Gray, John 2007. 'Neoconned! How Blair took New Labour for a ride'. *The Independent*, 22 June, 'Extra' Supplement, 1–5.

Greenwood, Keith M. 2003. *Robert College: The American Founders*. Istanbul: Boğaziçi University Press.

Hamel, Rainer Enrique 2003. 'Regional blocs as a barrier against English hegemony? The language policy of Mercosur in South America'. In *Languages in a Globalising World*. Maurais, Jacques and Michael A. Morris (eds.) Cambridge: Cambridge University Press, 111–42.

Hare, David 2005. *Obedience, Struggle and Revolt: Lectures on Theatre*. London: Faber and Faber.

Harvey, David 2005. *The New Imperialism*. Oxford: Oxford University Press.

Hobsbawm, Eric and Ranger, Terence (eds.) 1983. *The Invention of Tradition*. Cambridge: Cambridge University Press.

Jenkins, Jennifer 2007. *English as a Lingua Franca: Attitude and Identity*. Oxford: Oxford University Press.

Kant, Immanuel 2004. *Political Writings*, ed. Hans Reiss. Cambridge: Cambridge University Press.

Kayman, Martin A., Angela Locatelli and Ansgar Nünning 2006. Editorial: 'On being "European" in English'. *European Journal of English Studies* Vol. 10, 1–12.

Leonard, Mark, Catherine Stead and Conrad Smewing 2002. *Public Diplomacy*. London: Foreign Policy Centre, http://fpc.org.uk fsblob/35.pdf

Ljosland, Ragnhild 2005. Norway's misunderstanding of the Bologna process: when internationalisation becomes Anglicisation. Paper presented at the conference on Bi- and Multilingual Universities —Challenges and Future Prospects, Helsinki University, 1–3 Sept.

Mackey, William F. 2003. 'Forecasting the fate of languages'. In Jacques Maurais and Michael A. Morris (eds.) *Languages in a Globalising World*. Cambridge: Cambridge University Press, 64–81.

Morgan, Glyn 2005. *The Idea of a European Super-State: Public Justification and European Integration.* Princeton, NJ: Princeton University Press.

Morton, H.V. 1943. *Atlantic Meeting.* London: Methuen.

Ngũgĩ wa Thiong'o 1998. *Penpoints, Gunpoints, and Dreams: Towards a Critical Theory of the Arts and the State in Africa.* Oxford: Oxford University Press.

Ostler, Nicholas 2005. *Empires of the World: A Language History of the World.* London: HarperCollins.

Phillipson, Robert 1992. *Linguistic Imperialism.* Oxford: Oxford University Press.

Phillipson, Robert 2003. *English-Only Europe? Challenging Language Policy.* London: Routledge.

Phillipson, Robert 2006a. 'English, a cuckoo in the European higher education nest of languages?' *European Journal of English Studies,* Vol. 10, 13–32.

Phillipson, Robert 2006b. 'Figuring out the Englishisation of Europe'. In Constant Leung and Jennifer Jenkins (eds.) *Reconfiguring Europe: The Contribution of Applied Linguistics.* London: Equinox, 65–68.

Phillipson, Robert 2008. The linguistic imperialism of neoliberal empire. *Critical Inquiry in Language Studies,* Vol. 5, 1–43.

Pieterse, Jan N. 2004. *Globalization or Empire.* New York: Routledge.

Poole, Steven 2007. *Unspeak. Words are Weapons.* London: Abacus.

Rajadurai, Joanne 2007. 'Intelligibility studies: a consideration of empirical and ideological issues'. *World Englishes,* Vol. 26, 87–98.

Richards, I. A. 1968. *So Much Nearer: Essays toward a World English.* New York: Harcourt, Brace.

Rothkopf, David 1997. 'In praise of cultural imperialism'. *Foreign Policy,* 38–53.

Ruanni Tupas, T. 2001. Global politics and the Englishes of the world. In Coterill and Ife (eds.), *Language across Boundaries.* London: Continuum. 81–98

Rubdy, Rani and Mario Saraceni (eds.) 2006. *English in the World: Global Rules, Global Roles.* London: Continuum.

Russell, Bertrand 1960. *On Education, Especially in Early Childhood.* London: Unwin.

Seidlhofer, Barbara 2003. *Controversies in Applied Linguistics*. Oxford: Oxford University Press.

Seidlhofer, Barbara 2004. 'Research perspectives on teaching English as a lingua franca'. *Annual Review of Applied Linguistics*, Vol. 24, 209–39.

Skutnabb-Kangas, Tove 2000. *Linguistic Genocide in Education – Or Worldwide Diversity and Human Rights?* Mahwah, NJ: Erlbaum.

Swales, John 1996. English as 'Tyrannosaurus Rex'. *World Englishes*, Vol. 16, 373–82.

Task Force on Aboriginal Languages and Cultures 2005. *Towards a New Beginning: A Foundational Report for a Strategy to Revitalize First Nation, Inuit and Métis Languages and Cultures*. Report to the Minister of Canadian Heritage, June. Ottawa: Aboriginal Languages Directorate. www.aboriginallanguagestaskforce.ca

Wierzbicka, Anna 2006. *English: Meaning and Culture*. Oxford: Oxford University Press.

Winand, Pascaline 1993. *Eisenhower, Kennedy, and the United States of Europe*. New York: St. Martin's Press.

Comments

Comment 1

ADITI BHATIA

City University of Hong Kong. abhatia@cityu.edu.hk

Globalization or global dominance? Lingua franca or lingua Americana? Is English as lingua franca 'a neutral instrument for "international" communication' or a political tool used to create hegemony? Language is not entirely independent of culture and ideology: all three co-constitute each other, and thus supporting the belief that '*lingua franca* English is disconnected from the many "special purposes" it serves in key societal domains' is almost paramount to disbelieving the growing 'McDonaldization' (Ritzer, 2004) of society. The spread of *lingua franca* English may be seen as leading to the transfer by powerful nations of their values onto less powerful states, transforming lingua franca into what Phillipson refers to as *lingua cucula*. Experiences of reality are not only expressed through but also created by the language spoken. Language reflects our perception of reality, and the spread of English imperialism (cf. Phillipson, 1992) can be seen to an extent as suspending one's own repository of experiences in favour of another's (cf. Bhatia, 2007). 'Globalization' itself is a dubious term, and seems less an interconnection of nations and more their dependence on the 'American way of life'. The spread of *lingua franca* English does indeed seem like part of the New World Order agenda —one introduced by Bush Senior in an attempt to direct the world with the American moral compass.

However, despite the various strategies available for global dominance, to say that *lingua franca* is one of them because it transfers values of the West, more specially America's, seems in effect to accord

English the status of primary language as a single homogenized entity. Is this really the case, though? English may be spreading like wildfire, indeed, becoming the language of many key sectors in global societies, but Phillipson's (2008) constant reference to '*lingua franca* English' seems to gloss over the unique adaptations of the language by specific world communities, the melding and meshing of supposed American English into their own individual cultures. In doing so, Phillipson (2008) seems to relegate different world Englishes into the shadow of one universal, primary English. Take the example of 'Indian English', which has been adopted and stylized by one of the largest English-speaking nations in the world. English has been fused into Indian culture, taking on its values and expressions, borrowing and combining phrases from Punjabi, Urdu, and Hindi (Coughlan, 2006). The fusion of the so-called Standard English and Indian cultures produces a distinct variety of English which reflects the identities and thought processes of Indians across the globe. True, at the platinum hub of call centres many employees are expected to imitate American English for the sake of their job. Everyday speaking still consists of expressions that are coloured by Indian culture, which itself is a fusion of different ideologies. English is not accepted whole, nor has it blanketed its recipients with Westernisation. Instead, the 'collision of languages' has generated expressions that lead to the ability of people to 'shift seamlessly' between Hindi, Urdu, Punjabi, and English (Coughlan, 2006), building a plethora of identities for themselves and diversifying the organization and expression of their experiences.

References

Bhatia, Aditi 2007. Discourse of illusion: a critical study of the discourses of terrorism. Ph.D., Macquarie University.

Coughlan, Sean 2006. 'It's Hinglish, innit?' *BBC News Magazine*, 8 Nov. Retrieved 2 Jan. 2006 from http://news.bbc. co.uk/2/hi/uk_news/magazine/6122072.stm

Phillipson, Robert 1992. *Linguistic Imperialism*. Oxford: Oxford University Press.

Ritzer, George 2004. *The McDonaldization of Society*. Thousand Oaks, CA: Sage.

Comment 2

KINGSLEY BOLTON

Stockholm University, kingsley.bolton@english.su.se

There is much to admire in Robert Phillipson's article on English as *lingua franca*, not least the intoxicating sweep of the rhetoric, which is supported by a plethora of social and political facts and scholarly quotations from Theodore Roosevelt to John Pilger, from Kant to Umberto Eco, from Joseph Conrad to Bertrand Russell. All of which—through the various sections of the paper – draws the reader ever deeper into an examination of the central argument so vigorously expounded by the author.

At the core of the argument is concern at the current spread of English in Europe, an issue that Phillipson has discussed at some length earlier. This time, however, the main worry seems to be that the 'monster' of English, with lupine cunning, has dressed himself as a *lingua franca* lamb in order to do his dastardly works in the pleasant green woods and fields of Europe. The monster, it turns out is American, weaned from a British mother, and speaks 'Anglo English'.

Despite the rhetoric, there is much that merits serious comment in the paper (indeed, much more than there is space to deal with here), including Phillipson's comments on 'domain loss' in the Scandinavian context. However, while it is true that English is gaining ground as an academic language in the Nordic region, debates on this are often marked by layers of discursive schizophrenia. On the one hand, the leaders of many Scandinavian universities are campaigning actively for international engagement and urging many of their staff to publish internationally. On the other, some staff at the same institutions have grave concerns about the consequences such 'internationalization' may entail. Both discourses are emanating from the same institutions, and reflect different interest groups within those institutions.

My own view is that many of the concerns voiced with reference to English in Europe are rooted in issues far less linguistic than social and political, a view that Phillipson himself would perhaps endorse. Unlike him, however, I fail to see English *per se* as the major cause of such concerns, but would look to other readings of recent European history for an explanation.

One strand of that explanation would be the growth and development of the European Union over recent decades, and its continuing enlargement today. Another strand, crucially, would be immigration from outside Europe into the Nordic and western European context. What underpins the current paper seems to be the romantic longing for a European imaginary of nation-states with their languages and cultures organically intact. Meanwhile, reality takes other forms. In Stockholm, for example, schoolchildren now speak more than 150 languages at home, and the city has sizeable populations of political refugees from the Balkans. Iraq. Iran, Kurdistan, Somalia, and many other troubled points of the globe. Proficiency in Swedish in this context is much more important than in English, and (in a society whose immigrants account for 15 per cent of the total population) it is 'Swedish with an accent' that may cost you a job interview or fail to open other points of access to society, not English. Similar mechanisms doubtless operate in many other European countries, including once-liberal Holland, and even Denmark. In Europe today, 'structures and determinations of inequality' (to use Ruanni Tupas's words) adhere to national vernaculars, not to English, in a region of the world, it must be said, where mother tongue politics have had a long and bloody history.

Comment 3

BESSIE DENDRINOS

University of Athens, vdendrin@enl.uoa.gr

Dear Text,

I've been asked to converse with you, and I accepted the challenge knowing full well that it will be the sort of interaction that engages texts in unequal power relations. The participants here are the original text, which enjoys its integrity and sovereignty as its own thing, and the weak text, which is heteronomous as it is created from the flesh of the 'mother' text—fathered by my dear friend Robert Phillipson, who nonetheless celebrates equality and justice for all. The text to be born has to be, I was told, no bigger in size than 500 words and is doomed not to grow into adulthood.

Though I agreed to these terms, I now find it exceedingly difficult to select one problem to address because you, my dear, are not only amazingly rich with issues but also wilfully entertaining. In an effort to match your wit, I decided to use a 'stream of consciousness' technique in my writing and thus be true to my modernist subjectivity, which I have not been able to shake off, in fear that it might be replaced by the trendy, glitzy, Manhattanized postmodernism which monopolizes the terrain of cultural production and reception, as well as of the capitalist built environment. I am speaking about the type of environment in which the language you so well demonize flourishes.

This having been said, I must admit that I am skeptical with regard to your critique of the English language, which you call 'diabolic', among other names. What worries me is that, through your metaphors, human qualities are assigned to English which is, after all, *just* a language. It has no *ability* to do things by itself, nor does it bear the *responsibility* for its state of being. As I state elsewhere (and I am certain you agree): 'What a language is, or is not, depends on the historical and structural conditions for its maintenance and use, on the social conditions of its institutionalisation, on the symbolic value attached to it and to its users, and the support mechanisms available for its development, enrichment and promotion' (Karavanda and Mitsikopoulou, in press).

These conditions do include the role of agency which you acknowledge, suggesting that agents promoting or constraining the use of English be considered. But I am not sure who these agents are. On the contrary, I think that we can trace the discourses which promote the use of English as a global commodity—use which is interlocked with globalization. They are in fact embedded in discourses of globality. But to understand the discourses that promote English as a global language, it is essential to understand the counter-discourses which are connected also, but not exclusively, with discourses of multi-or plurilingualism and linguistic diversity.

The above is no easy task, because there are a variety of conflictual and competing meanings within both types of discourse – meanings that arise from historical, sociopolitical, and cultural conditions tightly linked to economic and neocolonial power relations. This being so, it is only natural that both discourses of English promotionism and monolingualism as well as of multi- or plurilingualism) are inscribed with the ideology formations of today's Western culture, driven by a global integrated economy based on the neoliberal model that entails the removal of the classical liberal division between market and society. In other words, as I have argued elsewhere, *both* discourses are commodified (Dendrinos, 2002). Our project, I suggest, could involve us in efforts to understand the ideological conflicts articulated therein (whether these are articulated in English, Danish, Portuguese, or Greek) so that our understanding can facilitate our move from critique of the product to practices of resistance against the conditions of production—the growing corporatism, militarization, and political fundamentalism which are having a deep-seated impact on our individual and collective experience.

References

Dendrinos, Bessie (2002) The marketisation of (counter) discourses of English as a global(ising) language. In M. Kalantzis, G. Varnava-Skoura, and B. Cope (eds.), *Learning for the Future: New Worlds, New Literacies, New Learning, New People*. Altona, Victoria, Australia: Common Ground (241–55). (Also available in Greek: G. Varnava-Skoura (ed.), *Ekpaideytikes Optikes, Ekpaideytikes Prooptikes* [Research views, educational perspectives]. University of Athens, 2003.)

Karavanda, M., and Mitsikopoulou, B. (eds.) (in press) Special Issue on New Englishes. *European Journal of Enlgish Studies*.

Comment 4

FATIMA ESSEILI

Purdue University, fesseili@purdue.edu

Phillipson's paper *Lingua franca or lingua frankensteinia?* addresses key concerns of linguists and politicians in the Outer and Expanding Circles, especially in relation to the spread of foreign languages and their threat to local languages, national aspirations, culture, religion, and identity. As a native of Lebanon, a multilingual country where Arabic, French, and English add to the linguistic complexity of Lebanese society, I agree with Phillipson that language policy-makers need to be aware of the dangers of the uncritical promotion of English and what he identifies as linguistic imperialism (Phillipson 1992). However, I am not convinced by specific arguments he makes with respect to identity, culture, and language. I will illustrate this by addressing Phillipson's notions of *lingua americana* and *lingua cucula*.

Phillipson seems to be treating English, or American English (*lingua americana*), to be more exact, as a sort of a Big Brother language that is going to brainwash people and force them to adopt it in what seems like a conspiracy theory. While it is true that the actions of language agencies and the speeches of politicians provide evidence of the underlying agendas of some countries, like the USA, this is not proof that people and nations are unaware of such agendas, or that the choices they are making are uninformed, rather than driven by practicality and economics in the first place. An example of this is the trilingualism policy in Lebanon (Shaaban and Ghaith, 1999).

Along the same line, Phillipson uses the cuckoo metaphor to refer to the situation of English (*lingua cucula*) in Europe. The metaphor goes like this: secret agents (cuckoo = politicians and/or policy-makers) sneak in and put the English language (cuckoo's egg) in the European nest (education system). Unaware that the egg they are incubating (English teaching and promotion) is not their own, Europeans are tricked into raising English, the fledgling that will eventually replace the thriving native birds (other European languages). The *lingua cucula* metaphor fails to take three important issues into consideration. First, it does not take into account identity, religion, and nationalism, which play a major role in the preservation of languages. Second, it is against factual evidence presented by many studies of world Englishes which reveal that countries adopt and adapt English as their own when they start using it (see e.g. Kachru, Kachru, and Nelson, 2006; Thumboo, 2001). Thus, it is no longer American English or British English, it is Indian English, Nigerian English, and so on. Third, and finally, if a policy does not serve a country's interests, people will speak out. The demonstrations and strikes in France and Greece against the Bologna initiative, which Phillipson references, are evidence that people are aware of their linguistic needs and their motivations for responding to them.

To his credit, Phillipson admits that the concepts of *lingua frankensteinia* and *lingua cucula* need further analysis; however, his underlying argument that 'the English monster' is hegemonizing other languages and cultures implies that this is what he believes to be the reality. To him, English is a *lingua frankensteinia* and a *lingua cucula*.

References

Kachru, Braj, Kachru, Yamuna, and Nelson, Cecil (2006) *The Handbook of World Englishes*. Oxford: Blackwell.

Phillipson, Robert 1992. *Linguistic Imperialism*. Oxford: Oxford University Press.

Shaaban, Kassem, and Ghaith, Ghazi 1999. Lebanon's language-in-education policies: from bilingualism to trilingualism. *Language Problems and Language Planning*, Vol. 23, 1–16.

Thumboo, Edwin (ed.) 2001. *The Three Circles of English: Language Specialists Talk about the English Language*. Singapore: UniPress.

Comment 5

MIKLÓS KONTRA

University of szeged, kontra@nytud.hu

The following news story was printed in Hungary's largest-selling daily newspaper *Népszabadság* on 22 December 2007 (my translation):

Hungary's FIDESZ Party Sees X-mas Specter

The local unit of Hungary's largest opposition party FIDESZ, in the ninth district of Budapest has called the 'Fuck the X-Mass (sic) Party 2' event held at Kultiplex Community Center last week the desecration of Christmas. FIDESZ demands that the community center should be closed down immediately. János Bácskai, the chairman of the ninth district FIDESZ unit has issued this communiqué: 'One does not need a lot of proficiency in English to establish the fact that our most intimate Christian holiday, the holiday of affection has been desecrated' and 'the preparations for the holiday of the Christian cultural complex have been placed in an unheard-of context by this obscene talk.' FIDESZ protests against what they call 'the primitive thoughts and deeds' which offend 'people cast of a Christian mind'. The local FIDESZ organization has also stated that Kultiplex Community Center is causing ever-increasing disturbance to local residents, its programs 'oftentimes end in scandals and hullabaloo, and the police routinely have to be called to the weekend riots.'

Journalist S.G. maintains that the word X-Mass—contrary to what the misinformed FIDESZ spokesmen believe—does not mean Christmas. Christmas, as is well known, is abbreviated X-Mas (sic). The word X-Mass is a play on words: it is the blend of Christmas and mass. 'The organizers of the program created this blend to refer to the large-scale commercialization of our most sacred holiday, and they intended to reject this phenomenon by this name.' said László Dirner, manager of the company which runs the Community Center. He added that during the program (which was not organized by his company) nothing was said that could hurt anybody's national, sexual, political or any other kind of identity. Nevertheless Mr Dirner extends his apologies to all who may have been offended in any way during the program.

Manager Dirner also stressed that Kultiplex Community Center is known as one of Budapest's most peaceful places of entertainment and any stories about riots during weekend nights are unfounded.

It is no exaggeration to assume that nine in ten readers missed crucial parts of this story printed in Hungarian, since out of the 27 member states of the European Union, Hungary's citizens have the lowest proficiency in foreign languages. In the 15-member-state EU every second citizen spoke English, every third spoke German, and every fourth French (if L1 and L2 speakers of a language are combined). In contrast, only one Hungarian out of ten could get by in *any foreign language* in 2002 (see Lukács, 2002), and that situation has not improved much in the last five years.

Hate speech looms rather large in Hungary these days. The name of an organization such as *Gój Motorosok* 'goy motorcyclists' can refer to social exclusion on the basis of identity, but the linguistic form of the name is such that legal sanctions cannot be imposed (see Kálmán, 2007, a linguist's expert testimony made for a recent court case).

The 'Fuck The X-Mass Party' story may be bad news for George Bush I, who thought that helping others to acquire English would appear to profit everyone, not least of all USA citizens. As Crawford (1992: 206) reported.

> George Bush espoused this latter view when he dispatched the Peace Corps into post-Communist Poland and Hungary. As much as dollars, the President suggested, the fledgling capitalists needed a world-class medium of communication. He told the departing volunteers:
>
> The key you carry with you will be the English language … the language of commerce and understanding. And just as national literacy has long been the key to power, so today English literacy has become the key to progress. Like your liberty, your language came to you as a birthright and a credit to the dreams and sacrifices of those who came before…Your investment is America's investment in the consolidation of democracy and independence in central and eastern Europe.

References

Crawford, James 1992. *Hold Your Tongue: Bilingualism and the Politics of 'English Only'*. Reading, MA: Addison-Wesley.

Kálmán László 2007. A Gój Motorosok elnevezésröl [A linguist's expert testimony on the name Gój Motorosok]. *Èlet és Irodalom*, 23 November 2007, 4.

Lukács, Krisztina 2002. Foreign language teaching in present-day Hungary: An EU perspective. *novELTy*, Vol. 9, No. 1, 4–26.

Comment 6

CHRISTIANE MEIERKORD

Universität Münster, Christiane.meierkord@uni-muensterde

In his current paper, Phillipson argues that *lingua franca* is a pernicious, misleading, and false term for the English language. This assessment seems to have resulted from a misconception of what communication in English as a lingua franca really entails. When a colleague of mine and I edited our volume on lingua franca communication in 2002, we concluded: 'Generally speaking, the term *'lingua franca'* is used with reference to a particular language's function only and…it is commonly held that *lingua francas* are second languages for their speakers' (Meierkord and Knapp, 2002: 10).

Empirical research over the last decade has demonstrated that lingua franca communication in English needs to be conceived as Interactions across Englishes (cf. Meierkord, 2004). These interactions are characterized by the fact that participants, for example, Nigerians or Germans, potentially bring their own individual, characteristic form of English into their interactions with others. Ideally, these different forms of English would all be on an equal footing in such interactions. However, since some forms of English have become a norm more than others, this is frequently not the case. Mastery or non-mastery of one of the standardized forms of English unfortunately often determines whether a participant is dominant or dominated in interactions conducted in English as a lingua franca.

This problem is, of course, not caused by the English language itself. Not only do English and other languages with similarly large user communities serve as lingua francas, but so too do languages such as Lingala, Afrikaans, or Kiswahili, whose function as a lingua franca extends across a smaller number of users. Since their use usually implies diglossia, all lingua francas potentially pose a threat to other languages. Thus, attempting to interpret the term *lingua franca* as indicting a 'neutral' or even 'liberating' use of a particular language is obviously a severe misinterpretation that most scholars will not subscribe to.

As a result of diglossia, languages may in fact die, but at the same time new forms of language tend to be born, such as Sheng and Engsh in Kenya.

These mixed codes, which consist of elements of Swahili, English, and a number of local languages, express their speakers' hybrid identities and are two examples of a *lingua franca* being creatively adapted to its speakers' needs.

Nevertheless, the lack of rigorously descriptive studies on the subject may in fact result in uncritical, and potentially dangerous, statements from all sides. Unfortunately, scholarly attention has, over the last few years, often concentrated on promoting a new form of English to be taught as a lingua franca, at the expense of empirical studies into what English as a lingua franca really is. Phillipson's call for intensive empirical research is therefore very timely. In order to better assess what these forms of interactions look like, descriptions of the different domains in which English is used are necessary. This should lead to a discussion of issues of (dis) empowerment, segregation, and marginalisation, to identify where English impedes access to social, political, and economic empowerment for individuals who do not command English. Furthermore, the results need to be interpreted in relation to language policy at a national as well as at a supranational level, such as the European Union, the Association of Southeast Asian Nations, or the African Union. At least for the former, Rampton's research (2005), for example, convincingly demonstrates that the use of English as a link language can hardly be taken to coincide with an Americanization of its speakers' identity. Rather, multilingual and multiethnic areas produce heterogeneous arrays of identities, many of which are hybrid and do not include 'American' facets at all.

References

Meierkord, Christiane, and Knapp, Karlfried 2002. Approaching lingua franca communication. In Karlfried Knapp and Christiane Meierkord (eds.), *Lingua Franca Communication*. Frankfurt a.M.: Lang. 9–28

Meierkord, Christiane 2004. Syntax in interactions across international Englishes. *English World-Wide*, 25(1), 109–32.

Rampton, Ben 2005. *Crossing: Language and Ethnicity among Adolescents*. Second edition. Manchester: St. Jerome.

Comment 7

MARIO SARACENI

University of Portsmouth, mario.saraceni@poit.ac.uk

In questioning the validity of the term *lingua franca*, Robert Phillipson reiterates in this paper the issues that he has brought to the fore and discussed in the last 15 years. He sees the English language as a vehicle of imperialism, and consequently expresses concern over its adoption as a pan-European lingua franca. In doing so, he explicitly and strongly condemns a form of globalisation that is purely driven by American corporate interests. He denounces the Americanization of the world and the uncritical acceptance of it. He criticizes the commodification of education. On that side of the discussion, it is easy to agree with him.

The problem with Phillipson's argument, however, is that it moves rather tortuously in a constant but precarious equilibrium between thesis and hypothesis. The foundations on which he bases his discussion are perilously shaky, as he indulges in anecdotal evidence and a patchwork of citations from a range of sources with very little or no grounding in sociolinguistics. Indeed, there is a bizarre paradox in Phillipson's contention: he attributes the highest degree of expertise, authority, and credibility concerning the English language to people who are by no means expert, authoritative, or credible about it. He quotes presidents and prime ministers even if he unequivocally states: 'It is well known that politicians lie.' He quotes a passing comment by David Rothkopf on the English language and elevates it to a piece of conclusive evidence of the link between American cultural imperialism and English in the world. He accepts, without question, the claims made throughout history by various politicians, rulers, missionaries, imperialists of all sorts about the role that *they* ascribe to the English language. Sociolinguistics, it seems, has very little to say about the matter.

Phillipson states that it is necessary to understand which agents promote English and why, but does not seem to recognize any agency in those who choose to add English to their linguistic repertoire. They are, presumably, the victims – unaware – of the subtle strategies of world domination encoded in English Language Teaching. The problem with this kind of conspiracy theory is precisely that it entails a complete absence of conscious, intelligent, and informed agency on the part of the stakeholders.

The Kachruvian take on the roles of English in postcolonial settings is dismissed with one stroke because it 'ignore[s] the constraints that affect the way languages are experienced and used'. This point seems to be of fundamental importance in Phillipson's argument, and merits much more attention than is devoted to it. Ruanni Tupas' quote is indeed very interesting, and it is unfortunate that the theme is not developed further.

Once the conspiracy theory is removed, it is possible to identify the paper's main claim: that English cannot be a neutral lingua franca if it is at one and the same time somebody's mother tongue and somebody else's foreign language. Fair enough. The conclusion, however, is surprisingly and anticlimatically tentative: a series of questions are asked, and in order to provide satisfactory answers Phillipson suggests that further empirical study is needed. This is undoubtedly true but, then, it invalidates his thesis at its core and reformulates it firmly as a hypothesis. A hypothesis that surely needs to be tested in a more systematic way.

Response

ROBERT PHILLIPSON

Copenhagen Business School, rp.isv@cbs.dk

I am grateful to the editors for commissioning a set of responses to my paper, and allowing me a brief final comment. Many thanks likewise to the commentators.

Two of them construe my analysis as a conspiracy theory. This is simplistic and false. I have at greater length elsewhere, in a paper that exposes the way Spolsky misrepresents my work (Phillipson 2007), argued against this put-down. A conspiracy smear (it has nothing to do with theory) is often, as a study of neoliberal agendas and ideologies shows, 'the standard invalidating predicate to block tracking of strategic decisions' (McMurtry 2002, 17, xiv). What critical scholarship should be concerned with is 'the deeper question of the life-and-death principles of regulating value systems which connect across and explain social orders' (ibid.). This is the overall context within which uses of 'global' English need exploration.

I refer in the paper to both push and pull factors influencing the way English is currently spreading. I don't accept that I ignore the agency of those who are opting to use English. English is invariably desirable for the society and the individual *provided that it is additive*. However, the acquisition of linguistic capital is structurally constrained by linguistic market forces—the 'practicalities and economics' that Esseili refers to—in such a way that complicity in using English is active but contingent rather than free. Does Saraceni really believe that the advance of English in the UK, North America, India, etc. has not been explicit government policy? The historical evidence is clear and not merely anecdotal. The problem is not English *per se*

(Bolton), but the language ideologies and practices associated with it. I endorse Dendrinos's suggestions for ways to move counter-discourses forward.

Kontra's report from Hungary demonstrates the infiltration of English vocabulary (a global phenomenon) that is comprehensible to only a fraction of those exposed to it (also widespread) and journalistic coverage, linking these to the way English is credited (here by Bush I) with exclusively positive traits (understanding, progress, democracy), whereas the language is also used for more subversive purposes (universally) and for imposing neoliberal agendas. Kontra's example touches the raw nerve of linguistic territorial space being occupied by an invasive language and culture.

Meierkord underlines the need to study whether lingua francas represent a threat, i.e. whether they are subtractive. Her focus on language functions, and analysis of domains of use, tallies well with study of the expansion of English in Scandinavia. Here the focus is moving away from words—languages have always borrowed words from each other—to domains, and scrutiny of whether marginalization and dispossession of Danish, Swedish, etc. is a reality. Definitions of the term *lingua franca*, and study of the diverse uses of English, nationally, worldwide, and in multilingual settings, need therefore to engage with and clarify inequality and hierarchies of language.

I agree with Bolton that the national mosaic of Scandinavian countries has been significantly influenced by Europeanization processes and by immigration. Reactions vary: in Denmark there is an atavistic rejection of immigrant cultures, whereas Americanization is imbibed virtually unnoticed. In Europe, alas, as elsewhere, language policy 'debates' tend to build on existential, nationalistic gut feelings rather than sober research findings.

Dendrinos stresses the complexity of the task of analysing the interlocking of English with globality, the commodification of the language, and local forms of resistance. There have throughout history been voices criticizing colonialism and imperialism, but there is a huge present-day challenge if we are to contribute to 'practices of resistance against the conditions of production', including linguistic production. This requires a fundamental rethinking of our professionalism and its role in society.

It is a problem if one's metaphors can be seen as attributing agency or human characteristics to a language rather than its users. *Lingua franca* is itself a synecdoche, but human communication is dependent on such abstractions and animations. *Pace* Esseili, my *lingua cucula* metaphor should not be treated too literally, even if there are common traits to linguistic and avian ecology. I hope that approaching the analysis of territory increasingly occupied by English through three lenses, projects, processes and products, will lead to holistic analysis of discourses and social and material realities.

Saraceni makes a plea for 'sociolinguistics', but macro-sociolinguistics needs political science, economics, law, and history if it is to escape the narrowness (Collini's hermeticism) that most empiricist, positivistic research is trapped in. Along with numerous misreadings of my paper, he suggests that it can be reduced to a single 'claim', namely inequality at the level of the individual. This standpoint considers personal choice the sole determinant of language behaviour and policy, and ignores social stratification, and language policies in education, the media, commerce, etc. that privilege one language above others—where the evidence is far from 'hypothetical'.

Bhatia's Hinglish involves distinctive lexis in contexts of 'banter', but this is worlds apart from the call centre economy. In this domain, young Indians are expected to expunge their Indian English accents and lexis, and even to adopt an Anglo-American name. This variant of intercultural communication entails subjection to external, US–UK norms. This fits snugly with English in India being the language of power, despite the warnings of Gandhi a century ago and Nehru fifty years ago. A great deal of Indian research indicates that '[o]ver the post-Independence years, English has become the single most important predictor of socio-economic mobility.…With the globalized economy, English education widens the discrepancy between the social classes' (Mohanty 2006, 268–69). Even if hybridity and glocalization are a reality—but presumably not in the examination system—*lingua frankensteinia* functions, such as young Indians not being well educated in Indian languages, represent a real threat.

Languages are not static, but distinctive, dynamic lexico-grammatical codes: 'each grammar can be seen as a repository of past experience, as the outcome of a very long process of adaptation to specific environmental conditions' (Mühlhäusler 2003, 120). These conditions and the world's languages are in collision with neoimperial forces and the dominant language. Varying approaches to such issues are brought together in Hornberger et al. (2008). Much of this work has been inspired by Braj Kachru's pioneering and creative rethinking of language policy issues, including pointing out (1997) the inadequacy of the term lingua franca. I assume that most readers of *World Englishes* wish to promote linguistic justice – through several languages and not least English(es). Those of us who are fortunate enough to be fluent in the Janus-faced *lingua divina/ lingua diabolica* have a particular obligation to work for this cause.

References

Hornberger, Nancy, et al. (eds.) 2008. *Encyclopedia of Language and Education*. 2nd edn. Vol. 1: *Language policy and political issues in education*; Vol. 9, *Ecology of Language*. New York: Springer.

Kachru, Braj B. 1997. World Englishes and English-using communities. *Annual Review of Applied Linguistics, 17*, 66–87.

McMurtry, John 2002. *Value Wars: The Global Market versus the Life Economy*. London: Pluto.

Mohanty, Ajit 2006. 'Multilingualism and predicaments of education in India'. In García, Skutnabb-Kangas, and Torres-Guzmán (eds.), *Imagining Multilingual Schools: Languages in Education and Glocalization*. Clevedon, Multilingual Matters, 262–283.

Mühlhäusler, Peter 2003. *Language of Environment, Environment of Language: A Course in Ecolinguistics*. London: Battlebridge.

Phillipson, Robert 2007. 'Linguistic imperialism: a conspiracy, or a conspiracy of silence?' *Language Policy*, Vol. 6, 377–83.

Chapter 8

English in higher education, panacea or pandemic?

The article[1] explores the term 'English-medium universities' in relation to current language policy trends worldwide. It situates universities and globalization historically, and assesses whether the continued use of English in postcolonial contexts and its current expansion in European higher education is purely positive—the lure of the panacea—or life-threatening for other languages and cultures, a pandemic symptom. It argues for the maintenance of multilingualism, with English in balance with other languages. It begins with a set of statements that serve to clarify factors that ought to determine university language policy.

> I am afraid our universities are the blotting-sheets of the West. We have borrowed the superficial features of the Western universities, and flattered ourselves that we have founded living universities here. Do they reflect or respond to the needs of the masses?
>
> *Gandhi*, 1942, in Gandhi 2008, 463

> Different cultures are thus interpreted in ways that reinforce the political conviction that Western civilization is somehow the main, perhaps the only, source of rationalistic and liberal ideas—among them analytical scrutiny, open debate, political tolerance and agreement to differ... science and evidence, liberty and tolerance, and of course rights and justice. ... Once we recognize that many ideas that are taken to be quintessentially Western have also flourished in other civilizations, we also see that these ideas are not as culture-specific as is sometimes claimed.
>
> *Amartya Sen*, 2005, 285, 287

... the written English prose medium which, in some 'standard' form, is the staple of the global medium is hardly a neutral or innocent instrument. It defines a discourse whose conventions of grammar and use are heavily vested ideologically, affirming and legitimising particular ways of seeing the world, particular forms of knowledge and particular relations of power, all of which work decidedly against the best interests of the disadvantaged countries.

Thiru Kandiah, 2001

... the right to education, teaching and research can only be fully enjoyed in an atmosphere of academic freedom and autonomy for institutions of higher education ...

Recognizing the diversity of cultures in the world ...

Teaching in higher education is a profession: it is a form of public service...

UNESCO Recommendation concerning the Status of Higher-Education Teaching Personnel, 11 November 1997

... University Language Policy is based on the following strategic precepts:

Languages are a resource within the academic community

The University's bilingual and multilingual environment and internationalisation are sources of enrichment for all and are a necessity for the international comparability of its research performance.

Language skills are a means to understanding foreign cultures and for making Finnish culture known to others. The university promotes the language proficiency of its students and staff as well as supports their knowledge of different cultures. Multilingual and multicultural communities promote creative thinking.

University of Helsinki, Finland, Language policy, 14 March 2007[2]

To provide a comprehensive education, developing fully the intellectual and personal strengths of its students while developing and extending lifelong learning opportunities for the community...

Take full advantage of the University's unique position as China's English-medium University.

Deliver courses and degree programmes in the English language, that are of the highest quality and in a comprehensive range of disciplines; where course content is up-to-date, relevant to community needs, and informed by current research; where teaching methods are appropriately student-centred; and develop skills and competencies that will enhance the graduates' contributions to society.

Strategic Development Plan 2003-2008, University of Hong Kong[3]

These glimpses of the complexity of higher education suggest that

1. universities should serve the entire society (Gandhi, Hong Kong)

2. the West should not be allowed to get away with claiming a monopoly of humane values, ideas, and 'civilisation' (Sen);

3. the use of English reflects and constitutes particular interests (Kandiah);

4. universities should function as a public good (UNESCO);

5. academic freedom and university autonomy are paramount (UNESCO);

6. universities should actively promote multilingualism (Finland);

7. English-medium education is a strategic asset (Hong Kong), but English needs to be seen in relation to multilingual competence (Finland) and cultural diversity (UNESCO) and is inherently problematical (Kandiah).

What the texts have in common is that they are available in English. This is as a result of the colonization of much of the world by the British, of twentieth century international organizations like UNESCO functioning in a limited set of politically influential languages, and of European universities increasingly functioning in English as well as national languages. The expansion of English worldwide has thus given it a special status in widely divergent contexts, to which many factors have contributed. It is therefore important for universities to know how this has come about, whose interests English serves, and what the implications are for other languages. We need to reflect on language policy past, present, and future.

The glimpses are not merely selected extracts from longer texts. They are also selective in that the *Finnish* university policy document is in three languages, with identical content also in Finnish and Swedish. The *Hong Kong* text is also in Chinese, though the Strategic Development Plan and Mission Statement make no mention of biliteracy, multilingualism, or any university language policy. The *UNESCO* document exists in the five other UN official languages. *Amartya Sen*, who has been Master of Trinity College, Cambridge and is currently at Harvard, is passionately committed to his mother tongue, Bengali, is a winner of the Nobel Prize for Economics, and is deeply knowledgeable about the cultural links over three millennia between the Indian, Chinese and Arab scholarly worlds. *Gandhi* attempted to limit the way English was used and idolized by elites in India in the hope that greater use of Hindustani and other Indian languages would lead to a more democratic society, one not so polarized along lines of language, religion and caste. Gandhi succeeded in the political struggle for independence but failed to prevent partition or the consolidation of an English-speaking elite class and English-medium universities in independent India, Pakistan and Bangladesh.

The concept 'university' derives from the Latin *universitas*, referring to the whole, the entirety, the universe.[4] Universities should be global in the sense that knowledge is sought after without constraint, taking the scholar into uncharted territory unimpeded by the dictates of the powerful, whether secular or religious. Students and their tutors need to create knowledge, and to know how and why it is created. There is a major challenge in maintaining universities of this sort when the institutions are increasingly regarded as businesses, and knowledge is treated as a commodity.

Is there a choice then between the panacea of English supposedly guaranteeing economic success, and the pandemic we are experiencing of corporate and military globalization, environmental degradation, energy and food crises, and an intensifying gap between global Haves and Never-to-haves, mediated and constituted by the key international language, English? Is Gordon Brown's plan to make British English the global language of 'choice' (announced on the occasion of his first visit as Prime Minister to China and India in February 2008) part of the problem or part of the solution to global language policy challenges? Is choice a reality, and if so, is it a *'free'* choice, living as we do in a world in which English is the primary language of the discourse of 'free' trade, the unfree neoliberal market, and the new imperialism (Harvey 2005)? Do universities still enjoy *academic freedom* in the global higher education market,[5] with many constraints that conflict with the principles propounded in UNESCO's *Recommendation concerning the Status of Higher-Education Teaching Personnel?*[6] I work at a university in a country that projects itself as progressive and liberal, but the trade union for Danish academics sent a formal complaint to UNESCO on 22 May 2008, accusing the Danish government of failing to live up to the Recommendations, in particular by restrictions on freedom of research, on institutional autonomy, and on collegiate governance.[7] We could also ask whether academic freedom is also being constrained by the expectation that virtually all Danish academics can function equally well in English and Danish, which is unreasonable.

'Free' universities in The Netherlands and Belgium are so designated because the particular institution is free of religious ties, affiliated neither with Roman Catholicism nor Protestantism, unlike many universities. How free is an 'American' university in the Arab world or a 'Christian' university in Japan? The Margaret Thatcher Center For Freedom, based at the Heritage Foundation in Washington DC, is explicit about the way it understands freedom: its goal is to ensure that the US and UK can 'lead and change the world'?[8] The 'free' of the Freie Universität Berlin means free of communism, so named because the university was established, with US funding, in the non-Soviet Union sector of Berlin.[9] Ironically the unfree university in communist east Berlin, the Humboldt University,[10] is named after the polymath scholar of the early nineteenth century whose higher education principles underpin the modern university ideal: university teaching should be delivered by active researchers, and academic freedom and the search for knowledge and truth should not be constrained by any orthodoxy. In the People's Republic of China an 'unwritten rule for academics is that there is no taboo for research but there are regulations governing what can be published and what cannot be published' (Zhou and Ross 2004, 10), i.e. the search for truth is encouraged but not its dissemination.

The magnificent chapels of Cambridge colleges, like the names of many of them (Christ's, Trinity) signify the close bond between the Church of England and scholarship in earlier centuries, others laud the state (King's, Queens') or mammon (Churchill, Wolfson) and occasionally science (Darwin). Christianity has been integral to the spread of Euro-American values and languages worldwide, and is at the heart of the Myth of America, the sense that the USA sees itself as having a Christian God-given right to spread its values worldwide by military and economic force, a warfare society, initially national, now global (Hixson 2008). Economic gospels underpin higher education activities in our more secular times, making it unlikely that universities are committed to the needs of the masses (Gandhi), to cultural diversity (Sen, Hong Kong), or to multilingualism (the University of Helsinki). What then of the 'English-medium university' —is it purely utilitarian, a practical necessity, a productive panacea? Or is English so imbued with the values and senses of an unjust world order that it needs to be controlled vigorously by well qualified people like any other infectious disease or pandemic?[11]

English-medium studies are a going concern in two senses: they are expanding in student numbers, and they are increasingly seen and run as businesses. Higher education is financially rewarding for the economies of the USA, the UK, Australia and New Zealand. English-medium education is also a reality elsewhere:

1. of mature vintage in some *former 'colonies'* (South Africa, the Indian sub-continent, the Philippines)

2. younger in *other postcolonial contexts* (Brunei Darussalam, Hong Kong, Singapore, South Pacific)

3. well established for some *elites* (Turkey, Egypt)

4. recent in parts of the *Arab world* (Saudi Arabia, United Arab Emirates)

5. even more recent in *continental Europe.*

In many other contexts worldwide, ranging from the Chinese mainland, Korea and Japan to Latin America, the former Soviet Union and many Arab countries, English is not the primary medium of instruction. A claim that English is globally relevant does not therefore mean that English-medium education is a present-day reality worldwide, even if academics everywhere may be concerned about scholarly publication in English and the acquisition of academic competence in English.

Category 5 is borderline, because there are no monolingual English-medium universities as such, whereas degree programmes are increasingly offered in English: in 2007, 774 in the Netherlands, in Germany 415, Finland 235, Sweden 123, figures that are high but small as compared with degrees in national languages (Wächter and Maiworm 2008). Questions are being asked in Scandinavia about whether the move into English for 'internationalization' purposes is wise if it means that vets, psychologists and other professionals are being educated entirely in English rather than the local language.

I assume that in categories 1–4, many or most universities are monolingual. The designation 'English-medium' excludes other languages—maybe from the lecture room and course materials, but hardly from the heads of the students or of local teaching and administrative staff, who are bi- or multilingual. Is the 'English-medium' label in reality a coded way of indicating that the medium is a foreign or second language for the students and some staff? One would not describe a British university as English-medium, but how about higher education in Singapore, where English is the sole medium of instruction throughout education in the country, unlike earlier, when there was also a Chinese-medium university? Is there now an assumption that English is the default medium of higher education, hegemonically projected as being 'normal'? Does the label only need to be used when the use of English is abnormal?

A recent survey of languages in Singapore concludes that after 'more than 40 years of independence, English is now firmly established as (i) the premier co-official language; (ii) the universally accepted working language; (iii) the only medium of instruction (language of education) at primary, secondary and tertiary levels; (iv) the *lingua franca* for inter-community as well as intra-community relations; (v) as the international *lingua franca* for global outreach; and (vi) increasingly the language of identity for a nation that has quickly shifted to English' (Pakir 2008, 194). 'There is still ambivalence towards English, which… is still seen as in some senses "foreign". At official and unofficial levels, for example, it is not accepted that a large proportion of Singaporeans are native speakers of English: when the government discusses the use of "native speakers of English" in education, they mean people from countries such as the UK, USA and Australia' (Gupta 2008, 109). We are clearly dealing here with perceptions of different Englishes and linguistic identities, and of the 'ownership' of English, some linguistic capital having wider currency than others.[12] Should Singapore now be seen as an 'English-dominant country'[13] like the USA or Australia (Herriman and Burnaby, 1996, 1), countries with a colonizing heritage that 'involved conquest of indigenous populations and denial, suppression or neglect of languages spoken by them in favour of English' (1996, 1)? The re-linguification of Singaporeans has involved a comparable process of nation-building, entailing subtractive language learning and language shift.[14]

Even if English is the dominant language of the UK and the USA, to label them as 'English-speaking countries' denies the diversity and multilingualism of their citizens, a discourse of historical amnesia. In colonial Hong Kong, British education entailed comparable deprivation of the residents' culture and history (Tsui 2007). A First Nations scholar in Canada, Andrea Bear Nicholas (2007), describes this as historicide, which in their case was combined with linguicide.

The question of appropriation of English for national, regional, or international purposes is explored insightfully in the contributions to Lin and Martin's *Decolonisation, Globalisation: Language-in-Education Policy and Practice* (2005, reviewed in Phillipson 2007b) and in Tsui and Tollefson's *Language Policy, Culture, and Identity in Asian Contexts* (2007), with exemplification from many contexts and a systematic attempt to explore whose interests English is currently serving. Neither deals specifically with university language policy, which makes our conference timely and important. The integration of the linguistic dimension with cultural and economic globalisation is revealingly explored in Rassool's *Global Issues in Language, Education and Development* (2007). The case study of Pakistan, written jointly with Sabiha Mansoor (ibid., 218–41), shows that the use of English as the sole medium of higher education (for only 2.63 per cent of the population) ensures the cultural alienation of the elite from the rest of the population. 'The global cultural economy is interdependent and, despite the dominant position occupied by English, in practice, it has an organically interactive multilingual base. A narrow monolingual nationalism (a reference to Urdu, RP), an under-resourced educational system as well as unequal access to English as international lingua franca, therefore, is counter-productive to national growth.' (ibid., 240). This confirms Tariq Rahman's analyses (1998).

The prevailing use of English in high-prestige domains such as scholarship has major implications, for democracy, a well-informed public sphere and population, and social cohesion, if local, more accessible languages are not *also* used. It is important not to think of democracy in purely Western terms, as though patented in ancient Greece, and invariably the norm in Western countries, which is simply untrue. Contact between China, India and Arabia flourished for two millennia, with translations between Chinese, Arabic and Sanskrit in many scholarly fields. The pre-eminence of Western science, in our unstable, inequitable, militarized world, is recent, and legitimated as though 'knowledge societies' are a late capitalist invention:

> science, mathematics, literature, linguistics, architecture, medicine and music. ... In so far as public reasoning is central to democracy ..., parts of the global roots of democracy can indeed be traced back to the tradition of public discussion that received much encouragement in both India and China (and also in Japan, Korea and elsewhere), from the dialogic commitment to Buddhist organization... The first printed book in the world with a date (corresponding to 868 AD), which was the Chinese translation of a Sanskrit treatise, the so-called 'Diamond Sutra' (Kumārajīva had translated it in 402 AD), carried the remarkable motivational explanation: 'for universal free distribution'. (Sen 2005 164, 182–3).

Dispensing monolingual education can be considered as in conflict with linguistic human rights principles. UNESCO's European Centre for Higher Education is on record, at a conference on the bilingual university, as stating that access to higher education in one's own language is, or can be considered, a basic human right.[15] This is a complicated area of international human rights law, sociolinguistics and language policy that would requires special investigation (see Skutnabb-Kangas 2000, Magga et al. 2007, Dunbar and Skutnabb-Kangas 2008).

We can provisionally conclude that universities must be able to operate with full academic freedom and university autonomy (UNESCO), which includes historical grounding (Sen), university language policies should address the issue of how to actively promote multilingualism

(Finland) and cultural diversity (UNESCO), and to address the tension between English-medium education as a strategic asset (Hong Kong) and what is inherently problematical about it for diverse societies (Kandiah). We need to reverse the historicide of colonial education (Tsui), in which the medium English played a decisive role.

Global capital, global English, local trauma

Well-funded US universities benefit by the fact that capitalism has reached its most extreme form in the US.[16] Along with a few universities elsewhere they are able to cream off top scholars from the entire world and give them exceptionally good working conditions. Their global impact is through the local language, English, which has consolidated more linguistic capital than any other language over the past two centuries. Capitalism was entrenched in the industrial revolution, colonial empires and global Europeanisation

> The system has set up that single unconscionable freedom—Free Trade. In a word, for exploitation, veiled by religious and political illusions, it has substituted naked, shameless, direct, brutal exploitation.
> … The need of a constantly expanding market for its products chases the bourgeoisie over the whole face of the globe. It must nestle everywhere, settle everywhere, establish connections everywhere. …
> In place of the old local and national seclusion and self-sufficiency, we have intercourse in every direction, a universal interdependence of nations. And as in material, so also in intellectual production. The intellectual creations of individual nations become common property.
> … It compels all nations, on pain of extinction, to adopt the bourgeois mode of production; it compels them to introduce what it calls civilization into their midst, i.e. to become bourgeois themselves. In one word, it creates a world after its own image. (reprinted in Mendel 1961, 15, 16, 17).

This was presciently described in *The Communist Manifesto* by Marx and Engels in 1848. It is thus historically incorrect to see globalization as a recent phenomenon, even if some of its late twentieth century forms were novel and its impact has been much greater. The bourgeoisie is no longer a privileged class in Europe and the USA but is more broadly and internationally based, the Haves with property, and an interest in the stock market. Financial globalization has changed the rules of the game over the past thirty years, with the sinister consequences of casino capitalism now visible. Cultural and linguistic globalization are aspects of what Marx already diagnosed as 'intercourse in every direction, a universal interdependence of nations'. Central to the global market is 'intellectual production', though current global educational trends have more to do with producing consumers rather than critical citizens. Corporate influence on universities goes back to the USA in the nineteeth century. Eighty years ago Bertrand Russell (1960, 166-68) expressed concern about the academic being limited by utilitarian constraints and an excessive influence on universities by business.

When contributing to an international conference entitled *Language Issues in English-Medium Universities: a Global Concern*, I experience the need to express my 'concern' about universities as 'concerns' in the contemporary capitalist world. The polysemy of the lexical item *concern* is explored in an appendix, so as to demonstrate that English is an intrinsically difficult language to learn and use unambiguously. The advocacy of English is analyzed in relation to the power of the language (the innate, resource and structural power of English, intrinsic, extrinsic and functional arguments) in chapter 9 of Phillipson 1992. The primary focus of the analysis in the present article is not on the linguistic forms of English that make for its intrinsic complexity but on the political, economic and ideological dimensions of English, and the functions that users of English perform. The appendix exemplifies the point that English is no panacea—but obviously the language cannot be ignored.

We need to clarify what the English in English-medium refers to, and how far it is global. Halliday (2006) makes a useful distinction between indigenized and standardized Englishes, which he categorizes as *international* and *global*:

> English has become a world language in both senses of the term, international and global: international, as a medium of literary and other forms of cultural life in (mainly) countries of the former British Empire; global, as the co-genitor of the new technological age, the age of information. … It is important, I think, to distinguish these two aspects, the international and the global, even though they obviously overlap. English has been expanding along both trajectories: globally, as English; internationally, as Englishes.

Both of these expansions involve what I have called semogenic strategies: ways of creating new meanings that are open-ended, like the various forms of metaphor, lexical and grammatical. But they differ. International English has expanded by becoming world Englishes, evolving so as to adapt to the meanings of other cultures. Global English has expanded—has become 'global'—by taking over, or being taken over by, the new information technology, which means everything from email and the internet to mass media advertising, news reporting, and all the other forms of political and commercial propaganda.

His 'international' is an unfortunate label, since he is in effect referring to *local* forms and uses of English, comprehensible within a country, for instance. His terms also elide the anchoring of *global* English in the English-dominant countries, where it is the primary *national* language, one that also opens international doors. Terminology in this area is a minefield which obscures power relations and hegemonic practices, nationally and internationally. For instance, the University of London optimistically advertises itself as 'the world's first global university' on the strength of administering examinations outside Britain for 150 years.[17]

Universities develop academic skills in the global, standard form, so far as *written* English is concerned, in order to generate graduates with international competence. This competence also represents linguistic capital nationally. In *spoken* academic English too, learning must be based on the lexis, grammar and much of the pragmatics of the global form, except for allowing considerable leeway so far as pronunciation or accent is concerned. This is precisely what David Li (2007) recommends for Hong Kong. I agree with Anna Wierzbicka that too many 'Publications on "global English", "international English", "world English", "standard English" and "English as a lingua franca" … neglect the Anglo cultural heritage … the semantics embedded in the words and grammar. … In the present-day world it is Anglo English that remains the touchstone and guarantor of English-based global communication' (2006, 13, 14).[18] Conformity to Anglo English norms also creates pressure to conform to the paradigms of academic activity in the Anglo world, which has serious consequences for alternative approaches embedded in academic cultures elsewhere.

A focus on global English forms and functions does not obviate the need for culturally appropriate pedagogy.

British analysts tend to endorse the increasing shift into English uncritically, even if they also celebrate its diversity and applaud multilingualism. I am not convinced by David Graddol's argument (1997, 2006) that the large number of second- and foreign-language users of English has reduced the influence of US–UK norms and speakers. Likewise when David Crystal surveys education worldwide (2004, 37), he states that 'English has become the normal medium of instruction in higher education for many countries —including several where the language has no official status. Advanced courses in The Netherlands, for example, are widely taught in English. No African country uses its indigenous language in higher education, English being used in the majority of cases. The English language teaching business has become one of the major growth industries around the world in the past 30 years.' In fact it is only the final sentence of this triumphalist discourse that is correct.[19] There is nothing 'normal' about the way English has become established—it is a survival strategy dictated by economic and political pressures, which dovetail with linguistic imperialism. There are causal factors and particular interests behind the expansion of English in the neoimperial world. The Africa generalization is patently false, granted the widespread use of Arabic, and some functions for Swahili and South African languages. The deplorable neglect of African languages is a direct result of colonization, neo-colonial 'aid' policies, and World Bank schemes imposed on African countries, with the complicity of corrupt leaders, English serving to isolate elites from the mass of population.

The South African experience is portrayed in an excellent survey of factors contributing to the dominance of English and the marginalization of other languages, as well as of criteria for promoting multilingual universities that would serve the community and students better (Webb 2007). Interview data reveal how the imposition of an English-only university zone in South Africa is experienced by multilinguals, and the clash of their identity with insensitive hegemonic teaching practices grounded in inappropriate native-speaker norms (Katunich 2006). The university's pedagogy clearly fails to promote the multilingualism that the state is officially committed to. It just so happens that the university's policies conform to World Bank loan policies that strengthen European languages and fail to allocate funding to African languages in education (Mazrui 1997). In this way, postcolonial education is functional for those that globalization benefits.

One of the instruments for implementing change is evaluation. A comparison of such procedures in higher education in two countries, the UK and Finland (Vartiainen 2004, reviewed in Phillipson 2007a), which stresses the significance of the legitimacy of such exercises for academics, diagnoses that British procedures are punitive (ranking that hierarchises and rewards accordingly), whereas Finnish ones actually encourage bottom-up quality control, evaluation serving to strengthen an institution's mission, management and follow-up. A key conclusion from the study is that university autonomy is a virtue that is in effect the norm in Finland (a country with an exceptionally successful economy and school system), whereas in England it is the privilege of elite universities.[20] The 'international quality' that all universities are supposed to strive for is not a gold standard but one that can be reached by many routes, and that coercive policies counteract.

Thiru Kandiah of Sri Lanka sees countries in the postcolonial world as trapped in a major contradiction—one which raises ethical issues for English-dominant countries. On the one hand, postcolonial countries need the 'indispensable global medium' for pragmatic purposes, even for survival in the global economy: a *panacea* for the privileged. On the other there is the fact that the medium is not culturally or ideologically neutral, far from it, so that its users run the 'apparently unavoidable risk of co-option, of acquiescing in the negation of their own understandings of reality and in the accompanying denial or even subversion of their own interests' (Kandiah 2001, 112): *pandemic*. What is therefore needed in relation to English is 'interrogating its formulations of reality, intervening in its modes of understanding, holding off its normalising tendencies, challenging its hegemonic designs and divesting it of the co-optive power which would render it a reproducing discourse' (ibid.). Kandiah advocates authentic local projections of reality, and emancipatory action.

Angel Lin (2005) makes the methodological point that a 'periphery' scholar should not merely take over 'centre' epistemologies, and argues that our research approaches risk being self-referential—purely 'academic'—and lack self-reflection. Lin echoes the denunciation of unreflective positivism and academic exhibitionism a century ago by one of the key founders of social science research, Max Weber (see Kim 2007, 130-31). Lin eloquently shows how critical discourse analysis unmasks the legitimation of an inequitable social structure. Proficiency in English remains an elusive goal for the many, but the education system is functional for the local elite, for China, and for global commerce. Here as in Pakistan and South Africa, the gap between scholarship and societal change remains wide. She endorses a challenge from Allan Luke: 'TESOL must do something other than what it currently does. Otherwise, it will remain a technology for domesticating the "other", whatever its scientific and humanitarian pretences' (ibid., 52, see also Edge 2006). Consulting the website of a successful and possibly representative British university with campuses in Malaysia and China gives the clear impression that what is being exported is not only the British English medium but also British content.[21]

An empirical study of 'Conceptions of a good tertiary EFL teacher in China' (Zhang and Watkins 2007) invited students and teaching staff, local and foreign, to state what they saw as important traits of the good teacher. A considerable number of features of personality, professional knowledge and communicative skills are identified, but there is surprisingly little focus on an expectation that foreign teachers should display familiarity with Chinese language and culture.[22]

The pedagogical challenges are considerable, and differ at each level of the education system. The need to critically evaluate how English is used and learned, and to decolonize our minds, is a task for people from both the centre and the periphery. For instance, the slippery term 'English as a lingua franca' is open to abuse, since its everyday use is so multifarious, and research into it tends to decontextualize users. It seems to imply symmetrical, equitable communication, which is often not the case, and fails to make a clear distinction between receptive and productive competence. It conceals the actual functions that the language performs, English as a *lingua academica, lingua bellica, lingua cultura, lingua economica*, etc. (Phillipson 2008b).

As researchers we need to ensure that the ethical principles and value judgements that underpin our activities are made clear, as a necessary foundation for valid, objective and enlightened analysis. Each of us should aim at being an 'interpretative specialist', whose 'virtues consist of passionate conviction, uncompromising intellectual integrity, and, most important of all, a Socratic knowledge of one's own self'—to cite the scholarly principles espoused by Max Weber (see Kim 2007, 130-31).

I would like to think that in our role as academics we can live up to Edward Said's goal of 'opposing and alleviating coercive domination, transforming the present by trying rationally and analytically to lift some of its burdens …secular intellectuals with the archival, expressive, elaborative, and moral responsibilities of that role' (Said 1993, 386). Said was dismayed by experiencing at a national university in one of the Persian Gulf states in the 1980s that the English Department taught orthodox British literature and practical language skills in an 'anachronistic and odd confluence of rote learning, uncritical teaching, and (to put it kindly) haphazard results' (ibid., 369). Students were learning the worldwide *lingua franca*, which 'terminally consigned English to the level of a technical language stripped of its expressive and aesthetic characteristics and denuded of any critical or self-conscious dimension' (ibid.). I fear that this sort of English teaching may still be with us, and that proficiency testing (TOEFL, Cambridge), which is big business,[23] does much to keep it that way.

If English learning is combined with a neglect of local languages, with these not being regarded as of equivalent significance, the likely result is cultural rootlessness, blind acceptance of the dominant world disorder, and an uncritical endorsement of more English, irrespective of the consequences for other languages. '*Global English*' does not refer to the totality of the globe's population. In popular and neoimperialist discourse, global English is a trope, a project, a representation that creates the impression that the language is universally relevant and that the whole of humanity should become proficient in the language. If *English-medium universities* are part of this 'global' project, they are unlikely to generate critical students with intercultural, multilingual competence. They are more likely merely to oil the wheels of the current inequitable economic system, contributing to social injustice and pandemic. I would claim that exclusively English-medium instruction, for instance a monolingual BA degree, in a former colony or in continental Europe, risks inculcating monolingual myopia and complicity in linguistic neoimperialism (Phillipson, 2006b, 2008a).[24]

The current expansion of English in higher education in Europe

European countries that consolidated 'national' languages as languages of instruction at all levels of education are currently under pressure to accord more space to English. There are a great many factors, structural and ideological, push and pull factors, influencing ongoing processes of Europeanization and Englishization (Phillipson 2003, chapter 3). The trend has created a good deal of alarm, even in countries where one would think that the main national language is impregnable. What does the expansion of English signify for the future of other languages of scholarship? How should the educational system create proficient users of English, and how can this goal be achieved in harmonious balance with proficiency in other languages?

An early pilot study (Phillipson and Skutnabb-Kangas 1999, first published in 1996) of how the pressure to increasingly function in English at a Danish university was experienced by academics identified three main types of scholars, English-only, Danish-mostly, and Multilingual. The characteristics of the three groups relate to such variables as their subject area, national and international networks, languages of publication, choice of paradigm, and sensitivity to language policy issues (the English-only academics were the least reflective!). The study noted a diversity of positions and a range of views, and concluded that 'multilingualism is entrenched in Danish higher education but that the general, although by no means sole, trend is towards a strengthening of English.'[25]

The gradual move into English-medium teaching in European higher education is surveyed by Coleman (2006), who assesses to what extent English is progressively becoming 'the language of higher education in

Europe'. He correctly notes the paucity of research studies. As 'drivers of Englishization' he identifies Content and Language Integrated Learning (CLIL—in experimental practice at the secondary level in several countries), internationalization, student exchanges, teaching and research materials, staff mobility, graduate employability, and the market in international students. Coleman fails, however, to point out that the European Union (EU), which largely follows the agenda of the corporate world, has been actively promoting all of these symptoms of Englishization in its policies to strengthen European integration. I dispute his claim that there is a consensus about the likelihood of global diglossia with English as the exclusive language of science, and that 'it seems inevitable that English, in some form, will definitely become *the* language of higher education' (ibid., 11, italics added).

Coleman also notes than when English is a medium of instruction in some MA programmes, particularly in northern Europe, there are serious problems in ensuring the quality of the English of students and lecturing staff. Many northern Europeans are able to function supremely well in English as a second language. They have learned the language in school as a foreign language. It is almost never the medium of instruction in state education in, say, Denmark, Finland or Germany. Many Europeans are exposed to the language in personal and professional life. School has to equip undergraduates in the Nordic countries to be able to read texts in English. The learning task is smaller for those whose mother tongue is a related Germanic language, as compared with speakers of a Romance or Finno-Ugric language, let alone an Asian one.

The internationalization of European higher education has gone under the label 'the Bologna Process' since 1999. The objective is 'within the framework of our institutional competences and taking full respect of the diversity of cultures, languages, national education systems and of University autonomy—to consolidate a European Higher Education Area at the latest by 2010'.

Forty-six European states are committed to it. The EU Commission largely sets the agenda, funds activities, and produces policy and planning documents. These are the foundation for the bi-annual Ministerial Meetings, which representatives of universities also attend.

At the most recent ones (Bergen in 2005, London in 2007), the main focus has been on structural uniformity (a single B.A., M.A. and Ph.D. system), on quality control (nationally and internationally), student mobility, recognition of qualifications, and joint degrees—all of which are demanding tasks for most countries—and making European universities attractive enough to compete with the USA and Australia. These countries are Bologna 'observers', out of self-interest, since foreign students in higher education are big business for them, and Europe is potentially a serious competitor.

What is striking is that not once in the lengthy communiqués from the ministerial meetings is there any reference to languages (even if the EU has twenty-three official languages). There is nothing on bilingual degrees or multilingualism. The language of virtually all documents and deliberations is English. This can perhaps be justified for practical reasons at a conference—though this does not guarantee equality in communication. However what emerges unambiguously is that in the Bologna process, 'internationalisation' means 'English-medium higher education' (Phillipson 2006a).

This European process is a direct result of education being increasingly considered a service that can be traded, under the aegis of the WTO, the World Trade Organisation, and more specifically of GATS, the General Agreement on Trade in Services. Member states have been legally committed to this 'liberalisation' process since 1995, but there is a fundamental unresolved tension between education as a human right and trading in educational services.[26] The pressures to reduce what are seen as national trading barriers are intense. Higher education is more vulnerable to international commercialization than is basic education, though this is also increasingly seen as a market rather than a public service.[27]

Prior to the bi-annual Ministerial Meeting taking stock of the Bologna Process in London, 17-18 May 2007, EU Commissioner Figel stated (press release IP/07/656):

> Bologna reforms are important but Europe should now go beyond them, as universities should also modernize the content of their curricula, create virtual campuses and reform their governance. They should also professionalize their management, diversify their funding

and open up to new types of learners, businesses and society at large, in
Europe and beyond. ... The Commission supports the global strategy
in concrete terms through its policies and programmes.

In other words, universities should no longer be seen as a public good
but should be run like businesses, should privatize, and let industry set
the agenda. The new buzzwords are that degrees must be 'certified' in
terms of the 'employability' of graduates. 'Accountability' no longer
refers to intellectual quality or truth-seeking but means acceptability to
corporate-driven neoliberalism. A recommendation that there should
be more 'student-centred learning' probably implies more e-learning
rather than a more dialogic, open-ended syllabus. Before *European*
integration has taken on any viable forms, universities are being told
to think and act *globally* rather than remain narrowly European—and
by implication use English rather than a national language. These ideas
are insulting to higher education in general and to all universities that
have been internationally oriented for decades, if not centuries.

I shall briefly cite a number of symptoms of English as pandemic.
There has been talk for several years in *Scandinavia* about the risk
of *domain loss*, when referring to an increased use of English in
research publication, or as the medium of instruction for higher
education, business, the media, etc. Invariably the assumption is that
any expansion in the use of English is at the expense of Danish,
Norwegian, or Swedish, which is by no means necessarily the case.
Such argumentation reflects a monolingual worldview, and is far
from the reality of much higher education teaching, especially in the
natural sciences. This is often bilingual, with textbooks written in
English, and a Scandinavian language as the language of the classroom
and examinations. The fact that natural scientists choose to publish
scholarly articles in English does not necessarily mean that they
are incapable of writing textbooks or popularizing articles on the
same topic in their mother tongue. How far domain loss is a reality
in Scandinavia has yet to be researched adequately, and preliminary
surveys are of limited theoretical and empirical validity. Existing
efforts are hampered by loose terminology, in that 'domain' may
refer to a vast range of activities or a narrow spectrum, and 'loss' is
inappropriate in that it obscures the agency of both the losers and
the gainers. In reality, domains are not 'lost': if and when it occurs,

it is when specific spoken or written activities are subjected to linguistic capital accumulation by dispossession due to forces behind an increased use of English, the result being the marginalization of other languages (Phillipson 2006a, 2008a).

Anecdotal evidence from Denmark suggests that less learning takes place when English is used, but there is a total absence of empirical studies. A small Swedish qualitative study of physics lecturing in Swedish and English indicates that pedagogical style and the quality of lecturing and of supporting activities are more significant than the medium of instruction (Airey and Linder 2006). While students do not see choice of language as important, their behaviour shows otherwise, and they are unaware of the differences.

In *France* a petition was signed by over 10,000 academics in the spring of 2008,[28] aimed at persuading French authorities, l'Agence d'Evaluation de la Recherche et de l'Enseignement Supérieur (Agency for the Evaluation of Research and Higher Education) that while publishing in English is a necessity, continuing to publish in French is essential for three reasons:

1. as higher education is funded through French national taxes, tax-payers have the right to access to research in French;

2. teaching through the medium of French requires that the writing of scholarly syntheses and textbooks in French should be seen as meritorious and necessary: 'how can one love a discipline by offering books only in English that are generally not at the right level or adapted to local teaching practices?'

3. learning to express oneself in a language other than one's mother tongue with equivalent semantic subtlety and complexity is very demanding; there is no better way of dialoguing with an authority than in one's own language.

The petition expresses concern that bibliometric research productivity exercises that give pride of place to publications in English disqualify research production in French (journals, books and textbooks). Petitioners insist that the assessment of qualifications for university appointments should not discriminate against publications in French.

German was the most influential language in the natural sciences and philosophy in Europe until the 1930s. German is the most important export language for Denmark, but its appeal to younger Danes has diminished as a result of the massive influence of English and Americanization in the media and youth culture, and the privileged place accorded to English in political discourse and in education at all levels. A colleague of mine, an eminent Professor of German in Denmark, reports that applicants for a higher education post recently were instructed to submit publications only if they were written in English or a Nordic language.[29] This is an example of the marginalization of publications in other 'international' languages, traditionally French and German, that scholars until twenty years ago were expected to be competent in. My colleague also speculated on the possibility that if Danish decision-makers were more familiar with the political scene in Germany and France, and followed how international relations issues are covered in the media there, Denmark might not have gone to war in Iraq as an uncritical ally of Bush II.

Spanish is another language, like German, French and Russian, in which a vast amount of scholarly activity takes place, in speech and writing. But philosophers from the Spanish-using world are experiencing that the large publishing conglomerates that dominate the scientific journal world (Taylor & Francis, Springer, Wiley-Blackwell, Elsevier) which publish benchmark encyclopedias, in English of course, have been known to refuse any references to Spanish-medium publications (Mendieta, Phillipson and Skutnabb-Kangas 2006).

A glance at the papers in a representative set of reference books, the nine volumes of the second edition of the *Encyclopedia of Language and Education*, edited by Nancy Hornberger and colleagues (2008) shows that however multilingual many of the individual contributors may be, reference is seldom made to languages other than English. 'Language' has been largely conflated with 'English'.

The Danish and Swedish governments have been promoting 'internationalisation' for decades, and have simultaneously been concerned to ensure the future of the national language while building up competence in English.[30] In both countries, committees have been appointed to look into the language policy issues. The Danes have conducted modest investigations, mainly concentrating on Danish, and largely undertaken by philologists with little familiarity with sociolinguistics or the international language planning and policy literature.[31] Danish vice-chancellors have advised strongly against any legislation that might restrict the right of universities to determine when each language should be used.[32] The Swedes have been more thorough: a succession of parliamentary investigations culminated in a 2008 White Paper of 265 pages that articulates a case for legislating on the status of Swedish, and for consolidating the linguistic human rights of two sets of minority language users—speakers of five legally recognized minority languages, and users of Swedish Sign language —as well as providing for the maintenance of the languages and cultures of immigrants.[33] The clauses of the proposed Swedish legislation relate to the following points:

- declaring Swedish the *principal* ('huvud' = main, chief) language of the country, a formulation that deliberately avoids the terms *official* and *national,* Swedish being the language that unites all residents of the country, irrespective of mother tongue;

- creating obligations for the society, including its agents in all sectors, its legislators and administrators, to see that language rights are realized;

- in higher education and in dealings with EU institutions, ensuring that Swedish should be used whenever possible;

- institutions having a duty to work out how best the pre-eminence of Swedish can be maintained (e.g. ensuring terminology development).

The Swedish White Paper refers to the risk of *capacity loss* when Swedes are obliged to function in English rather than their mother tongue, whether in higher education or in the EU system (ibid., 220). In other words people's linguistic or communicative competence may be reduced, and if this is allowed to take place, this erodes the main instrument of a well-functioning democracy, in speech and in writing. Effectively what is happening here is capacity dispossession of the individual, in the worst case in both languages. One means of combating this is to oblige budding academics who write a Ph.D. thesis in an 'international' language to produce a detailed summary in the national language. This is generally required in the Nordic countries. Another example: two of my younger colleagues, whose Ph.D. theses are in English, are writing a book on language testing—in Danish. There are plenty of examples in Europe of academics with eminent competence in at least two languages, one of which now tends to be English. English need not be either panacea or pandemic.

Towards the multilingual university?

Continued faith in monolingualism reflects a belief in what I formulated in *Linguistic Imperialism* (1992, chapter 7) as five tenets that were influential in postcolonial education policy:

- English is best taught monolingually,
- The ideal teacher of English is a native speaker,
- The earlier English is taught, the better the results,
- The more English is taught, the better the results,
- If other languages are used much, standards of English will drop.

The book documents in considerable detail that each is in fact a fallacy:

- the monolingual fallacy
- the native speaker fallacy
- the early start fallacy
- the maximum exposure fallacy
- the subtractive fallacy.

It is relevant to consider how far any of these fallacies are adhered to at university level, and with what consequences. Adherence to the five tenets contributes to former colonies remaining in a state of dependency on norms of the centre, assists the British economy, and supports the myth that English is a panacea. There is therefore a need for explicit multilingualism policies, as recommended for all Nordic universities. Boosting the learning of a variety of languages should be part of a strategy for ensuring that national languages are not submerged under English and for openness to a variety of cultures and markets. Ensuring balanced cohabitation with additive (as opposed to subtractive) English is a real challenge for higher education worldwide. Policies for strengthening competence in English must be one dimension of maintaining cultural and linguistic diversity, locally and globally, and resisting an unsustainable capitalist world 'order'.

If universities aim that their staff and students should be 'equally competent' in two or more languages, there need to be policies for attaining and maintaining 'parallel competence'. Whether this will be achieved widely in Nordic universities is an open question, and unpredictable. One dimension of explicit language policies must be raising awareness about functioning multilingually. There should be an incentive structure to reward those who are able to teach and publish in more than one language. The present tendency is to associate higher prestige and rewards for articles in 'international' in the sense of English-medium journals, this affecting careers, promotion prospects, and financial outcomes.

An issue that ought to be of considerable concern to any 'English-medium' university is that if competence in English is becoming more widespread, in similar ways to basic literacy and computer skills, it is likely that fluency in English alone will no longer represent a competitive advantage in the job market. It is a basic principle in economics that the market value drops for anything that is widely available.

The University of Hong Kong's mission statement and strategic development plan are laudable and visionary. Unlike Helsinki University, there is no commitment on language policy, despite the centrality of languages for all faculties—architecture, education, medicine, psychology, public administration, all. When the university offers 'courses and degree programmes in the English language', how can one ensure that this will 'enhance the graduates' contributions to society' if most citizens function in Cantonese? Precisely the same concern applies worldwide, where the risk is that elites will have an advanced command of English, and become increasingly detached from their ordinary citizens operating in Arabic/Bengali/Catalan/ Dutch/…

The challenges of linguistic pandemic control are comparable worldwide. English has for centuries had some pandemic traits and consequences on several continents. It is no panacea in the modern world. If vibrant local cultures and languages are to continue, language policy efforts need to be concentrated on diverse local language ecologies and maintaining a healthy balance between English and other languages. Universities must contribute to this. Some national and international laws and practices serve to protect threatened minority languages (Skutnabb-Kangas 2000, chapter 7) but there are no international law mechanisms for controlling dominant international languages. What happens in each country and each institution is therefore of decisive importance. In view of the major challenges that universities face, the efforts of academia are needed more than ever before, and can lead to English not being experienced as either pandemic or panacea.

Notes

[1]   The article was produced in preparation for a keynote lecture at the International Conference, *Language issues in English-medium universities: a global concern*, held at the University of Hong Kong, 18–20 June 2008. Conference papers are accessible on http://www.hku.hk/clear/conference08/index.html.

[2]   http//www.helsinki.fi/inbrief/strategy/HYn_kieliperiaatteet.pdf

[3]   http://www.hku.hk/strategic_booklet/english/fs-academic.htm.

[4]   When the first European university emerged in Bologna in the eleventh and twelves centuries, *universitates* initially referred to associations of students, and only later of professors, rather than to the institutions. Latin terms like *rector, facultates*, and *collegium doctorum* also evolved as seats of learning became established throughout western Europe. I am grateful to Hartmut Haberland for this clarification, which dictionary etymologies generally ignore.

[5]   A petition in Denmark by academics (signed by over 1600 within three months in early 2008) calls for reform of a 2003 law governing higher education. Specific complaints are that university administration is now top-down management without proper consultation procedures, with the Ministry of Higher Education dictating what should be taught and learned, and which research areas should be given priority. Societal accountability has been replaced by dependence on the

business world; research policy has been replaced by industrial policy, which is incompatible with the role of the university as a public good in a democracy, and with academic freedom for the individual researcher.

6   Academic freedom both for the institution and for the individual are enshrined in a 1997 declaration of UNESCO, declarations of the Council of Europe, and in the Charter of Fundamental Rights of the European Union. This states (Article II-73) that 'The arts and scientific research shall be free of constraint. Academic freedom shall be respected', which it sees as 'extensions of the freedoms of thought and expression'. The UNESCO declaration is very detailed (13 pages):

> Autonomy is the institutional form of academic freedom and a necessary precondition to guarantee the proper fulfilment of the functions entrusted to higher-education teaching personnel and institutions.

> Higher-education teaching personnel are entitled to the maintenance of academic freedom, that is to say, the right, without constriction by prescribed doctrine, to freedom of teaching and discussion, freedom in carrying out research and disseminating and publishing the results hereof, freedom to express freely their opinion about the institution or system in which they work, freedom from institutional censorship and freedom to participate in professional or representative academic bodies.

The Royal Danish Academy of Sciences and Letters published a report (in Danish) for its 2007 annual general meeting entitled 'Freedom of research and expression at universities'. The report concludes that there is a general tendency for these freedoms to be constrained in western Europe, that the rights are protected better in legislation in certain countries than in Denmark. There is an increasing degree of control of teaching and research by the state and business interests (e.g. the Senates of Danish universities have a majority of non-academics), with less freedom of choice for the academic. The general climate in which universities are run and experienced is unfree. The report exemplifies through fictitious cases that build on actual experience that traditional values are being undermined through a variety of insidious and crude pressures.

7   The complaint is accessible on http://www.dm.dk/.

8   The website (http://www.thatchercenter.org/) states that it was established in 2005, following a substantial donation from the Margaret Thatcher Foundation to the Heritage Foundation. It claims to be the only public policy centre in the world dedicated to advancing the vision and ideals of Lady Thatcher. Its key aims are to focus on how the United States and Great Britain can lead and change the world, to strengthen the relationship between the United States and Great Britain, and link conservatives in the US, UK and Europe who are committed to the transatlantic alliance and the cause of freedom across the world.

9   The university was founded in 1948. Its website states that in the first decade the primary academic focus was on political science, sociology, Eastern European Studies and American Studies, a clear statement of its prioirities. The website has photos of the Henry Ford building (I recently also saw one at Koc University, Istanbul), and of John F. Kennedy, see http://www.hu-berlin.de/ueberblick-en/history/huben_html.

10 The university was founded in Berlin in 1810, inspired by Wilhelm von Humboldt's concept of a 'Universitas litterarum' which would achieve a unity of teaching and research and provide students with an all-round humanist education. This concept spread throughout the world and gave rise to the foundation of many universities of the same type over the following 150 years. See http://www.hu-berlin. de/ueberblick-en/history/huben_html.

11 I wrote an article with Tove Skutnabb-Kangas in 1994 entitled 'English, panacea or pandemic' (*Sociolinguistica* 8. English only? in Europa/in Europe/en Europe, 73–87). It expressed scepticism at the hubris of the way English was being marketed as a panacea in the post-communist world, along with the free market and human rights. English was conflated with democracy and all things good, backed up by fraudulent claims for what the language would achieve.

12 The 'ownership' of English in Singapore is explored in a study that challenges the conventional way in which the country is characterised (an 'Outer circle' country), granted that English has become the primary language of the younger generation and increasingly the language of both formal and informal situations (Rubdy et al 2008).

The study elicits reactions to samples of language so as to verify the ability of informants to 'make confident judgements and their willingness to rely on their intuitions', proof of which is interpreted as indicating ownership of English. The study provides useful evidence of the limitations of our terminology (static concepts like the three circles and native speaker), and critiques the way politicians disparage local linguistic forms.

13 The applied linguistic classification of Singaporeans hitherto has been as English-knowing bilinguals.

14 There are several articles on the sociolinguistics of Singapore in Tan and Rubdy in press.

15 The 'Centre Europeén pour l'enseignement supérieur' (CEPES) conference in 2000 on the bilingual university, its origins, mission and functioning, drew on the experience of universities in Finland, Canada, Switzerland and elsewhere (it noted that bilingual universities are becoming more widespread world-wide), identified the following principles: any bilingual university needs to take serious account of the influence of the specific political and social environment in which the university operates; the mission of bilingual universities should be community bridge-building, promoting a wider outlook, promoting bilingualism as an objective for all students, such policies permeating all university organisational matters.

16 US national identity was forged through massive violence, the dispossession and extermination of the indigenous peoples, the myth of unoccupied territory, the surplus value extorted from slave labour, and an active process of national imagination to form a common identity, one deeply permeated by religion (Hixson 2008). The nationalist revolt of 1776 and the ensuing state formation and constitution privileged white male slave-owning Euro-Americans. These founding fathers devised a constitution in which ' "We, the people" elided hierarchies of race, class, and gender' (ibid., 39), the Other being stigmatized as sub-human and therefore exterminable. The architects of the American Revolution were highly literate, 75% were English-speaking, seeing themselves as involved in 'a sacred event ordained by God for the redemption of all of mankind. Even Benjamin Franklin, the leading scientific rationalist, declared, "Our cause is the cause of all mankind, and we are fighting for their

liberty in defending our own. It is a glorious task assigned us by Providence" ' (ibid., 37). This Myth of America has been echoed continuously over three centuries, currently in the rhetoric of Bush II, and we are all affected by it, wherever we live: the Myth is being implemented universally. There is considerable debate within the TESOL organization about the ethics of evangelization when it is integrated, often covertly into English teaching.

[17] In *The Guardian Weekly*, 30 May 2008, <www.londonexternal.ac.uk>. This is as bombastic and pretentious as the title of a related book, *Examining the world. A History of the University of Cambridge Local Examinations Syndicate* (Raban 2008).

[18] See the appendix for an example.

[19] Neil Kinnock, Chair of the British Council, reports (in a Foreword to Graddol 2006): 'The English language teaching sector directly earns nearly £1.3 billion for the UK in invisible exports and our other education related exports earn up to £10 billion a year more.'

[20] On the commodification of education, and the marketisation discourses, see Holborrow 2006, reflecting experience in Ireland.

[21] Sensitivity to local cultural and linguistic factors seems to be totally absent from the content of the School of Education of the University of Nottingham's Malaysia campus (http://www.nottingham.edu. my/Faculties/Social/Education/Pages/default.aspx), including the M.A. degrees in TESOL and in Teaching Content Through a Foreign Language. Courses are 'elaborated in the UK and taught by UK staff'. The University of Nottingham at Ningbo, China states in its mission statement that its goal is 'Academic Excellence in the Service of Global Citizenship', and this means that the University of Nottingham Ningbo, China has committed itself to developing subjects that combine internationally ranked teaching and research excellence at the University of Nottingham UK with Chinese needs for internationalization and globalization. This allows Chinese students to enjoy a world-class international education without the major expense of studying abroad. All undergraduate and postgraduate programmes in Ningbo are conducted entirely in English with the same teaching and evaluation standards as at Nottingham UK.' This means that there is UK content in the three MA programmes in English Studies.

The Centre for Research in Applied Linguistics is an outpost of the Nottingham, UK centre.

22 Mainstream 'development aid' to education has an appalling track record, which ought to make one sceptical about whether the British English Language Teaching (ELT) sector can solve educational learning problems in India or anywhere else. Most British people are notoriously monolingual; ELT qualifications in the major 'English-speaking countries' typically do not require evidence of successful foreign language learning or experience of multilingualism. Educational language projects in Asia in the 1990s are surveyed in an admirable collection of papers *Language and Development. Teachers in a Changing World* (Kenny and Savage 1997). It contains a fund of reflective analysis of the factors contributing to the triumphs and, more frequently, the failures of development aid projects. But it is striking that the title of the book itself seems to assume that English is a panacea. 'Language' refers exclusively to English. All 'teachers' in our changing world are apparently teachers of English. This invisibilization of the rest of the relevant languages is a re-run of much colonial and postcolonial language-in-education policy, which, as is well known, has served European languages well and other languages much less well. It reflects investment being put into English, an infrastructure and ideology that discursively construct English as the handmaiden of globalization, the universal medium. Such is linguistic imperialism.

23 Over 6 million students took the TOEFL test or its sister test of business English in 2007. Over 1 million took the Cambridge IELTS test in 2007, an increase of 300 per cent since 2004 (reported in *The Guardian Weekly*, 20 June 2008).

24 Phillipson 2008a. The article explores the transition from the linguistic imperialism of the colonial and postcolonial ages to the increasingly dominant role of English as a neoimperial language. It analyses 'global' English as a key dimension of USA empire. US expansionism is a fundamental principle of the foreign policy of the US that can be traced back over two centuries. Linguistic imperialism and neoimperialism are exemplified at the micro and macro levels, and some key defining traits explored, as are cultural and institutional links between the UK and the USA, and the role of foundations in

promoting 'world' English. The article explores the role of language in corporate-driven globalization and theorizes linguistic neoimperialism by situating discourses and cultural politics in the material realities of neoimperial market pressures.

25 A number of studies of Englishization in the Nordic countries are referred to in Phillipson 2006c, 70–71.

26 Devidal 2004 is a very detailed analysis from the perspective of international human rights law of the implications of education falling within GATS, with many references to resistance, and a strong plea for all education to be excluded. De Siqueira 2005 is a thorough historical analysis of the GATS process with a special focus on education.

27 For the reports of the Special Rapporteur on the Right to Education of the UN's Commission on Human Rights, see <www.right-to-education.org>. For an analysis of the attack on universities as a public good, as falling within GATS and outside human rights law, for instance by the US-dominated European Association for International Education, see Phillipson 2006a.

28 Lettre ouverte aux responsables de l'Evaluation Scientifique. Les scientifiques doivent-ils continuer à écrire en français? < http://petition.hermespublishing.com>.

29 Per Øhrgaard, at a language policy conference held at Copenhagen Business School on 9 December 2007. A report of the conference, plus recommendations for action has been published (Hansen and Phillipson 2008). A recording of the entire day's proceedings can be downloaded from www.cbs.dk/forskning_viden/institutter_centre/institutter/isv.

30 Norwegian academics have produced a sensitive policy statement on maintaining a balance between Norwegian and English: *Framlegg til ein språkpolitikk for universitet og høgskolar i Noreg*, 2006. www.uhr.no/documents/Framlegg_til_ein_språkpolitikk_for_UHsektoren_1.pdf.

31 *Sprog til tiden. Rapport fra Sprogudvalget*, København, Kulturministeriet, 2008 http://www.kum.dk/sw69654.asp. It is a weakness of the Danish policy document that Danish and English are only seen as in competition with each other. The argumentation is entirely either/or, a zero sum game. This falsely reflects the reality that much B.A. level teaching is in fact hybrid or bilingual, with English-language

texts being taught through the medium of Danish. The report also suffers from serious gaps: there is nothing on experience in other Nordic countries, on the Bologna process, on types of pedagogy, on bilingualism or language awareness.

[32] Press release from Danske Universiteter ('Universities Denmark'), 22 April 2008.

[33] *Värna språken – förslag till språklag. Betänkande av Språklagsutredningen* 2008. Stockhom: Statens Offentliga Utredningar. SOU 2008:26. www. regeringen.se/content/1/c6/10/09/59/4ad5deaa.pdf. The White Paper also has substantial sections on many aspects of the use and learning of English. So far as higher education is concerned, the focus is on internationalization (incoming students as much as the mobility of Swedish students), the need for quality in school and higher education, and the realization that higher education institutions need to formulate explicit language policies. Reference is made to The University of Gothenburg, Sweden's language policy (2007), which states that

- The official language of communication of Göteborg University is Swedish...

- Göteborg University should strive towards linguistic diversity and see to it that competence in languages other than Swedish and English is seen as an additional qualification for employment at Göteborg University.

- Göteborg University should disseminate research findings to society in general in clear and intelligible Swedish and English.

[34] Another example. When Chris Patten entitles his memoirs *Not quite the diplomat. Home truths about world affairs* (2005), he is playing on the way 'diplomacy' has positive connotations that the reality of functioning in international relations conflicts with. The core meaning of the noun *diplomat*, a functional ascription for a government representative, differs from the metaphorical meaning that the adjectival form *diplomatic* generally has, tactful considerate. 'Home truths' have nothing to do with the core meaning of a 'home', but imply revealing secrets that the public is not aware of. His fascinating book describes how the Chinese treated him very differently when his role switched from Governor of Hong Kong (an ex-colony which he praises highly) to European Union Commissioner with responsibility

for international or 'diplomatic' affairs. A primary thrust of his book is to denounce the policies of Bush II and Blair—although he is relatively uncritical of the USA's global role—in the hope that more enlightened policies, a balance between American, European and Asian interests, may emerge in a multi-polar world.

[35] This reminds me of my only previous visit to Hong Kong in 1996, for an excellent language rights conference, when I was alarmed to see that my participation, according to the programme, was '*sponsored*' by Oxford University Press. It is true that OUP covered my flight costs, but my sense of shock was due to a gut feeling that somehow my academic freedom was being impugned if my scholarly activity was sponsored by a commercial undertaking.

References

Airey, John and Cedric Linder 2006. 'Language and the experience of learning university physics in Sweden'. *European Journal of Physics,* Vol. 27, 553–560.

Coleman, James A. 2006. 'English-medium teaching in European higher education'. *Language Teaching,* Vol. 39, 1–14.

Crystal, David 2004. 'The past, present, and future of World English'. In *Globalization and the future of German,* Andreas Gardt and Bernd Hüppauf (eds). Berlin: Mouton de Gruyter, 27–45.

De Sequira, Angela C. 2005. 'The regulation of education through the WTO/GATS'. *The Journal for Critical Education Policy Studies,* Vol. 3, No. 1, 12 <www.jceps.com>

Devidal, Pierrick 2004. 'Trading away human rights? The GATS and the right to education: a legal perspective'. *The Journal for Critical Education Policy Studies,* Vol. 2, No. 2, 22 <www.jceps.com>.

Dunbar, Robert and Skutnabb-Kangas, Tove 2008. *Forms of Education of Indigenous Children as Crimes Against Humanity?* Expert paper written for the United Nations Permanent Forum on Indigenous Issues (PFII). New York: PFII. [In PFII' system: "Presented by Lars-Anders Baer, in collaboration with Robert Dunbar, Tove Skutnabb-Kangas and Ole Henrik Magga"]. http://www.un.org/esa/socdev/unpfii/documents/E_C19_2008_7.pdf

Edge, Julian (ed.) 2006. *(Re-)Locating TESOL in an Age of Empire.* Basingstoke: Palgrave Macmillan.

Gandhi, Gopalkrishna (ed.) 2008. *The Oxford India Gandhi: Essential writings.* Delhi: Oxford University Press.

Graddol, David 1997. *The Future of English?* London: The British Council.

Graddol, David 2006. *English Next: Why global English may mean the end of 'English as a Foreign Language'.* London: The British Council.

Gupta, Anthea Fraser 2008. 'The language ecology of Singapore'. In Angel Creese, Peter Martin and Nancy H. Hornberger (eds). *Ecology of Language, Encyclopedia of Language and Education,* Vol. 9, Second edition, New York: Springer, 99–111.

Halliday, Michael A. K. 2006. 'Written language, standard language, global language'. In Braj B. Kachru, Yamuna Kachru and Cecil B. Nelson (eds.), *The Handbook of World Englishes.* Malden, MA and Oxford: Blackwell, 349–365.

Hansen, Lisbeth Verstraete and Robert Phillipson (eds) 2008. *Fremmedsprog til fremtiden. Sprogpolitiske udfordringer for Danmark* (Foreign languages for the future. Language policy challenges for Denmark). Copenhagen: Department of International Language Studies and Computational Linguistics, Copenhagen Business School.

Harvey, David 2005. *The New Imperialism.* Oxford: Oxford University Press.

Herriman, Michael and Barbara Burnaby (eds.) 1996. *Language Policies in English-Dominant Countries. Six Case Studies.* Clevedon: Multilingual Matters.

Hixson, Walter L. 2008. *The Myth of American diplomacy. National identity and U.S. foreign policy.* New Haven: Yale University Press.

Holborrow, Marnie 2006. 'Ideology and language: Interconnections between neo-liberalism and English'. In Edge, (ed.), 84-103.

Kandiah, Thiru 2001. 'Whose meanings? Probing the dialectics of English as a global language'. In Robbie Goh et al (eds.) *Ariels – departures and returns: a Festschrift for Edwin Thumboo.* Singapore: Oxford University Press.

Katunich, John 2006. 'Equity and English in South African higher education: Ambiguity and colonial language legacy.' In Julian Edge (ed.) 139–157.

Kenny, Brian and William Savage (eds.) 1997. *Language and Development. Teachers in a changing world.* Harlow and New York: Addison Wesley Longman.

Kim, Sung Ho 2007. *Max Weber's Politics of Civil Society.* Cambridge: Cambridge University Press.

Li, David C. S. 2007. 'Researching and teaching China and Hong Kong English.' *English Today,* 91/92, Vol. 23, No. 3 and 4, 11–17.

Lin, Angel M.Y. 2005. 'Critical, transdisciplinary perspectives on language-in-education policy and practice in postcolonial contexts: the case of Hong Kong.' In Lin and Martin (eds), 38–54.

Lin, Angel M.Y and Peter W. Martin (eds.) 2005. *Decolonisation, Globalisation: Language-in-Education Policy and Practice.* Clevedon: Multilingual Matters, 2005.

Magga, Ole Henrik, Ida Nicolaisen, Mililani Trask, Robert Dunbar and Tove Skutnabb-Kangas 2005. *Indigenous Children's Education and Indigenous Languages.* Expert paper written for the United Nations Permanent Forum on Indigenous Issues. New York: United Nations.

Mazrui, Alamin A. 1997. 'The World Bank, the language question and the future of African education.' *Race & Class*, Vol. 38, No. 3, 35-48.

Mendel, Arthur P. (ed.) 1961. *Essential works of Marxism*, New York: Bantam.

Mendieta, Eduardo, Robert Phillipson and Tove Skutnabb-Kangas 2006. 'English in the geopolitics of knowledge'. *Revista Canaria de Estudios Ingleses*, Vol. 53, 15-26.

Nicholas, Andrea Bear 2007. 'Historicide and linguicide.' *Shunpiking. Nova Scotia's Discovery Magazine* 49. Mi'kmaq and Maliseet First Nations Supplement, October 2007, 20-21.

Pakir, Anne 2008. 'Bilingual education in Singapore'. In Jim Cummins and Nancy H. Hornberger (eds.), *Bilingual Education*, volume 5 of *Encyclopedia of Language and Education*, second edition, New York: Springer, 191–203.

Patten, Chris 2005. *Not Quite the Diplomat. Home Truths about World Affairs.* London: Allen Lane/Penguin.

Phillipson, Robert 1992. *Linguistic Imperialism.* Oxford: Oxford University Press. Also published since 2001 by the Shanghai Foreign Language Education Press, and since 2007 by Oxford University Press in New Delhi.

Phillipson, Robert 2003. *English-Only Europe? Challenging language policy.* London: Routledge.

Phillipson, Robert 2006a. 'English, a cuckoo in the European higher education nest of languages?' *European Journal of English Studies*, Vol. 10, No. 1, 13-32.

Phillipson, Robert 2006b. Language policy and linguistic imperialism. In Thomas Ricento, (ed.). *An Introduction to Language Policy. Theory and Method.* Oxford: Blackwell, 346-361.

Phillipson, Robert 2006c. 'Figuring out the Englishisation of Europe'. In Constant Leung, Constant and Jenkins, and Jennifer (eds). *Reconfiguring Europe: The Contribution of Applied Linguistics.* London: Equinox, and British Association for Applied Linguistics, 65-86.

Phillipson, Robert 2007a. Review of Vartiainen 2004. 'The legitimacy of evaluation. A comparison of Finnish and English institutional evaluations of higher education'. *Language and Education*, Vol. 21, No. 4: 360–361.

Phillipson, Robert 2007b. Review of Angel M.Y. Lin and Peter W. Martin (eds) 2005 'Decolonisation, globalisation: Language-in-education policy and practice'. *Studies in Second Language Acquisition*, Vol. 29, No. 1, 139-141.

Phillipson, Robert 2008a. 'The linguistic imperialism of neoliberal empire.' *Critical Inquiry in Language Studies*, Vol. 5, No. 1, 2008, 1-43.

Phillipson, Robert 2008b. 'Lingua franca or lingua frankensteinia? English in European integration and globalisation.' *World Englishes*, Vol. 27, No. 2, 250-284, a 'Forum' consisting of the article, responses by seven scholars, and a closing word by Robert Phillipson.

Phillipson, Robert and Tove Skutnabb-Kangas 1994. 'English, panacea or pandemic.' *Sociolinguistica*, Vol. 8. English only? in Europa/in Europe/en Europe, 73-87.

Phillipson, Robert and Tove Skutnabb-Kangas 1999. 'Englishization: one dimension of globalization'. In David Graddol and Ulrike H. Meinhof, (eds.) *English in a changing world. AILA Review* 13, 19–36.

Raban, Sandra (ed.) 2008. *Examining the World. A History of the University of Cambridge Local Examinations Syndicate*. Cambridge: Cambridge University Press.

Rahman, Tariq 1998. *Language and Politics in Pakistan*. Karachi: Oxford University Press and Orient Longman, New Delhi, 2007.

Rassool, Naz 2007. *Global Issues in Language, Education and Development: Perspectives from postcolonial countries*. Clevedon: Multilingual Matters and Orient Longman, New Delhi.

Rubdy, Rani, Sandra Lee McKay, Lubna Alsagoff and Wendy D. Bokhurst-Heng 2008. 'Enacting English language ownership in the Outer Circle: a study of Singaporean Indians' orientations to English norms.' *World Englishes* Vol. 27, No. 1, 40–67.

Russell, Bertrand 1960. *On Education, Especially in Early Childhood*. London: Unwin.

Sen, Amartya 2005. *The Argumentative Indian. Writings on Indian Culture, History and Identity*. London: Penguin.

Skutnabb-Kangas, Tove 2000. *Linguistic Genocide in Education—Or Worldwide Diversity and Human Rights?*: Lawrence Erlbaum Associates and Delhi: Orient Longman.

Smith, Ross 2005. 'Global English: gift or curse. "The case against English as the world's lingua franca" '. *English Today* 82, Vol. 32, No. 2, 56–62.

Tan, Peter K. W. and Rani Rubdy (eds) in press. *Language as commodity. Global structures, local marketplaces*. London: Continuum.

Tsui, Amy B.M. 2007. 'Language policy and the social construction of identity: the case of Hong Kong'. In Tsui and Tollefson (eds.), 121–141.

Tsui, Amy B.M. and James W. Tollefson (eds.) 2007. *Language Policy, Culture, and Identity in Asian Contexts*. Mahwah, N.J.: Lawrence Erlbaum Associates.

Vartiainen, Pirkko 2004. *The Legitimacy of Evaluation. A Comparison of Finnish and English Institutional Evaluations of Higher Education*. Frankfurt am Main: Peter Lang.

Wächter, Bernd and Friedhelm Maiworm 2008. *English-taught programmes in European higher education. The picture in 2007*. Bonn: Lemmens Medien.

Webb, Vic 2007. 'English in higher education in South Africa: exclusion or inclusion?' In Pol Cuvelier, Theodorus du Plessis, Michael Meeuwis and Lut Teck (eds). *Multilingualism and Exclusion, Policy, Practice and Prospects*. Hatfield, Pretoria: van Schaik, 287–301.

Wierzbicka, Anna 2006. *English: Meaning and Culture*. Oxford: Oxford University Press.

Zhang, Qunying and David Watkins 2007. 'Conceptions of a good tertiary EFL teacher in China.' *TESOL Quarterly* Vol. 41, No. 4: 781–790.

Zhou, Minglang and Heidi A. Ross 2004. 'Introduction: The Context of the Theory and Practice of China's language policy. In Zhou and Sun (eds.), 1–18.

Zhou, Minglang and Hongkai Sun (eds) 2004. *Language Policy in the People's Republic of China. Theory and Practice since 1949*. Boston: Kluwer Academic Publishers.

Websites

UNESCO Recommendation concerning the Status of Higher-Education Teaching Personnel, 11 November 1997. http://portal.unesco.org/en/ev.php-URL_ID=13144&URL_DO=DO_TOPIC&URL_SECTION=201.html

European Commission

A new framework strategy for multilingualism. http://europa.eu/languages/servlets/Doc?id=1037

Report on the implementation of the Action Plan 2004-2006 'Promoting language learning and linguistic diversity'. http://ec.europa.eu/education/polices/lang/policy/report_en.html.

Recommendations of the High Level Group on Multilingualism. http://ec.europa.eu/education/policies/lang/doc/multireport_en.pdf

European Language Indicator. http://ec.europa.eu/education/policies/lang/key/legislation en.html.

Bologna process. http://ec.europa.eu/education/policies/educ/bologna/bologna/en.html

Council of Europe, Language Policy Division http://www.coe.int/T/DG4/Linguistic/Default en.asp

See *Policy guide and studies; Language Education Policy Profiles; Common European Framework of Reference for Language Learning; European Language Portfolio*

Skutnabb-Kangas, Tove (compiler). *Bibliography on multilingual education, linguistic human rights, etc.* Almost 300 pages; updated regularly. http://www.samiskhs.no/index.php?c=307&kat=Research+%26+Science. Click on Bibliography, under Tove's name on the right-hand side.

Appendix

A semiotic interlude: why English is no panacea. An exploration by analysis of the word **concern** *of the suitability of English to function as an international language.*

Criteria that should be met by any language in use for international purposes can be identified, as they have been by the inventors of planned languages like Esperanto. Smith (2005, 58) focuses on six features:

1. Maximum speakability, i.e. a range of phonemes as small as is feasible without restricting communicative capacity

2. Sensible orthography, i.e. words being spelt as they are pronounced, and vice versa

3. Regular inflection rules (such as no irregular verbs)

4. Uncomplicated grammar (that is, the absence of complexities which contribute little or nothing while making learning more difficult, as with the verbs *avoir* and *être* in French)

5. Freedom from ambiguity. […]

6. The ideal *lingua franca* should be easy to learn.

The *Encarta World English Dictionary* (Bloomsbury 1999, also Microsoft) lists five semantic categories for **concern**. I have supplemented the examples in the dictionary with university-oriented ones in types 1 and 4: Noun

1. WORRY OR STH CAUSING IT, a reason to worry, or sth that causes worry. *The changes in the university are giving rise to concern.*

2. AFFAIR THAT SHOULD INVOLVE SB a matter that affects sb, or that sb has the right to be involved with. *It's no concern of yours.*

3. CARING FEELINGS, emotions such as worry. Compassion, sympathy, or regard for sb or sth. *I shall express my concern by sending some flowers.*

4. BUSINESS a commercial enterprise. *Universities may have been seats of learning once, but now they have to be run like commercial concerns.*

5. (*dated*; etymological information on semantic shift from Latin via French).

Verb

Four semantic fields, corresponding to 1, 2, and 3 (that the adjectival form *concerned* pairs off with), nothing corresponding to nominal 4, but has a fourth meaning:

BE ON THE SUBJECT OF to be about a particular topic, *This concerns academic freedom.*

In short, the English lexical item *concern* has five distinct meanings.

The New Shorter Oxford English Dictionary (1993) lists no fewer than nine distinct meanings, in two groups, for the noun, in one case requiring it to be in the plural, with considerable detail in explaining and exemplifying the headword.

Conclusions

- English is intrinsically a confusingly difficult language, especially for second language users.

- This complexity, and the polysemy of individual lexical items—English having many homonyms and homophones, generally grounded in the hybrid origins of modern English—means that the language is *prima facie* unsuitable for use as an international language. Its properties lead to misunderstandings and represent a huge learning task.[34]

- The flexibility of the same form functioning as both Noun and Verb (rather than these being categorically marked, for instance by a morphological form, as in many languages) is an additional complication for second language users.

- The current clout of English has nothing to do with any intrinsic properties, and everything to do with the power of its users, and the uses to which the language has been put.

As a multilingual, I am alert to the way other languages borrow from English (and vice versa, I learned a great deal about English through learning a post-Viking language, Danish). The word *concern* has been borrowed from English into Danish, but the meaning is subtly different. A standard monolingual reference work (*Politikens Nudansk Ordbog*, fifteenth edition, 1992) defines the noun, *koncern*, as exclusively meaning a group of companies, a cartel or combine, but in more recent years the term is used to refer simply to a company, alongside the older term *selskab*.

Living in Denmark as I do, it is possible that I am influenced by hearing the word '*koncern*' used in a Danish context and sense, which could trigger other denotations than a monolingual English-user would initially bring into play.[35] In-depth familiarity with several languages is a major cognitive and cultural advantage, which our ancestors seem to have appreciated when Latin and Greek played a central role in the school curriculum.

English falls down on all of Ross's six counts. My purpose in exemplifying the semiotic and grammatical complexity of English is to demonstrate that it is unlikely to function as an efficient or symmetrical language of international communication. It is no panacea. But even if English is no panacea, clearly the language cannot be ignored.

Book Reviews

A.L.Khanna, Mahendra K. Verma, R.K. Agnihotri and S.K. Sinha *Adult ESOL Learners in Britain*

Far too many adult immigrants in Europe have not become sufficiently proficient in the locally dominant language for access to the job market and genuine integration. This study provides lucid documentation of the language provision offered in England to adult immigrants from a variety of backgrounds, and the experience of a broad range of learners of English of the genus ESOL (English for Speakers of Other Languages), and their teachers and administrators.

The findings make grim reading. There is unambiguous evidence of a wish to learn English, for instrumental, functional reasons, but the teaching on offer is limited in scope; the teachers are mostly well-intentioned but under-qualified English people, with no familiarity with the mother tongues or cultures of the learners; courses do not lead to accredited qualifications. At root the entire provision is deeply embedded in a racist, assimilationist tradition that serves to maintain the learners in a stigmatised, dependent position.

It is a short, crisp, wide-ranging book, 93 pages of text, appendices reproducing 11 pages of questionnaire and other research instruments, and a detailed bibliography. The text begins with a rapid but significant historical analysis of the way English has been taught monolingually within Britain and abroad. Subtractive language learning was imposed on Celtic language speakers, Huguenot immigrants, and successive generations of refugees and labour migrants, culminating in 'English for our coloured citizens' from the 1950s. English has always been taught as the one-way route to the English way of life.

The trend since the 1970s has been for ESOL to be instigated informally in an effort to reach immigrant women with little English or familiarity with things British. This missionary or pastoral service was often idealistic but seldom addressed the underlying racism, ethnocentrism and stereotyping. In ESOL, which faithfully reflects the values and prejudices of the wider community, minority mother tongues are invalidated, and bilingualism is seen as something foreign and un-British. Masses of sources of many types are cited to justify this description and analysis. It is all the more powerful as it comes from eminent academics, two resident in Britain and two in India, who have in-depth familiarity with immigrant communities. The questionnaire itself was translated into Urdu, Hindi, Bengali and Chinese. One minor grouse is that it is unfortunate that all the researchers were males, particularly since most of the ESOL learners are female (sensitivity to the gender issue in ESOL is evident in the analysis, p. 84), and there is no shortage of well qualified female academics from the sub-continent.

Chapter 2 represents a quick run-through of 'trends in second language research'. This involves brief summaries of the major influences on language pedagogy since 1945, from behaviourism to cognitivism, via SLA, communicative approaches, sociolinguistic perspectives, learner variables, attitudes and motivation. The prevailing Western research traditions are faithfully recorded, a presentation that is useful to those familiar with the work reported on, but probably rather arcane for any newcomers. This is unfortunate if one of the target audiences for the book is the professionally under-qualified teachers who actually do ESOL. The research team would prefer teaching that demonstrates 'understanding, respect and equality', and this is only marginally advanced by familiarizing the reader with fads of recent decades, particularly since the learners under investigation in this study were taught by people with virtually no teacher training. Their pedagogical loyalty must be assumed to derive primarily from the language teaching (French? Latin? English?) that they were at the receiving end of long ago. In addition, one of the weaknesses of the atomistic categories of positivistic second language research is that general educational principles seldom loom large, and the more humane, culturally and linguistic empathetic approach advocated in this book is invisible in such research traditions.

Chapter 3 is an illuminating presentation of the research methods employed for the study (which draws only selectively on chapter 2). The small scale of the research is stressed: 133 informants of the 200 contacted, at seven centres scattered throughout the United Kingdom. The individual and social variables recorded are presented, including rating and self-rating of language competence in L1 and English, types of use and exposure to English, and attitudinal factors. The teachers are also profiled. This set of variables could be invaluable for any future work of a similar kind, in whatever country. They are also impressively drawn on in the later, more analytical chapters.

Chapter 4 provides a detailed characterization of the learners, covering their countries of origin, age, gender, age at arrival, length of stay, occupation (nearly half were housewives), and teachers' evaluations of their language proficiency. Areas where language difficulties were particularly severe include the reading of newspapers and official documents, and negotiations with officials, although many South Asians were able to use their mother tongue with doctors, because most of the doctors in inner city areas come from the same country. Fascinating statistical detail is provided for the use of the mother tongue in a wide range of domestic and external settings. The authors note that one of the most striking figures is the 'rapidly decreasing number of informants who use the mother tongue with children' (57), though this generalisation does not apply to the Bengalis. The finding is, however, counter-balanced by a wish for mother tongue teaching for the children.

When it comes to attitudes to English, there is a universal pragmatic wish for instrumental proficiency, but when tested for traits associated with the language, few are positive. Few rate English as being 'civilised' or 'scientific'. Likewise the host society is seen as far from 'friendly', this reflecting the uncertain social status of ESOL learners, and mixed support from their own group.

In Chapter 5 many of these findings are correlated with a substantial number of variables, providing a wealth of detail that those directly involved should reflect on. The classic dichotomy of instrumental and integrative motivation is explored, and the conclusion drawn that the 'migrant groups would like to learn the language of the host society without at the same time losing their identity' (67) or losing their mother tongues. This ought to go without saying, but stating it is evidently necessary. If the informants have experienced racist abuse and marginalization, it is not surprising that they do not identify with the dominant group. Apparently Bangladeshis experience the 'potent threat of racial discrimination' (76) more intensely than Indians or Pakistanis, even if their language proficiency and measures of integrative motivation are relatively higher. Age at arrival also seems to have a decisive influence.

While the voices of the learners are mostly muffled behind the clinical data of questionnaire statistics, correlations, and abstract categories, the ESOL teachers are given a voice in Chapter 6. What comes out clearly is the low status of the ESOL profession, and the undermining of their honourable efforts by the institutional racism of the contexts within which the teaching operates. One cannot really speak of a 'profession', just as the ideal of bilingual teachers, that most endorse as desirable, is seldom a reality. One manifest conclusion from the study is the need for practitioners to work with professional development of all kinds, and for the real needs of these learners to be met more adequately.

Chapter 7 briefly concludes the book by stressing that ESOL needs to be 'more sensitive to the socioeconomic, cultural and linguistic backgrounds of the ESOL learners' (91). Any reliance on 'market forces' is unlikely to improve matters. A key ESOL administrator is cited as stressing 'both anger at the inequity of the current situation and a feeling of powerlessness in the midst of it' (Tom Jupp in 1995, 93). What is therefore needed is 'a national strategy for ESOL which recognises the sociolinguistic and pedagogic value of the development of skills in both mother tongue and English'. One can't help wondering why no such strategy has been forthcoming, as it would manifestly make sense politically, economically and culturally. The Nuffield Languages Inquiry, *Languages, the next generation* (2000) is a key national policy document that speaks of 'neglect of the nation's linguistic wealth' and pleads for more multilingualism for all in Britain. Lifelong language learning is also advocated. And even if the explicit Nuffield agenda is improving the prospects for 'business', surely this is one field where a reformed ESOL could have much to offer. How can one make policy-makers understand that it is in their interest, as well as that of the adult migrants, that ESOL should be properly funded, organized and professionalized? This book provides a coherent rationale for this purpose.

Ulrich Ammon (ed.), *The Dominance of English as a Language of Science. Effects on other languages and Language Communities.*
Berlin & New York: Mouton de Gruyter, 2001. xiii + 478 pp.

The book contains 22 papers, in four sections, one on general issues, and three on various types of country, those with English as the sole language of science, those traditionally oriented towards several scientific languages, and countries with their own language of science.

Ulrich Ammon's introduction is a brief run-through of some of the themes of the anthology, with reflections on dominance and the injustice of some scholars having to use a foreign language of science. The underlying issue is whether the pre-eminence of English in the scientific world is occurring at the expense of other languages of scholarship, real or potential, and whether a privileged language, along with the paradigms associated with it, represents a threat to other ways of thinking and their expression. This is a major issue for the contemporary scientific world, one that native speakers of English have quite probably not given much thought to. The book provides a wealth of description, but generalization, comparison and synthesis are tricky (and not undertaken by the editor) because the individual contributors handle their topics in such differing ways, often without the theoretical underpinning being explicit. Some studies are presented in great detail, others more cryptically. The focus in some is an entire country, in others a single university or discipline, others deal with researchers' assessment of their competence in foreign languages, etc. I found the first half of the book uneven and frustrating, as my comments will show, whereas much of the second half is admirable.

The more general papers are a very mixed bag. *Robert Kaplan's* article ranges widely in the history of language and science, but seems deeply ambivalent about what explains American and English dominance. It is curious that someone who engages in language planning and policy, and expresses concern for threatened languages, and who notes many influences and factors, regards none as causal: English has become a dominant language by 'accident'. He notes the role of native speakers as journal gate-keepers and guardians of standards ('there is nothing insidious about the actions of English-speakers; it is simply a matter of more or less benevolent self-interest'!), but questions the existence of standard English. His American worldview is epitomized by incorrect nomenclature for European institutions and false statements about the official and working languages of the European Union, which he refers to as the 'European Council' (11), which does not exist, and as the Council of Europe (18), which is a totally different body.

Kaplan distances himself from research that shows how Western nations have promoted English as one element of commercial, political and military influence, whereas the following paper, by *Angéline Martel*, reports on how OECD countries have harnessed science, technology and innovation to the interests of the state and the economy. She presents in some detail the active language policy measures undertaken in Québec, and reveals the intermeshing of language with many variables while communication trends and commerce are changing the nature of research communities and national languages. An elaborate heuristic model of language policy dynamics in a wider sociopolitical context is presented and exemplified, for instance, statistics on research productivity and impact via French and English. The paper is one of the few that strives to assess how well our concepts capture the complexity of the relationship between science and technology, national interests and languages, and language planning measures. A sophisticated multi-dimensional analysis emerges, one which is unfortunately marred by a multitude of small errors, mostly of language (English not being her first language), a few of fact (a 1945 document is reported as being for President Theodore Roosevelt, a book by Bourdieu appeared in 1945, …). Such shortcomings are to be found in many of the articles in the book.

Miguel Siguan's paper explores the paradox of a search for 'strictly rational, and thus universally valid, knowledge' (67) and the fact that no language, English included, is perfect or strictly rational. He accepts the pre-eminence of English but is concerned about the dominance of English weakening other languages and cultures, to the point where these will be 'deformed or destroyed' (68). Similar contradictions in Siguan's analysis appear at the textual level: he claims that a text on atomic physics, law, or economics 'can be thought of in the same way' (64) in European languages, but he sees translation between culturally embedded languages as 'difficult' (66), even as regards terminology, and effectively impossible in the case of philosophical texts. His brief reflections on Western scientific thought contain a number of debatable generalizations and are punctuated by comments on other languages ('primitive' ones, and 'Inuki' - presumably Inuktitut- as a purely oral language) that demonstrate a profoundly Eurocentric rationality.

Abram de Swaan's paper on English in the social sciences also seems to be deeply self-contradictory. There is an unabashed celebration of the joys of English as an international elite language: 'English has come to serve a number of linking functions, in fact almost all of them and almost everywhere' (74), yet editors of social science journals are seen as imposing an Anglo-American vision of the world that masquerades as 'universal human destiny' (78). He states that 'students cannot be effectively taught the social sciences in one language only, whether it be their mother tongue or a foreign, world language, e.g. English' (77), yet looks to monolingual American social science as the norm. de Swaan believes that 'the entirety of human experience and history' (78) can be expressed in English, but notes that translation is often insuperably difficult (75). So in fact while rejoicing in English as the 'true world language of science, technology, media and business' (71), a language that offers no threat to other languages, he advocates an adjustment of the social sciences and humanities paradigm that accepts 'American and British conceptions and practices' (79). de Swaan's political science approach does not take up issues of domain loss, language shift, diglossia, and linguistic hierarchization. This is frustrating, since it is in the social sciences that pressures to publish in English rather than a local language are a serious existential issue, as the following article makes clear.

Heather Murray and Silvia Dingwall's paper on 'The dominance of English at European universities: Switzerland and Sweden compared', provides a substantial amount of data on these two demographically small states, both of which are also covered elsewhere in the volume. Some of the key variables are the amount of English used at undergraduate and graduate levels, the language used in doctoral dissertations and other research publications, and attitudes to English and whether its use puts one at a disadvantage. Light is shed on whether the expanding use of English is occurring additively or subtractively. The concluding reflections assess that diglossia does not involve a threat to Swiss German, since its speakers are used to operating in two variants of German and Swiss national identity is connected to bilingualism, though vigilance is needed to maintain democratic communication channels open within the country.

Grant McConnell's paper is on English in countries in East and Southeast Asia. It draws on a range of demographic data, and figures for the use of English or a local language as medium of education, all presented in maps and diagrams. He admits that the data is incomplete and inconclusive, which suggests that data collection needs to be vastly more focused if it is to produce explanatory results. This study seems to be less illuminating than other studies of the 'spread' of English and 'post-imperial' English, and I have difficulty in seeing the relevance of it to the book as a whole.

The problem of conflicting interpretations of what is understood as falling within 'English as a language of science', or remaining outside it, recurs in the next section. This is on 'Countries with a History of English-Language Dominance' and brings together Australia, three former colonies, and Israel.

Bernard Spolsky and Elana Shohamy in fact relate that Israel does not have a history of English-language dominance. The only language that has been privileged is Hebrew, to the exclusion of 'big' European languages and Yiddish—though the utilitarian value of English is increasing here, as elsewhere.

Richard Baldauf acknowledges the relevance of historical, economic and technological factors for the expansion of English, but echoes Kaplan's 'accidental' interpretation of the expansion of English. He reproduces statistical tables on the use of several languages in scholarly databases over successive decades, but admits that the figures are unrepresentative. There are sensible reflections aimed at making individuals from 'English-speaking' countries more multilingual (his endorsement of languages other than English rings a trifle hollow when the five words of French used in his text contain a gross grammatical error, 158), but whether this could impact significantly on linguistic hierarchies and the forces that underpin these remains unexplored. His detailed presentation of Australian language policy cannot be said to advance the understanding of English dominance in science.

My worry about why certain papers have been included recurs with *Rodolfo Jacobson's* article on Malaysia. His data demonstrate code-switching at a faculty meeting, but might have derived from countless other settings, and the central issue of choice of a local language, or English, or a hybrid amalgam, as the medium of communication for scientific discourse, is not addressed. Little evidence is cited for the claim that switching to and from English is 'not a product of cultural awareness' (189) and that English is merely 'a neutral linguistic tool' (190). Post-colonialism studies would be unlikely to corroborate this interpretation.

William Wu, Dennis Chan and Björn Jernudd's modest study of 'English in science communication in Hong Kong: educational research output' explores language choice over three decades of articles, and hypotheses about use of English or Chinese. Far more data would be needed for firm conclusions about the nature of the relationship between the two languages to be drawn.

The article by *Jerzy Smolicz, Iluminado Nical* and *Margaret Secombe* on 'English as the medium of instruction for science and its effects on the languages of the Philippines' reports on a small empirical study of attitudes to language use by schoolchildren. Ammon, in his introduction, apparently thinks that the study relates to tertiary education. Although the study usefully documents perceptions of trilingualism, in effect triglossia, it is not concerned with English as a language of scholarship.

The 'countries' in this section are thus strange bedfellows, and some of them ought to be in a different bed.

The following section, 'Countries with a history of foreign languages for science other than, or in addition to, English' has papers from

Finland, Hungary, and Sweden. *Harald Haarman and Eugene Holman's* analysis of Finland is a masterly analysis of scholarly languages past and present, macro and micro issues. Finland has a history of scholarly multilingualism and openness to intercultural contact (one likely result of the country having been colonized). Finland now contributes to global technical standards and innovation, especially in telecommunications, and is a pioneer network society. This economic and cultural success builds on a healthy balance between several local languages (e.g. doctoral dissertations in Finnish, Swedish and the first in an indigenous language, Saami) and major use of English domestically and externally (doctoral dissertations predominantly in English in some fields, primarily in Finnish in others, a few in French and German) and confirms that 'technological modernization in Finland is evolving within the framework of high standards of living, whereas in the USA, modernization is intensifying at the cost of the quality of life' (Manuel Castells, cited 257). The article is a sophisticated intellectual history of languages in Finland that provides significant documentation of trends, and permits optimistic generalizations about how a demographically small country can try to strike a balance between the maintenance of strong local cultural and linguistic values and being an active participant in, and contributor to, globalisation and americanisation.

Péter Medgyes and Monika László present a detailed empirical study of the foreign language competence of Hungarian academics, with comparison between 1989 and 1999. There is a wealth of detail, on types of proficiency, contact (also with L2 users of English), bi- and multilingual competence, and commitment to international communication and the strengthening of the main national language.

Britt-Louise Gunnarsson's article is a detailed study of the use of English in all faculties at a single Swedish university, with statistics for many variables, including attitudes. It shows the depth of penetration by English in different faculties, and concludes that diglossia represents a threat to Swedish culture. There is a careful diagnosis of current trends, but strictly speaking the proposed remedies (increased use of French and German, better training in reading comprehension and writing skills in English, strong measures to strengthen Swedish) do not derive from the data but are policy and value-oriented. Unfortunately no mention is made of the measures that the Swedish government is currently undertaking to ensure that Swedish is not further marginalized. The governments of the Nordic countries commissioned research in 2001 designed to assess whether domain loss represents a serious threat to the Nordic languages.

The final section includes six richly informative articles on European countries (*Claude Truchot, Roland Willemyns, Ulrich Ammon, Rudolf de Cillia and Teresa Schweiger, Urs Dürmüller, Tatjana Kryuchkova*). Rather than commenting on each individually, I will point out some of the many cross-cutting sub-themes that permeate these studies and earlier articles:

- Use of English in research publications and in university teaching is expanding almost everywhere. In some subjects, typically the natural sciences, technology and medicine, it is the norm except in French-speaking areas. A diglossic division of labour, with English for specialist scholarship and the local language for popularization is seen as a problem (Sweden), no problem at all (Belgium, German-speaking Switzerland), or up to the reader to decide (Hungary).

- Attitudes to the dominance of English vary considerably. Some assume that a single global language of science is all to the good, others bewail the marginalization of other languages and the cultural, political and economic knock-on effects. The use of German and French internationally is diminishing. Russian is likely to suffer the same fate, as Russian scholars become more competent in English.

- Legislation to counteract the invasion of English (France) can partially influence a symbiosis with English as a scientific language, but few governments appear to have explicit language maintenance policies other than traditional national ones that predate globalisation (Austria, Germany).

- Proficiency in English has improved radically in some countries (Hungary, Finland, Russia), but possibly not in others (Austria, Belgium, France, Germany). These divergent outcomes may correlate with the degree of use of English as a medium of education, or at least extensive use of textbooks, in some cases beginning at undergraduate level, some not until doctoral level, and in some barely at all.

• The advance of English involves opening up to freedom of information (Russia, Hungary), and has led to a greater acceptance of Americanization (France), but there is no simple correlation between English as an international language of science and English as a national language.

• The status of English as the benchmarking medium for scientific activity leads to the writing of scholars in other languages being ignored. Thus Ferguson and Fishman were pioneers in establishing diglossia and the sociology of language internationally, but there were significant predecessors on precisely these topics who wrote in French (see Willemyns, 338).

The final two articles cover English in Brazil (*Vera Lúcia Meneses de Oliveira e Paiva* and *Adriana Silvina Pagano*), which has little on scientific language, and the evolution of scientific language in Japan (*Fumio Inoue*), including terminology development and many dimensions of language planning.

The book provides a wealth of description of the use of English as a scientific language. It confirms that there is an as yet unmet need for a theoretical framework covering relations between scientific languages, their use and users, the structures, local and global (states not being sovereign in this area) within which they operate, factors leading to the contraction or expansion of scientific languages and linguistic power, and the individual scholar's agency, access to and production of scientific languages, some form of bilingualism being the norm outside 'English-speaking' countries. The book draws little on social theory, even in the more general articles, and it is unfortunate that eminent scholars in contrastive scientific rhetoric, its characteristics and determinants (such as John Swales and Anna Mauranen) are not represented. Nor is there any presentation of whether the activities of supranational bodies such as the European Union, the Council of Europe, and counterparts elsewhere in the world, can strengthen a range of scientific languages.

Ammon unfortunately does the cause of scholarly quality and equality no good by not giving the entire manuscript the meticulous care that editing requires. At the macro level there is the problem of the inclusion of articles which only marginally elucidate the general theme of the book. At the micro level the irritating symptoms include bibliographical gaps and errors (one book is published in 'An Arbor' by 'The America of Chicago Press', 76; two different titles are given to one book of mine: x, 360), French accents are missing, an article credited to two authors refers to 'me' in the singular, etc, etc. Virtually every article has blemishes of some kind. Several of the papers by people for whom English is not the mother tongue contain language errors that affect comprehension, including his own ('politics' and 'policy' used interchangeably, 'drail' for 'trail, 357; 'no tuition' where what is presumably intended is 'no fees', 357), over and above countless German-influenced forms that disrupt, without perhaps impeding, comprehensibility. Ammon ends his own paper with some constructive proposals about non-native international English, and bias in native speaker gate-keeping, but his message would have been much more persuasive if the book as a whole had been more focused and been guided by an unstinting insistence on precision.

Words of the World: The Global Language System.
Cambridge: Polity Press, 2001, 253 + xi pages.
David Block and Deborah Cameron (ed.).
Globalization and Language Teaching. London
& New York: Routledge, 2002, 196 pages.
Janina Brutt-Griffler. *World English: A Study of its
Development.* Clevedon: Multilingual Matters, 2002,
215 + xiii pages.

I reviewed books on the global reach of English (Fishman, Conrad & Rubal-Lopez, 1996; Graddol, 1997; Crystal, 1997) in a volume that reflects a diversity of approaches to the pre-eminence of English (Phillipson, 2000a). This review article concerns three further books that situate English in broader socio-political analytical frameworks. Two are unconvinced about linguistic imperialism, past or present, while the third looks at its contemporary manifestations.

Abram de Swaan's (AdS) wide-ranging book, *Words of the World: The Global Language System*, elaborates an analytical framework that draws on political economy and political sociology in order to explore why people learn powerful languages. Five chapters explore languages in India, Indonesia, South Africa, selected former French and British colonies in Africa, and the European Union. The book builds on a largely descriptive, historical foundation, and employs a mathematical template that measures the 'communicative value' (Q-value) of a language. AdS's global language 'system' essentially sees language as being a matter of individual choice, of self-interest, that assumes that the greater the range of potential language uses and users, the more reason there is for the individual to shift language 'upwards'.

In AdS's constellation of languages, multilinguals are the key link between languages that are isolated and languages higher up in the hierarchy. While about one hundred languages occupy a 'central' position, twelve are supercentral: Arabic, Chinese, English, French, German, Hindi, Japanese, Malay, Portuguese, Russian, Spanish and Swahili. English is the 'hypercentral' language. One wonders whether Japanese connects the speakers of 'a series of central languages,' and why Bengali, which manifestly serves such purposes, and has more speakers than several of the languages included, has been excluded.

Linguists will react sceptically to AdS's claim that it is intelligibility that makes languages distinct. Sociolinguists will be surprised to read that 'Languages are the creation of no-one in particular and they are nobody's property' (30). For AdS, language death is not due to policies that eliminate minority languages, they merely 'wither away' (15). Hierarchy is seen as a sliding scale of options for the upwardly mobile, nationally and internationally. These cosmopolitans are unconcerned about whether their language learning is additive or subtractive (concepts that he does not use). By relying on choice, and the individual's wish to learn a language that is seen as a collective good, AdS ignores the role of the state in providing an infrastructure in education that constrains choices, and the role of the media in transmitting discourses that generate national linguistic cultures, norms and status.

AdS's theoretical foundations are surprisingly selective. Thus a book on 'the global language system' has little on globalization. AdS nods occasionally in the direction of linguistic and cultural capital, but does not link this to class or linguistically defined social stratification (linguicism) or linguistic inequality. There is no analysis of the cultural dimensions of North–South relations, global cultural flows, or McDonaldization. One would expect there to be serious consideration of how border-crossing languages, English in particular, serve to integrate particular communities (states, or professions), and how particular interest groups (finance capital, corporations, media and educational products) are connected in the world system. But this side of things is unexplored, since the focus is on individual countries rather than the wider networks of late modernism. AdS's layered language 'constellation' is essentially a simple model of triglossia, wrapped in algebraic game theory. Like most work in diglossia, it is loosely anchored in (neo)liberal social theory (Williams 1992). Key concepts in the sociology of language, language maintenance and shift, and language spread are scarcely mentioned. Fishman et al's work (1996) on English as a 'post-imperial' language, and how this connects to global economic and political interests, is untouched. There is occasional sniping at work on linguistic imperialism, but no serious attempt to engage with dominance and hierarchy.

The privileged position of English is rightly seen as according benefits to native speakers, because of the large communicative potential of users of the language. AdS sees resistance to the hegemony of English as misguided. A language rights 'movement' is falsely represented as working for 'the right of human beings to speak whatever language they wish.' This is a misreading of the thrust of efforts to codify and implement language rights, and the commitment of UNESCO, and many communities and NGOs, to maintaining the world's linguistic and cultural diversity. He seems unaware of the role of international law, particularly in human rights conventions, in seeking to constrain an oppressive state and protect language rights (de Varennes 2000).

The descriptive chapters are relatively richer, which is not surprising considering the voluminous wealth of macro-sociolinguistic studies. But there are inevitably major problems in condensing the narrative into a few pages on each country.

Much of the description of languages in India is stimulating, with sensitive presentation of the complexities of the many languages and of the privileged but contested status of Hindi and English. However I doubt whether many Indian sociolinguists would agree with the claim that 'Indians are an extremely unilingual people' (p.63), and AdS does not appreciate that the promotion of Hindi as an all-India language was not seen as entailing a shift from other Indian languages. AdS suggests that elite status in India can be achieved through either Hindi or English, and that each is as good as the other (p.78). This interpretation ignores the reality that in many domains, English is emphatically the top language, and that this supremacy is consolidated at all levels of education. The stark choice is typically between education through the medium of English (a policy that the World Bank is consolidating) or through the medium of an Indian language in under-funded schools. This has produced what Nehru claimed he was working to avoid, namely an English-speaking caste at the summit of the Indian social system. The massive brain drain and the internationalization of computer service industries reinforce these processes. When AdS's figures for the Q-value of English are inconveniently low as compared with the figure for Hindi, he brings in the added value of English as an international language as a weighting factor (p.79). This doubtless tallies with what happens in reality, but this scholarly legerdemain suggests that the Q-value figures have little explanatory power, not least when the unit of analysis is a single state.

A striking feature of the chapter is that western researchers are drawn on extensively in the main body of the text, whereas Indian researchers are relegated to footnotes. This eurocentricity is an insult to Indian scholars.

The chapter on Indonesia draws on Dutch-language sources, but the same eurocentricity recurs. Indonesian independence in 1945, after centuries of Dutch colonisation and three years of Japanese occupation, was presumably a cause for rejoicing by Indonesians, but not for AdS: 'the Dutch presence in Asia came to an unhappy end' (p.87). However, AdS rightly underlines the significance of the emergence of a single state language, Bahasa, as an exception to the general pattern of colonial languages remaining in place in postcolonial states. Nor is Bahasa the mother tongue of the dominant group, which is Javanese.

Three types of former French/Belgian and British colonies are contrasted, countries with a single dominant local language (Rwanda/Kinyarwanda, Botswana/Tswana), with a widespread African second language (Senegal/Wolof, Tanzania/Swahili), and countries with a range of local languages (Zaire, Nigeria). However, the conclusion in each case is that elites have clung to the former colonial language, since its limited accessibility to the mass of the population gives its users a hegemonic position that is convertible into prestige and influence. This explains why even widely used languages like Wolof and Swahili do not open the top doors. AdS does not refer to the ambivalence of the Tanzanian government about introducing Swahili as the main medium of education at secondary level. It is also incorrect to state that vernacular languages are used as a primary school medium of education (120). AdS fails to report the clear evidence of British aid organizations strongly backing the maintenance of English, and the key role of the World Bank, here as elsewhere in Africa, in putting funding into the former colonial languages rather than African languages. These pressures have been thoroughly documented in a succession of studies. Yahya-Othman and Batibo (in Fishman et. al., 1996), whom AdS cites, are in no doubt that neo-colonialism and linguistic imperialism have been in force and continue to be so.

It does not seem to have occurred to AdS to consider what the wealth of these elites derives from, or the role of African oil and raw materials in the global economy. To state blithely that education for a large proportion of the population is not available for 'lack of funds' ignores the unfair trading terms that the North imposes on the South, and the misappropriated fortunes that end up in Western banks. To write as though English and French serve exclusively local purposes ignores how elites in the South are in hock to North interests, and how corruption and clientism are often channelled along ethnolinguistic fault lines.

For AdS: 'a policy ostensibly aimed at promoting a diversity of languages will actually further the hegemony of English. That is the recurrent paradox of contemporary language politics: the more languages, the more English' (127). Post-apartheid language policy envisages a break with the linguicist policies of the past, though how the struggle between English and African languages that have inherited low prestige will evolve is unclear, and relates to wider political and economic inequalities and policies (Alexander 2002). AdS's Q-value table for African languages fails to note that languages such as Zulu and Xhosa are strongly represented in the east and south respectively. In most regions, language policy aims at trilingualism rather than an unattainable competence in all eleven official languages. Language rights are enshrined in the Constitution because of a wish to respect diversity, and not because of the efforts of misguided sociolinguists, as AdS suggests (139). Nor does the right to learn and use the mother tongue in any way conflict with the right to learn other languages, and in particular those that are seen to open doors.

What then explains the grip of English? For AdS 'the spread of English is the mostly unintended outcome of expectations held and decisions made accordingly by hundreds of millions of people across the globe…. especially with a view to employment chances' (142). He concedes though that this 'free choice' is triggered by 'multinational entrepreneurs, who orient themselves to national and worldwide markets' and involves 'collusion' with the global economic system (142). This merry tale of linguistic freedom is then exemplified: 'Wherever different people speak different languages for example in business, in the mines and industry, in the schools, in the courts, in government and the churches—problems of communication are almost unfailingly resolved by adopting English' (142). This is wishful thinking. Of South Africa's 40.6 million population, 3.45 million have English as their mother tongue, and 7 million are estimated as having some competence in English as a second language, though there are higher estimates (1996 census figures, quoted in Lass, 2002, 104 and de Klerk and Gough, 2002, 358–59). On the challenges of multilingualism, see Heugh, 2002.

The coverage of language policy in the EU contains many questionable statements. The chapter is not a useful source of basic information on the diversity of language traditions in the member states or the functioning of EU institutions (for which see Phillipson 2003). There are points of detail that can be queried on virtually every page, but three examples will have to suffice. With reference to the eleven official EU languages, AdS states: 'Everyone agrees that this is a completely unmanageable number' (184). But the translation and interpretation services of each of the EU institutions maintain precisely the opposite. Their political masters show no inclination to accept a reduction in language rights, which are administered in a complex system that has successfully coped with each enlargement. AdS goes on to predict that members of the European Parliament will be 'likely to waive their right to speak their own language' (185). Quite the contrary, all the planning documents that this cardinal principle is non-negotiable. Finally, AdS states that it is 'linguists' who endorse a policy of learning two foreign languages, whereas in fact it is politicians at the Council of Europe who embraced the idea many years ago, and it is now the official policy of the EU and its member states.

AdS's concluding chapter is mostly a summing-up of points made earlier, but he does admit that languages other than English are in 'precarious coexistence' with it (189), and that the globalization of science via English means that American norms apply (192). The over-generalizations continue to the end: 'Everywhere people must cope with several languages' (193). Everywhere? Does this apply to US citizens? The statement is not even true of EU institutions: the translation and interpretation services permit senior people to function monolingually. For the rest of us, a diversity of tongues is 'choice' within the constraints permitted by the nation-state and globalization in a rapidly changing world, in which communication respects state borders less and less. We live in a much more complex world linguistic constellation than AdS presents.

It is disturbing that Abram de Swaan and his publishers have produced a work which, despite being written by one of the few political scientists who work on macro-sociolinguistic issues, fails to do justice to a wealth of ongoing work and is marred by basic errors of fact. The book reads like an apologia for English come what may, with a few minor worries as afterthoughts. It is perhaps ironic that a scholar who is impressively articulate in English as a foreign language seems to be guilty of what Ngugi wa Thiong'o warns against (1986, 20): 'It is the final triumph of a system of domination when the dominated start singing its virtues.' One would have hoped for something better from political science and Polity Press.

The second book, *Globalization and Language Teaching*, features an important collection of articles that traces some of the many ways that globalization impacts on language policy and language teaching. A short introduction by the editors ties together many of the themes that link articles in sections headed 'The global and the local,' 'Zones of contact,' and 'Methods and materials.'

That gobalization entails cultural homogenization and triggers conflicting responses locally is made clear in the article on language teaching in Japan (*Kubota*). This adheres to a naïve, essentialized belief in English as *the* international language, symbolized by white Anglo-American teachers and native speaker norms. In parallel with this cultural and linguistic self-colonization, a discourse of reactionary nationalism has evolved, partly as a result of the government proposing to make English a 'second official' language. These tensions are sensitively portrayed, and Kubota pleads for policies to respond more positively to linguistic diversity internally and externally.

The paper on language education in Britain (*Harris, Leung and Rampton*) reports on the many challenges to traditional norms of language, the state, and ethnicity that migration and globalization entail. New transnational means of communication, de-territorialization, and hybrid linguistic identities characterize urban centres (56.5% ethnic minorities in inner London, with 350 home languages). The Thatcherite-Blairite neoliberal economic order has implemented an authoritarian educational 'national' curriculum with a strict focus on Standard English. Schools thus ignore the real complexity and diversity of language uses and needs: language in education policy is in denial, ignoring at its peril the 'moral, cultural and political grounds now emerging at the intersection of globalization and diaspora processes' (45). The article powerfully blends acute social analysis with lucid exemplification.

Heller analyses how the significance of French and English language proficiency in Canada has shifted as traditionalism gave way to modernism and, thereafter, globalization. The shift is from language as community to language as a key commodity for employment. Francophones have acquired more economic and political power, and, significantly, 'both French and English are growing in importance in the service and information sectors of the globalized economy' (49). Bilingual skills are not necessarily essential for elite jobs, though they often are for lower level ones. Identities are shifting, as battles in communities over education (exemplified in Ontario) and employment show. Language struggles essentially represent competition over resources, a reality that the network and information society has not changed: 'language is more obviously tied into processes of construction of social difference and inequality, not less, as globalization utopianists would have it' (62). The article has a wealth of exemplification, drawing on extensive fieldwork, and is conceptually stringent and illuminating.

Cameron traces the shift from linguistic imperialism to communicative imperialism. 'Language becomes a global product available in different local flavours....The dissemination of "global" communicative norms and genres, like the dissemination of international languages, involves a one-way flow of expert knowledge from dominant to subaltern cultures' (70). Cameron argues that the modern focus on communication skills, defined by 'experts,' entails the dissemination of American ways of speaking, which are being extended worldwide, often without their ethnocentricity being perceived. The forms of communication, genres and styles of the dominant consumerist culture have the willing but possibly unwitting support of teachers of English and communication skills.

Kramsch and *Thorne* are less concerned with the dissemination of US cultural norms than with their interaction with French ones, when foreign language learners (in Berkeley and a lycée) interact by e-mail in a global communication network. The language learning efforts of both groups (of respectively French and English) reflect authentic communication, but analysis of the interaction reveals insensitive ignorance of different dimensions of communication, both factual and phatic/trust-building. Lack of awareness of cultural differences (in basic knowledge, and in the pragmatics of questioning, responding, and meshing into an effective shared interactive genre) was aggravated by the technology and the 'myth of the internet as a person-to-person mode of communication, free from national and institutional constraints and ideologies' (95). These difficulties were reciprocal, so it is unfortunate that the authors, in a richly reflective empirical paper that is theoretically insightful, state that 'genre is the mediator between the global and the local' (99), when also noting that both genres are local, in this particular interaction involving two languages, both as foreign languages. The medium is global, but that does not guarantee neutrality, unlike Esperanto, which is an authentic 'inter-local' language (Dasgupta 2000). Though perhaps US norms are the global default norms, since globalization fundamentally means Americanization (Bourdieu, 2001, 84; RP's translation):

> 'Globalization' serves as a password, a watchword, while in effect it is the legitimatory mask of a policy aiming to universalize particular interests and the particular tradition of the economically and politically dominant powers, above all the United States. It aims to extend to the entire world the economic and cultural model that favours these powers most, while simultaneously presenting it as a norm, a requirement, and a fatality, a universal destiny, in such a manner as to obtain adherence or, at the least, universal resignation.

The remaining papers all address the downside of a globalizing, Englishizing language pedagogy agenda.

- There is a strong plea (*Wallace*) for a critical re-think of literacies and of the thrust of language teaching, so that learners of English as a second or foreign language can 'participate in its critique and recreation' (114).

- In similar vein, *Block* critiques second language acquisition theory for under-rating the complexity of language learning, due to a technical-rational approach that is consonant with McDonaldization in many domains. The profession needs to escape from dehumanizing 'McCommunication' approaches to research and learning.

• *Canagarajah* articulately stresses the inequalities of the global pedagogical village, and the inappropriacy of teaching materials and methods exported worldwide. By working through strategies and activities that represent bottom-up, eclectic but focused ways of empowering learners in meta-communicative awareness, his 'postmethod' approach explicitly and persuasively goes beyond mono approaches of language, culture and method.

• *Gray* analyzes the 'one size fits all' global English teaching textbook, which is gender-inclusive but sanitized of any sensitive topics (politics, religion, sex,…) that could limit marketability. The vast British textbook business thus uncritically endorses materialism and Western values. This paper also contains significant empirical verification of these conclusions, which are situated reflectively in relation to the many complex manifestations of globalization and glocalization.

As language specialists, I feel we have an obligation to tease out the links between globalization, Americanization, and Englishization. The book as a whole contributes substantially to this task, even though only a few contexts are covered; for instance, there is no mention of regional trends such as the increased use of English in Europe. It is also ironical that the 'language teaching' of the title is largely confined to a concern with English, even if the balance between English and other languages is a key issue globally and in many local contexts.

Janina Brutt-Griffler (JBG) is also concerned with globalization and language learning in her *World English: A Study of its Development*. She seeks to establish that 'English owes its existence as a world language in large part to the struggle against imperialism' (ix), arguing that the spread of English 'requires primarily linguistic analysis rather than socio-political' (ix). One wonders how these parameters can be separated from each other, not least when JBG's unit of analysis is the bilingual speech community. And while I strongly approve of the historical record being further explored, and of our concepts and research paradigms being refined and challenged, greater validity will only emerge through impeccable scholarship, which I regretfully feel

JBG's work does not live up to. I suspect that Pennycook's warning about the need to draw lessons from the historical record with 'great care' (2000, 50) has not been heeded. Although the book demonstrates an impressive range of reading and empirical documentation, the theoretical task that JBG has set herself is vastly complex and perhaps impossibly difficult.

JBG's book has, in my view, a very poor fit between two halves that are only tenuously integrated. There is little theoretical or empirical glue binding together the two colonial case studies and the modern world. The glue is a conviction based on an exclusive focus on demand for English at the expense of supply. But supply and demand do not exclude each other, and to claim that the 'impetus and agency for English language spread lies (stet) outside Center nations' (28) ignores the reality of North–South relations, past and present, in the global economy as much as in global English. Colonial empires were kept within English/French/Portuguese spheres of influence, where trade and language followed the flag, so it is false and anachronistic to suggest that worldwide 'one language had to develop as the commercial lingua franca' (49). According to JBG, Anglo-American hegemony in the world market has 'declined' (112), though twelve pages later the US and the UK are back again 'dominating the world market', and World English (WE) is the 'dominant socio-political language form' (114).

According to JBG, WE consists of language *spread* (a process) and language *change* (products). We are presumably dealing with one English rather than world Englishes. The claim is made—though not substantiated—that by switching agency from the individual to the group ('the essential actor is the acquiring speech community', 23), one can create a theoretically adequate foundation for the phenomenon of WE. World English is 'superseding national languages' entirely as a result of a 'world historical process' (124) that is presumed to be universally democratic and beneficial, even when JBG states that the need for a commercial *lingua franca* 'springs from the economic basis of society' (49). This being so, presumably the functions that the 'new' variants of English perform in multilingual societies, internally and externally, must be of central relevance, but JBG sees WE as doing away with 'hierarchy among speech communities' (180), and non-Western nations 'take equal part in the creation of the world econocultural system and its linguistic expression, WE' (108). Does JBG really think that the World Trade Organization, the World Bank, and the North American Free Trade Association and their like serve the whole of humanity equally and equitably? Alas, there is not one shred of evidence for this (International Forum on Globalization, 2002). In JBG's WE, 'national distinctions dissolve,' so the notion of a standard is redundant. Though as this process is supposed to be similar to the development of national languages (180), it is curious that norms are somehow no longer in place. These contradictions and inconsistencies do not add up to a valid analysis.

The first two chapters of JBG's book review much of the relevant literature (in doctoral thesis fashion) in making a case for the ubiquity of English being due to 'the process of second language acquisition by speech communities' (11), which JBG terms macroacquisition. She distances herself from a linguistic imperialism approach (Phillipson 1992), which she regards as entailing English being spread 'entirely or mainly for its own sake' (27), a uniform policy of 'universal and exclusive education in English' in colonies (29). I write precisely the opposite at several points in my book. It is intriguing that JBG can read my work as detaching language from context like this, when the *sine qua non* of colonialism was profit, and when some commentators regard my approach as Marxist. JBG refers with approval to critics of my work, but not to my rebuttals (Phillipson 1996, 1997, 1999, the latter a review of Fishman, Conrad and Rubal-Lopez, a volume in which scholars from all over the world were invited to relate to my work, and in which none questioned the validity of the concept linguistic imperialism except one of the American editors) or to more recent statements (e.g. papers by myself and others in Ricento 2000), which would have inconvenienced her analysis. JBG seldom refers to African or Asian scholars. Where are Gandhi and Ngugi on linguistic imperialism? Not there, since they would undermine JBG's claim that English was 'not unilaterally *imposed on* passive subjects, but *wrested from* an unwilling imperial authority as part of the struggle by them against colonialism' (31, italics in the original). Ali Mazrui has written (1975) revealingly about the dialectic and deeply ambivalent process for the African intelligentsia of functioning primarily in English.

JBG's thorough descriptions of Basutoland and Sri Lanka are in fact entirely compatible with my analysis of colonial education, even if Basutoland was an extreme case, since the country was exclusively a labour reserve for the South African mining industry, an exploitation colony in territorial juxtaposition with a settler colony (Mufwene, 2002). Obviously much policy was reactive and ad hoc in a large empire. Clearly, genuine education can lead to resistance to an oppressive system, and colonizers sought to control minds as well as markets, irrespective of language.

JBG considers the influence of a number of key British colonial planners, and regards the twin systems of vernacular education for the masses and English-medium for the privileged as forming 'bilingual education'. But colonial education was modelled on what was done in the UK: it replicated its content, and used its exams. I have written that Macaulay's importance tends to be exaggerated (Phillipson, 1992, 133), and to write that I saw him 'imposing English as the language of all education in India' is a misreading of page 111 and the book as a whole. Far from Macaulay being a minor colonial official, as JBG suggests (40), he was near the top of the colonial hierarchy, and paid an astronomic salary (£10,000 p.a.). In contemporary terms, Macaulay would be described as a spin doctor, someone with a talent for penning quickly what others wished, with a tendency to the bombastic. Macaulay's primary achievement in his short stay in India was writing the Indian Penal Code.

My reference to a 'massive drive to establish English' relates explicitly (132) to 'the past 30 years', i.e. the postcolonial period from roughly 1960 onwards, the time when the sacred cows and false tenets of ELT/ESL (Kachru 1997, Phillipson 1992) were being articulated, and which continued the colonial education language hierarchy, with English as the linguistic holy grail, a language that eludes the masses in Asia and Africa, however much coveted. JBG's comforting reassurance that 'there is no indication that English is supplanting other languages where it has spread as a world language' (121) is contradicted by the evidence among elites in India, parts of Africa, and potentially in Scandinavia.

Far from JBG's writing being 'balanced and dispassionate' (as ELT luminaries label it in the blurb on the back of the volume), it creates a one-sided case for the global status quo, even while proclaiming a commitment to multilingualism and equal rights for all users of English. It is a complex, ambitious book covering a vast range of topics and sources, many elements that in my view simply do not form a coherent, valid whole (and I also have queries or corrections about countless points of detail). If English professionals are to work for a more just world, and this goal probably unites many applied linguists, the links between economic, linguistic and other forms of globalization still need much more intensive study.

References

Alexander, N. 2002. *An Ordinary Country: Issues in the Transition from Apartheid to Democracy in South Africa.* Pietermaritzburg: University of Natal Press.

Bourdieu, P. 2001. *Contre-feux 2.* Paris: Raisons d'agir.

Crystal, D. 1997. *English as a Global Language,* Cambridge: Cambridge University Press.

Dasgupta, P. 2000. 'Culture, sharing and language'. In Phillipson (ed.), *Rights to Language: Equity, Power and Education* (49–51). Mahwah, NJ: Lawrence Erlbaum.

De Klerk, V., and Gough, D. 2002. 'Black South African English'. In R. Mesthrie (ed.), *Language in South Africa* (356–378). Cambridge: Cambridge University Press.

De Varennes, F. 2000. Tolerance and inclusion: The convergence of human rights and the work of Tove Skutnabb-Kangas. In Phillipson (Ed.), *Rights to Language: Equity, Power and Education* (67–71). Mahwah, NJ: Lawrence Erlbaum..

Heugh, K. 2002. Recovering multilingualism: Recent language-policy developments. In R. Mesthrie (ed.), *Language in South Africa* (449–475). Cambridge: Cambridge University Press.

International Forum on Globalization 2002. *Alternatives to Economic Globalization. A better world is possible.* San Francisco: Berrett-Koehler.

Kachru, B. B. 1997. World Englishes and English-using communities. *Annual Review of Applied Linguistics,* Vol. 17, 66–87.

Lass, R. (2002). South African English. In R. Mesthrie (ed.), *Language in South Africa* (104–126). Cambridge: Cambridge University Press.

Fishman, J., Conrad, A., and Rubal-Lopez, A (eds.) (1996). *Post-imperial English. Status change in former British and American colonies, 1940-1990.* Berlin and New York: Mouton de Gruyter.

Graddol, D. (1997). *The Future of English?* London: The British Council.

Mazrui, A. A. (1975). *The Political Sociology of the English Language: An African perspective.* The Hague: Mouton.

Mufwene, S. (2002). Colonization, globalization and the plight of 'weak' languages. *Journal of Linguistics,* Vol. 38, No. 2, 375–395.

Ngugi wa Thiong'o (1986). *Decolonising the Mind: The Politics of Language in African Literature.* London: James Currey.

Pennycook, A. (2000). Language, ideology and hindsight: Lessons from colonial language policies. In T. Ricento (ed.), *Ideology, Politics and Language Policies: Focus on English* (49–66). Amsterdam: John Benjamins.

Phillipson, R. (1992). *Linguistic Imperialism.* Oxford: Oxford University Press.

Phillipson, R. (1996). Linguistic imperialism – African perspectives. *English Language Teaching Journal,* Vol. 50, No. 2, 160–167.

Phillipson, R. (1997). Realities and myths of linguistic imperialism. *Journal of Multilingual and Multicultural Development,* Vol. 18, No. 3, 238–247.

Phillipson, R. (1999) Review of Fishman, Conrad & Rubal-Lopez, Eds. (1996). *Language,* Vol. 75, No. 2, 375–378.

Phillipson, R. (2000a). English in the new world order: Variations on a theme of linguistic imperialism and 'world' English. In T. Ricento (Ed.), *Ideology, Politics and Language Policies: Focus on English* (87–106). Amsterdam: John Benjamins.

Phillipson, R. (ed.). (2000b). *Rights to Language: Equity, Power and Education.* Mahwah, NJ: Lawrence Erlbaum.

Phillipson, R. (2003). *English-Only Europe? Challenging Language Policy.* London & New York: Routledge.

Ricento, T. (ed.) (2000). *Ideology, Politics and Language Policies: Focus on English.* Amsterdam: John Benjamins.

Williams, G. (1992). *Sociolinguistics: A Sociological Critique.* London: Routledge.

Michael Cronin, *Translation and Globalization.*
London: Routledge, 2003, x + 197 pp.

Cronin's book makes a strong case for translation playing a decisive role in maintaining linguistic diversity worldwide. It is a learned, lively, wide-ranging book that should interest not only translators but all who are concerned with language policy. There is manifestly a need, since textbooks on language policy typically ignore translation.

Cronin's 'Introduction' presents the themes of each of the five chapters, and explores lucidly and appetisingly why globalization and technological change make it important to see non-literary translation as far more than merely instrumental. Translation has multiple social and cultural roles, and in a globalizing age, is ever more important. A critical translation studies needs to address the functions of translation in mediating between cultures and in maintaining or constraining biocultural diversity.

Chapter 1, 'Translation and the global economy', takes translation analysis beyond contrasting texts, or a focus on translators, to the world portrayed in translation products. Globalization, information technology, and the knowledge economy have transformed working processes. Translation is at the heart of localization processes, for example, when a software manual is produced fast in a large number of languages. The translation industry, dominated now by large international companies, is conservatively estimated as employing over 300,000 people. Multilingual websites need constant and rapid updating, for e-commerce and other purposes. Marketing and documentation blend into each other. Corporations (e.g. Symantec of Norton Antivirus) operate globally, and provide instant service in many languages.

Translators need a historical understanding of texts as a wider reference system, especially with the shift from stone to paper to electronic sign, and with present-day dependence on automated systems. Cronin traces the medium back to the origins of literacy, and its symbiosis with translation for several thousand years (Alexandria, the Bible), and while the tools have changed over time, the underlying processes of refining translation through cross-lingual intertextual comparison remain the same. The 'fundamental complicity between language and the technical in human development' (28) reminds us that the functions that tools serve are decisive. For translation to flourish requires support from the state's representatives, which Cronin exemplifies with multilingualism in post-apartheid South Africa (but without drawing on the extensive South African literature on difficulties of implementation). Translation itself may be seen as universalizing the culturally specific (e.g. a literary text) or particularising the universal (e.g. a factual text).

This profound point is then connected to the tension between a global US-driven thrust towards cultural homogeneity and the reality of multiple modernities in different contexts. Cronin sees a need to counteract 'monoglot diffusionism (English is the Language of the Future) which masquerades as an absolute truth' (34). Cronin refers to *globalization as translation*, since 'translation is not simply a bi-product of globalization but is a constituent part of how the phenomenon both operates and makes sense of itself' (34), an insight that critical discourse analysts would endorse. Historically translators have played a key role in bridging cultures, but their activity tends to be hidden, and is not culturally neutral.

Chapter 2, 'Globalization and new translation paradigms', deals with the economic reality of the consolidation of translation activities in large corporations aiming at sensitive localization, central surveillance, and economies of scale through technological networking. The competing tensions of centralization ('gigantism') and national economies at different points of development impacts on a translation industry in which 'projects are managed across countries, continents, cultures and languages' (45). Economic trends often mean that non-English speakers have the double task of translation into and from English, and the translation process 'is erased from public view in the global parochialism of Anglophone monoglossia' (60). But even Microsoft has had to realize that localization is not a purely technical, uncreative process (Gates: 'just linguistic', 62). EU efforts to promote multilingual translation have also probably contributed to sensitivity to local appropriacy, though Cronin may be over-optimistic about the nature of EU texts, since there is evidence that these are departing from national norms and cultures, and that databanks aggravate this process (Koskinen 2000, Tosi 2005). Some efforts have been made by

European governments to fund literary translations across languages, but EU investment in this has been minimal.

Cronin's description of global players seeking 'to eliminate the costs of translation by moving the debt across to the translated who then become invisible in the linguistic accounts of the powerful' (60) tallies with François Grin's study of the way the costs of foreign language education in continental Europe represent a massive subsidy to the Anglo-American economy, to the tune of at least €10 billion per year, and more probably about €16 to 17 billion (Grin 2005).

Cronin pleads for the emergence of a more reflective translator, who contributes to public debate, an intercultural broker who is consulted in the media just like historians and economists. This would be a valid task for professional associations of translators, which exist worldwide.

The requirement of fidelity in translation entails transforming material from other cultures or earlier periods, oscillating between a role as *guardians*, keepers of tradition through the power of remembrance, and one as *traders* seeking out the new and opening up for the circulation of new commodities and ideas. The demands of immediacy in the market (instantaneous time) have to be balanced against memory and complexity (mnemonic time).

Cronin cites ongoing work on the co-articulation of biodiversity with cultural and linguistic diversity, languages being extinguished, and with them the cultural knowledge embedded in them. Translation comes in for three reasons: it is essential for understanding what is unique about others; it can serve to counteract monocultural myopia; and the future of the planet depends on tapping into memories in each culture. It is impressive that Cronin brings in this new multi-disciplinary perspective (see <www.terralingua.org>), which is evolving fast in an effort to resist some of the negative effects of corporate globalisation.

Chapter 3, 'Globalization and the new geography of translation', is thematically unified by linking several threads: new realities of space and time radically changing the task of translation; Ireland's experience of linguistic oppression and renewal, building on two millennia of diaspora linguistic activity; the factors that contributed to US capital investing in software translation in Ireland; the translator as Houdini, a linguistic escapologist, the tricks of the trade being obscured from the public's view, which leads in turn to translating being under-rated in the wider society; the tension that pits the forces of global cultural homogenization against diversity and new hybridities. There is some overlap with earlier chapters, but the chapter usefully draws on Irish history, China and India, and theories of globalization, hegemony, and the multilingual global city. The descriptions of the software translation exercise effectively exemplify how the 'knowledge economy', outsourcing and localization function in practice, and why translation is important for the maintenance of difference.

Chapter 4, 'Globalization and the new politics of translation', goes into more depth on issues of time and space, and pressures of time and complexity, for instance, when translating legal documents for supranational organizations or corporate product descriptions (Caterpillar services dealerships in 35 languages and publishes 800 pages per day). Cronin sees translation as relational, since humans and machines complement each other rather than the one substituting for the other. This cyborg thinking parallels the way social scientists see the integration of minorities as relational, a reciprocal process that also engages the dominant group.

Since the pressures behind translation memory and conversion systems are primarily economic and institutional, the risk is the 'virtual absence of a critical political economy of translation' (119). This definitely applies to the world's largest translation services, in the European Union, which tend to be seen as having purely subservient functions, even if these are crucial for democratic legitimacy (Phillipson 2003). As a result of criticism, and to counteract its low esteem, the EU translation service now aims to occupy 'the centre stage of policy-making and must be integrated into the preparatory process from the outset in order to prevent it [translation] from becoming a constraint on the Commission's work' (press release IP/05/976 of 20/07/05, DG Translation of the European Commission).

In a fascinating section exploring what translation does to translators, Cronin, drawing mainly on French theoreticians, Dostoevsky and Koestler, speculates on whether the imperative to be faithful entails an element of fraudulence. This is because ideally a translation is as good as the original, producing a cloned text, a duplicate posing as the original. To achieve this bilingual rapprochement, the translator constantly balances between translation as homogenization and as creativity, the capacity to stand outside experience and reproduce it afresh. Achieving this is elusive, because of the intrinsic inadequacy of words to grasp reality, but also because translation is inevitably selective, partial, metonymic. The asymmetrical relationship between English and other languages means that English is constantly being enriched by postcolonial writers, but only 3% of US publications are translations. Babel is a warning of the hubris of thinking that one language can ever be enough.

Chapter 5, 'Minority languages in a global setting', is concerned with how dominant languages affect minority languages: while translation can lead to assimilation (of content and form), it can be a route to maintaining vitality and diversity. The advance of English, in cyberspace, the EU and globally, means that all other languages are in effect minority languages, even those that translation theory has hitherto considered as equal (French, Russian, etc). Language use at international conferences is a good example of English linguistic hegemony being uncritically confirmed. It is surprising for someone pleading the cause of critical scholarship (who correctly notes that minority status is not a given but reflects a relation between languages) to refer to languages 'dying, disappearing', terms that make the agents of linguicide invisible.

A major weakness of translation studies and theory has been the neglect of non-European languages and lack of attention to powerless languages. Failure to do so may result in a concentration on pragmatic, technical aspects of the translation process, to the neglect of aesthetic and political factors that influence minority language use.

The concluding section presents a rationale for an ecology of translation, implying a healthy balance between all languages. This is a somewhat pious hope, albeit one that the book as a whole argues for convincingly. Having analysed many ways in which English impacts in earlier chapters, here he quotes evidence that the threat to most languages comes from big local languages rather than European ones. Although he rightly underlines that maintaining diversity must be driven by local forces, and hopes that homogenizing globalization forces can be contained, one crucial element is missing in his analysis, namely how education can promote multi- and bilingualism. This is where translation studies would benefit from more familiarity with sociolinguistics, and language (in education) policy. Other work in translation studies, such as Anderman and Rogers 2005, is even less well informed about wider language policy issues, and seems crude compared with Cronin's intellectual brilliance and wide reading.

In underlining the importance of translation, Cronin seems over-optimistic in assigning it a major role in social and cultural reproduction. But his richly allusive, thought-provoking text is an articulate portrait of modern translators, and powerfully portrays how they have far more social roles than is appreciated. The book returns to many of the same themes in each chapter (making the chapter headings suggestive rather than accurate), which entails a certain amount of repetition. But Cronin has fleshed out the meaning in the modern world of Victor Hugo's 'translators are bridges between peoples'. He brings to life Goethe's insight: 'whatever people say about the shortcomings of translation, it remains one of the most important and meritorious tasks in international communication.'

References

Anderman, Gunilla and Margaret Rogers (eds) 2005. *In and out of English: For better, for worse?* Clevedon: Multilingual Matters.

Grin, François 2005. *L'enseignement des langues étrangères comme politique publique.* Rapport au Haut Conseil de l'évaluation de l'école, Paris, http://cisad.adc.education.fr/hcee/documents/rapport_Grin.pdf

Koskinen, Kaisa 2000. Institutional illusions. Translating in the EU Commission. *The Translator,* Vol. 6, No. 1, 49–65.

Phillipson, Robert 2003. *English-Only Europe? Challenging Language Policy.* London: Routledge.

Tosi, Arturo 2005. The devil in the kaleidoscope Can Europe speak with a single voice in many languages? In *Reconfiguring Europe: The Contribution of Applied Linguistics,* ed. Constant Leung and Jennifer Jenkins. London: Equinox, 5–20.

Viv Edwards, *Multilingualism in the English-Speaking world*
Oxford: Blackwell, 2004, 253 pp.

This is a richly documented presentation of the considerable linguistic diversity of countries which are often described as 'English-speaking'. It presents a vivid array of examples of multilingualism as a distinctive feature of the British Isles, the USA, Canada, Australia and New Zealand. The extent of this linguistic diversity is charted from its roots in languages of ancient and more recent origin to ongoing contemporary activities and struggles for recognition. There are chapters on the provision of language services (translation and interpretation), language in the family, education past and present, and the extent to which both minority and majority populations are adding languages to their repertoires. There is coverage of the rights of indigenous peoples, Sign language users, and immigrant populations, the same topic often being dealt with through examples that contrast the way challenges have been addressed in each of the countries. There are chapters on languages in the economy (with data on, for instance, the way Welsh and South Indian languages in the United Kingdom have financial clout), the media (use of minority languages in TV, radio, etc), the arts, diplomacy and defence. A concluding chapter is tantalisingly entitled 'Is life really too short to learn German?', a question put by a blinkered scholar, to which the resounding answer is that all can benefit by developing multilingual competence.

It is a challenge to be even-handed in treating minorities as dissimilar as the French-speaking groups in Canada alongside vulnerable indigenous peoples and diaspora immigrant minority groups in both settler states and Britain. At root there are the same issues of cultural maintenance, adaptation to new contexts and technologies, multiple identities, and an often uneasy alliance with the dominant English-speaking forces of the wider community. Edwards is persuasive in presenting the wide diversity of situations on different continents in such a way that the wealth of detailed exemplification brings out similarities and overall trends (often summarized at the end of a chapter) which hammer home the message that we are experiencing a major consolidation of multiple forms of bilingual and bicultural life. The picture that emerges is of increasing hybridity as struggles for cultural recognition achieve some of their goals. It is perhaps a little disappointing that these diversification processes in the entire English-speaking world are not explored in relation to the massive pressures of cultural homogenization (McDonaldization) that US corporate dominance in key domains, economic, military and cultural, entails.

Edwards invariably writes Indigenous with a capital letter, signifying that the original inhabitants of a territory are a special case requiring positive semiotic recognition. The designation used has consequences for how we perceive and refer to such groups, and is of major significance in international law, which grants rights to Indigenous Peoples, including the right to self-determination. Referring to native Americans as 'Aboriginals' entails risks, since this term may reinforce stereotypes, and does not imply recognition in international law. Indigenous Peoples in North America refer to themselves as 'First nations', a term that is more evocative and potentially empowering that the anonymous generality of 'groups'.

Edwards frequently refers to 'ethnic' groups as though this term is synonymous with 'ethnic minority' groups. This conflation unfortunately serves to normalize the difference between minorities and the majority, who by implication lack any ethnic identity. This is precisely the way racist discourse continues to marginalize those who differ from mainstream. Paradoxically, adopting and legitimating journalistic discourse of this kind is inconsistent with Edwards' passionate commitment to the cause of minority languages. This is grounded in a deep understanding of what membership of the Welsh language community has meant over decades of relatively successful struggle, along with a deep understanding of the cultural vitality of Sign languages and many immigrant language communities in the UK. The examples from Australasia and North America also reflect a profound familiarity with developments over several decades, only some of which provide cause for satisfaction.

The book demonstrates how key decisions on choice of language have to be taken in all of the contexts explored. When a media channel, a musical product or play is commissioned, there is invariably the dilemma that the market for English is so much larger than a minority language community. However, Edwards show with many examples how either/or thinking is often invalid. An instructive example is that when bilingual readers are considered, with the minority language on one page and English on the other, there are competing and conflicting reactions to the desirability of such a format. Edwards is able to conclude that such books can in fact be significant for the majority-language English speakers in a classroom. The use of the minority language is not merely symbolic but can shift awareness significantly, and build bridges between majority and minority.

This is not a book for the specialist, and inevitably the coverage of topics tends to be brief. For instance, Edwards' coverage of the language needs of diplomatic and security services is selective and the wider context is obscured. Foreign language competence has always been of paramount important to diplomacy (though countries like Australia were apparently slow to recognize this), and career diplomats generally have the incentive of a bonus payment for certified language proficiency. Although the 9/11 attack and US military and political responses since then have revealed acute gaps in high-level competence in languages seen as of strategic importance (Arabic, Pashtu, Farsi etc), there has been a series of US surveys of national foreign language needs over the past fifty years. Quite apart from failure to implement appropriate decisions, what would also need consideration is the fact that the 'intelligence' community is served by the huge secretive Echelon spying service. This is firmly anchored in 'English-speaking' states worldwide, plus a few other vassal states like Denmark/Greenland. Echelon makes it possible to listen in on all electronic communication worldwide, your allies and your assumed 'enemies', in whatever form, including personal emails, anything that may be of economic, political or military interest to the imperial state, the USA. Whether efficient use is made of such 'intelligence' is another story. The current increased investment in foreign languages and what the Pentagon refers to as 'Strategic communication' merely signifies that the super-state that has taken upon itself to impose its values and economic system worldwide has been obliged to recognise that linguistic diversity cannot be ignored.

Edwards does not attempt to cover what British membership of the EU means for languages, but notes that involvement in EU affairs requires foreign language competence (there is one error: Irish is an EU treaty language, not an official language). All EU governments are committed to making schoolchildren competent in two foreign languages, but the shocking reality is that education in Britain is aiming at nothing of the kind. Building on the new forms of multilingualism that are evolving in Britain would make a significant contribution towards achieving the educational goals that the EU advocates and new forms of trilingualism, through using globalization and migration processes constructively. This would open up for access to markets and cultural interchange worldwide. It would also represent a break with the sub-title of the book, 'The pedigree of nations', which is reminiscent of what Donald Rumsfeld once arrogantly referred to as 'old Europe'. It is the new evolving Europe and multilingually diverse 'English-speaking' countries that this book richly describes.

Angel M.Y. Lin and Peter W. Martin (eds.)
*Decolonisation, Globalisation: Language-in-Education
Policy and Practice.*
Clevedon: Multilingual Matters, 2005. 204 + xix pp.

This collection of ten studies from Asian and African contexts begins with a general introduction by Allan Luke that links many strands and challenges to current radical educational thinking, and another by the two editors, and concludes with reflections by Suresh Canagarajah. The editors present an intellectually challenging framework for reading the country studies, and appetisingly draw in themes to articulate a case for re-thinking much language-in-education policy. Their hope is that the volume goes beyond state-art-of-the art description and theorization, and can lead from coherent deconstruction to proactive reconstruction. This is needed since many of our analytical categories remain simplistic, and inadequate educational policy leads to the perpetuation of social inequalities. A key paradox is the widespread demand for 'more English' although English stratifies and is elusive. Dominant groups/classes are groomed for the economy of globalization that has dashed most decolonization hopes. Across differing country reports, the pattern is of an 'emptying-out of the "linguistic local" and the one-sided pursuit of the "linguistic-global"' (9).

Annamalai makes a rich, subtle presentation of educational language policy in colonial and postcolonial India. Most useful for SLA is remarks on how English nativization processes are taken on board in education, and what the implications are for mobility nationally, for inclusion or exclusion, and for participation in the global economy. He also stresses various decolonization needs, both in terms of attitudes (escaping from ingrained orientalism at all levels of education) and teacher competence.

Lin's paper on Hong Kong makes the methodological point that a 'Periphery' scholar should not merely take over 'Centre' epistemologies, and argues that our research approaches risk being self-referential (purely 'academic') and lack self-reflection. Lin eloquently shows how critical discourse analysis unmasks the legitimation of an inequitable social structure (now under Chinese management). Proficiency in English remains an elusive goal for the many, but the education system is functional for the local elite, for China, and for global commerce. But even if her ethnographic data unearth the attitudes of the marginal (those who know their life chances are adversely affected by not knowing English), the gap between scholarship and societal change remains wide. She ends by endorsing a challenge from Luke: 'TESOL must do something other than what it currently does. Otherwise, it will remain a technology for domesticating the "other", whatever its scientific and humanitarian pretences.'

The analysis of 40 years of independent Singapore, by Rubdy, vividly reveals an activist approach to language policy, the conscious replacement of mother tongues by the key language of global capitalism, English, and to a lesser extent Mandarin, in order to create and cement a new national identity and ensure the economy. The overtly elitist educational policies give the lie to the notion of English being 'neutral', since losers are condemned to the variant of English, Singlish, which, however authentic, is considered irrelevant by an authoritarian state. One current challenge is the need, because of changes in the global economy, for education to produce more critical, creative citizens while retaining their loyalty to the top-down national project.

Martin's paper presents classroom discourse samples in multilingual Sarawak. These suggest that very little learning of any kind is taking place. Though Martin makes the connection to national educational and economic goals, it is unlikely that teachers or pupils can do so, and failing to provide literacy in the minority languages looks like slavish adherence to a western modernist agenda.

Abdolmehdi Riazi's run-through of four millennia of Iranian history is a more general article, but fascinating on major cultural and linguistic influences. In recent decades, globalization pressures have created a massive demand for English, which the Islamic state tolerates. It is extensively taught in schools in a 'quantitative' grammar-translation way. Riazi bemoans an almost total lack of language planning for status purposes.

The article on a Turkish higher education institution by two US scholars, Reagan and Schreffler, unfortunately devotes much of the text to a general language policy and planning survey. The issue of striking a balance between an increased use of English as the medium of instruction (with serious problems in ensuring quality) and maintaining the vitality of the local language is a key issue in northern Europe too (Phillipson 2006). This article is exceptional in addressing the ideological implications of assigning English a greater role. The authors acknowledge that the awareness of their Turkish colleagues of wider issues of linguistic imperialism and globalization is generally limited.

Three articles present language-in-education analyses in Africa, which, with the exception of part of the South African economy, experiences the downside effects of globalization, unlike Hong Kong and Singapore, key players in financial globalization. The three are grim reading, as the classroom evidence from Kenya (Bunyi), Tanzania and South Africa (Brock-Utne citing local scholars) is of inappropriate pedagogy and little learning. Probyn's summary of the complexities and contradictions of South African language policy is eminently lucid. The case for bilingual education has been made strongly by African researchers for over thirty years, so that the present picture of waste merely confirms a stranglehold that keeps Africans in a dependent, largely semi-literate state, with elites buying themselves into English-medium education. Aggravating factors are the perception of English as a panacea, poor policy implementation, insufficient resources for work on African languages, and the inappropriate donor policies.

Canagarajah teases out some of the main tensions revealed, and relates them to top-down language policy—which he regards as a failure—and education, stressing the potential of integrating learning with language ecology, multiliteracies, and bottom-up approaches that recognise that globalization has overtaken decolonization. (Does this mean SLA should transform into Multiple Language Acquisition?) Although the volume is exceptionally coherent and inspiring, there still remains a gap between sophisticated analysis, and proactive policies that explicitly explore what incorporation by globalization and more English actually entail. It would be invalid to conclude that, by analogy with educational sociology recognising that 'education cannot change society', TESOL cannot change globalization. The learning of English globally is a precondition for the functioning of corporate globalization: how and why the language is learned and used ought therefore to be a major concern in the neo-imperial age we now live in.

Phillipson, Robert 2006. English, a cuckoo in the European higher education nest of languages? *European Journal of English Studies*, Vol. 10, No. 1, 13–32.

Index